LORENZO SNOW

Lorenzo Snow, about 1898

LORENZO SNOW

SPIRITUAL GIANT   PROPHET OF GOD

FRANCIS M. GIBBONS

Deseret Book Company
Salt Lake City, Utah

To my mentor

Second printing March 1983

Contents

Preface

All nature is characterized by a certain duality, a combination of spirit and matter, whose highest expression is man. Man's outward form has its counterpart in the spiritual being that his body houses. And in his maturity, man's physical aspect reflects the condition of this interior being who, shielded from the natural eye, functions ceaselessly and in silence to mold the body to its own likeness. It is a law of nature, therefore, that the qualities of godliness or depravity existing in the spirit of a man will at last fight their way through his outer shell and etch themselves on his countenance and in his demeanor for all to see. By these signs we can accurately gauge the condition, the maturity, and the stature of a man's spirit.

We can use these signs to make a reasoned judgment about the spiritual stature of the subject of this work, Lorenzo Snow, the fifth President of The Church of Jesus Christ of Latter-day Saints, thanks to a description of his appearance left by a protestant minister, who "was startled to see the holiest face but one" he had ever beheld. "His face," the minister wrote, "was a poem of peace. In the tranquil depths of his eyes were the 'home of silent prayer' and the abode of spiritual strength. . . . I watched the play of emotion and studied with fascinated attention, the subtle shades of expression which spoke so plainly the workings of his soul; and the strangest feeling stole over me, that I stood on holy ground; that this man did not act from the commonplace motives of policy, interest or expediency, but he acted from a far off center." As this writer reflected upon his visit with the prophet, he concluded, "The picture of that slight, venerable form hallowed with the aura of an ineffable peace will haunt my heart like the vision of a celestial picture thrown upon the camera . . . of my dreaming soul."

Although Lorenzo Snow was well born, he did not at birth, nor in the early and middle years of his life, manifest the heavenly qualities this observer described. He did have within him the seeds of greatness, as did many of his contemporaries who failed to grow and mature as he did. The difference lay in the processes through which this man passed in reaching the state of development he attained before death.

The object of this biography is not so much to describe the events, conditions, and achievements in Lorenzo Snow's life (although it will contain a great deal of these) as it is to probe into the reasons, the motivations, and the disciplines that produced such unusual results, that converted a young, obscure boy into a powerful, accomplished man with a celestial character and bearing.

Chapter One

The Early Years

Lorenzo Snow was the offspring of solid Puritan stock, his first paternal ancestor to reach America, Richard Snow, having settled in Woburn, Massachusetts, within two decades after the Pilgrim landing. The family put down deep roots in the hardy New England soil, remaining there until Oliver Snow III moved to what was then the new American frontier, Ohio. There, on April 3, 1814, in Mantua, Portage County, Rosetta L. Pettibone Snow, Oliver's wife, gave birth to her fifth child and first son, Lorenzo.

His parents were Baptists, so Lorenzo was raised in a religious atmosphere. However, according to his elder sister, Eliza R. Snow, the parents were not Baptists of the "rigid, iron-bedstead order." More liberal in their views than most, the Oliver Snows created a home that, according to Eliza, "was a resort for the good and intelligent of all denominations."

The parents being gregarious and hospitable, the Snow family was exposed to the diverse views of many religious sects. Not being fettered by rigid orthodoxy, it was inevitable that the Snows, living so close to Kirtland, Ohio, the first major gathering place of members of The Church of Jesus Christ of Latter-day Saints, would have had contact with the Mormon missionaries who aggressively proselyted throughout the area from the early part of 1831. As a consequence, Lorenzo's mother and his sister Leonora were baptized into the Church in 1831, and his sister Eliza followed them into the waters of baptism in the spring of 1835.

At the time of Eliza's conversion, Lorenzo was mature in every sense of the word. He had reached his twenty-first birthday; he was physically strong through years of strenuous work on his father's farm, work that lay in large part on his shoulders by reason of his status as the eldest of three sons; and he was mentally tough and resilient as the result of his innate abilities and the training he had received at home.

Lorenzo had early shown an aptitude for study and reflection and, strangely enough, an almost inordinate fascination for military affairs. So pronounced were these interests that they crowded out any inclination toward religion during his early years. Despite the fact he was regularly exposed to the doctrines of the Church from about age seventeen due to the conversion of his mother and sister, he showed little awareness of their importance, or even of their existence.

At age twenty-one, Lorenzo, to further his ambitions for a military career, decided to attend Oberlin Collegiate Institute (later designated Oberlin College), then the most respectable institution of higher learning in the area. His preparatory schooling consisted of independent studies, elementary school, and a term at the high school in Ravenna, Ohio. Disposing of what sister Eliza referred to as his "paternal inheritance" to acquire the means to finance his education, Lorenzo left Mantua in September 1835 for Oberlin, which lay about fifty miles to the west.

A trip that began as merely an exciting prelude to his academic career turned into one of the most significant and far-reaching experiences of his entire life. En route to Oberlin, Lorenzo fell in company with David W. Patten, a highly intelligent and articulate man who, only seven months before, had been ordained as one of the original twelve apostles of The Church of Jesus Christ of Latter-day Saints. Working out of Kirtland, a small Ohio town about as far north of Mantua as Oberlin is west of it, Elder Patten was fulfilling one of the numerous "missions" of his apostolic career, which was to be cut short little more than three years later by the guns of a mob at the so-called Battle of Crooked River in Missouri.

Birthplace of Lorenzo Snow, Mantua, Ohio

While Lorenzo had previously known many brilliant men, never before had he met one who combined keen intelligence with deep spirituality, as did this man. Nor had he ever heard one who spoke with such certainty about other-worldly things, about a pre-mortal state and about the celestial status hereafter of those who, in life, accept and live the commandments of God.

While we are left to conjecture about the extent to which Lorenzo may have received hints and impressions about his future associations with this man and with the organization he represented, there is no doubt that the experience—seemingly fortuitous, yet having about it the marks of a destined encounter—had a profound and lingering effect upon him. "From that time," Eliza was to write later, "a new field, with a new train of reflection, was open to my brother's mind, the impress of which has never been erased."

Lorenzo applied himself to his studies and did well; but they did not produce the satisfaction and fulfillment he had confidently expected to receive. While he had enrolled at Oberlin to advance his military ambitions, it was inevitable that he would there experience a wide exposure to religion, as the school was a Presbyterian institution and was used by that sect to train its clergy. This fact, coupled with the provocative thoughts that had been sown in his mind by David W. Patten, drew him to another purpose than the one that had taken him there. For the first time in his life, Lorenzo began to seek after spiritual enlightenment through a systematic study of religion. He brought an open mind to the task and focused upon it the same objective analysis and precision that he applied to a mathematical or military problem. But the results were discouraging. Writing to Eliza in Kirtland, where she had moved after her baptism, he observed gloomily: "If there is nothing better than is to be found here in Oberlin College, good bye to all religions."

Eliza, imbued with the missionary zeal of most converts to the Church, a zeal intensified by the fact that the target was her brother, saw an opportunity to bring Lorenzo closer to the conversion she earnestly sought for him. She invited him to come to Kirtland to enroll in a Hebrew school under the tutelage of a Jewish scholar, Joshua Seixas, who had been persuaded by the Prophet Joseph Smith to establish his school there as a means of training Church leaders. By the spring of 1836, Lorenzo was settled in Kirtland and attending Professor Seixas's school. His classmates included not only Joseph Smith, but most of the other principal leaders of the Church, who were preparing to build up an organization they confidently expected would revolutionize the world and prepare for the Second Coming.

Chapter Two

Conversion

At the time of Lorenzo's arrival in Kirtland, its populace was engulfed by a wave of spiritual fervor comparable to the fiery excitement on the Day of Pentecost. In January of that year, the Prophet Joseph Smith began to administer "endowments" in the Kirtland Temple, spiritual ordinances.

Of his experiences on the twenty-first of that month, Joseph recorded, "The heavens were opened upon us, and I beheld the celestial kingdom of God, and the glory thereof, whether in the body or out I cannot tell. I saw the transcendent beauty of the gate through which the heirs of that kingdom will enter, which was like unto circling flames of fire; also the blazing throne of God, whereon was seated the Father and the Son. I saw the beautiful streets of that kingdom, which had the appearance of being paved with gold."

Others who were in the temple the same day had a similar experience. "The visions of heaven were opened to them also," Joseph wrote. "Some of them saw the face of the Savior, and others were ministered unto by holy angels, and the spirit of prophecy and revelation was poured out in mighty power; and loud hosannas, and glory to God in the highest, saluted the heavens, for we all communed with the heavenly host."

These electrifying incidents foreshadowed the phenomenal outpouring of the Spirit the Saints were to experience at the dedication of the temple, which took place the last of

March and first of April. Of a special meeting that followed the first dedicatory session, Joseph wrote, "A noise was heard like the sound of a rushing mighty wind, which filled the Temple, and all the congregation simultaneously arose, being moved upon by an invisible power; many began to speak in tongues and prophesy; others saw glorious visions; and I beheld the Temple was filled with angels, which fact I declared to the congregation. The people of the neighborhood came running together (hearing an unusual sound within, and seeing a bright light like a pillar of fire resting upon the Temple), and were astonished at what was taking place. This continued until the meeting closed at eleven p.m."

The climax of these manifestations came on Sunday, April 3, 1836, when Joseph Smith and his associate, Oliver Cowdery, retired alone to the pulpit of the temple, "the veils being dropped," to engage in "solemn and silent prayer." As they arose, four visions were opened to their minds when, in succession, the Savior, Moses, Elias, and Elijah appeared to them. The description of the Savior on this occasion was quite detailed: "We saw the Lord standing upon the breastwork of the pulpit, before us," Joseph wrote, "and under his feet was a paved work of pure gold, in color like amber. His eyes were as a flame of fire; the hair of his head was white like the pure snow; his countenance shone above the brightness of the sun; and his voice was as the sound of the rushing of great waters."

Thus, at the time of Lorenzo's arrival in Kirtland, accounts of visions, speaking in tongues, and prophesyings were on everyone's lips. While these reports must have piqued Lorenzo's interest and curiosity because of his recent but unsuccessful foray into religion, what must have especially attracted him was the measured, analytical demeanor of the people who reported these extraordinary events. Absent was any element of frenzy or irrationality, qualities too often evident among the extreme sects that abounded on the frontier of that day, sects with which Lorenzo had frequent contact. The Latter-day Saints did not fit into the traditional mold of those who had been touched by a spiritual fervor. Their demeanor more nearly coincided with that of the academicians with whom Lorenzo had associated at Oberlin.

Because of the false and malicious reports that had been circulated about the Saints, Lorenzo probably was surprised at their reasonableness. In fact, that religion could be reasonable may have been something of a new idea to Lorenzo. He had come to Kirtland to cultivate his mind. He now began to realize that in this place, unexpectedly, his spiritual horizons might also be expanded. This important shift in focus is reflected in a chance encounter Lorenzo and Eliza had with Joseph Smith on a Kirtland street one day. Joseph suggested that Eliza bring her brother to dinner some evening. Intently watching the Prophet as he walked away from them, Lorenzo said, "Joseph Smith is a most remarkable man. I want to get better acquainted with him. Perhaps, after all, there is something more to Joseph Smith and to Mormonism than I have ever dreamed."

Lorenzo fed his growing interest in the doctrines of the Church as he began to study more, to reflect, to pray, and to attend meetings of the Saints. Of the many he attended before his conversion, none made a more profound impression upon him than a "patriarchal blessing meeting" in the temple presided over by Joseph Smith, Sr., the Prophet's father. Lorenzo said that in his appearance and demeanor, Joseph Smith, Sr., resembled his mental image of Father Abraham. "I had never before seen age so prepossessing," he wrote of the Patriarch. At the conclusion of the meeting, in visiting with Lorenzo, the Patriarch said, "Why, brother Snow, I discover that you are trying to understand the principles of Mormonism. Well, do not worry, but pray to the Lord and satisfy yourself; study the matter over, compare the scriptures with what we are teaching; talk with the brethren that you are acquainted with, and after a time you will be convinced that 'Mormonism' is of God, and you will be baptized."

It is doubtful the wise patriarch could have given a better admonition to hasten the conversion of this promising young man. There was no element of coercion or manipulation in it. Nor was there a hint of an ulterior motive. It represented nothing more than the effort of a new-found friend to help with a puzzle that had perplexed Lorenzo for many months, a puzzle that cried out for a speedy solution. And the calm certitude with which his friend had spoken must have given him confidence that he could find the answers he sought.

Within weeks after this incident, Lorenzo's knowledge had progressed to the point that he was prepared for baptism. But it still was not the sure knowledge he felt the need to obtain. It was tentative, founded upon reasoning and analysis, upon his confidence in the mentors who had led him thus far, and upon the feelings that had begun that day on the road with David W. Patten.

Lorenzo was baptized by John F. Boynton, another of the original twelve apostles of this dispensation. The ordinance was performed in June 1836 in the Chagrin River that flows through Kirtland. With this initiatory step, and the confirmation that followed soon after, Lorenzo was officially accepted into fellowship in the Church. But something was lacking. All the essential formalities had been complied with, but the new convert felt uneasy and dissatisfied because no significant inner change had taken place. The young man who emerged from the river with the apostle at his side was no different in his spiritual perceptions from the young man who had descended into it. He was not the "new man" he had hoped to be, and this troubled him because he had heard reports of, had even witnessed, the joy that had filled others as they had been filled with the Holy Ghost. Why had not the same phenomenon occurred in his case? As he looked within himself for the answer, he realized that he had not yet paid the price for such a manifestation. Determined to remedy this defect, the new member, recalling the experience of Joseph Smith in going into the grove for enlightenment, and remembering the admonition of James that had taken him there, sought a secret place in the woods that surrounded Kirtland. There, alone, Lorenzo prayed mightily for the spiritual witness and confirmation he desired. "I had no sooner opened my lips," he later recorded, "than I heard a sound, just above my head, like the rustling of silken robes, and immediately the Spirit of God descended upon me, completely enveloping my whole person, filling me from the crown of my head to the soles of my feet. . . . No language can describe the almost instantaneous transition from a dense cloud of mental and spiritual darkness into a refulgence of light and knowledge, as it was at that time imparted to my understanding. I then received a perfect knowledge that God lives, that Jesus Christ is the Son of God, and of the restoration of the holy Priesthood, and the fulness of the Gospel. It was a complete baptism—a tangible immersion in the heavenly principle or element, the Holy Ghost; and even more real and physical in its effect upon every part of my system than the immersion by water."

In the twilight of life, reflecting upon the events that had shaped his character, Lorenzo pointed to this one as having had a most profound influence. It marked his conversion from a state bordering on intellectual agnosticism to one of spiritual certainty and commitment. He no longer needed to live on borrowed light.

The spiritual elevation that accompanied Lorenzo's conversion continued for several minutes until at last "the celestial element which filled and surrounded [him] began gradually to withdraw." In assessing what had taken place, he wrote, "On arising from my kneeling posture, with my heart swelling with gratitude to God, beyond the power of expression, I felt—I knew that He had conferred on me what only an omnipotent being can confer—that which is of greater value than all the wealth and honors worlds can bestow."

As Lorenzo retired that night, the same spiritual phenomenon was repeated, as it was for several nights thereafter, like the ebb and flow of a celestial tide. "The sweet remembrance of these glorious experiences," he reflected in his later years, "from that time to the present, bring them fresh before me, imparting an inspiring influence which pervades my whole being, and I trust will to the close of my earthly existence."

This experience radically altered Lorenzo's course. But another experience provided much of the thrust that carried him to the pinnacle of achievement he ultimately attained. It occurred several months after his baptism when he went to Father Joseph Smith for a patriarchal blessing. Now that he had a personal knowledge that God reveals his mind and will to and through his servants, he had perfect confidence that the Patriarch would disclose what lay ahead for him. The blessing that his aged and benign friend conferred was all he had hoped for: "Thou hast a great work to perform in thy day and generation. God has called thee to the ministry. Thou must preach the gospel of thy Savior to the inhabitants of the earth. Thou shalt have faith even like that of the brother of Jared. . . . There shall not be a mightier man on earth than thou. . . . Thou shalt have power over unclean spirits—at thy command the powers of darkness shall stand back and devils shall flee away. If expedient the dead shall rise and come forth at thy bidding. . . . Thou shalt have long life. The vigor of thy mind shall not be abated and the vigor of thy body shall be preserved."

At the date this blessing was given, there was nothing in Lorenzo's demeanor or past performance to prompt the patriarch to make such extravagant promises. And yet, looking back upon Lorenzo's life, one is struck with awe at the precise way in which the various aspects of this blessing were fulfilled.

The life of Lorenzo Snow, following the conferral of his patriarchal blessing, shows a perfect coincidence between his conduct and the blessings of the patriarch. Through his faithfulness, his blessing was fulfilled. This symmetry between promise and performance lends an added fascination to a life whose course was radically altered by the unusual conversion he experienced in Kirtland in the spring and summer of 1836.

Chapter Three

The First Mission

During the remainder of 1836 and the early part of the following year, Lorenzo received many confirmations of the powerful testimony that had descended upon him in answer to his fervent prayers. In Kirtland, he witnessed many spiritual manifestations, such as prophesying and speaking in tongues.

Filled with the spirit of his religion, and in fulfillment of his patriarchal blessing, he set out on foot upon his first mission in the spring of 1837, having been ordained an elder and designated as a missionary a short time before. As was customary in those early days of the Church, he began his journey with no detailed preparations, with no specific plan for proselyting other than to bear testimony, and he carried no money. This last aspect of his mission was the most difficult for him to reconcile. Having a genteel, almost patrician temperament, he was embarrassed to have to beg for food and shelter. The only thing that enabled him to overcome these deep-seated feelings was "a positive knowledge that God required it." Reflection convinced him that if this was required of the early disciples as an act of humility and subservience, he could not in good conscience refuse to comply with the same requirement imposed by one whom he sustained as a prophet of God.

The first night out posed no problem as he was accommodated in the home of Mrs. Granger, his father's sister, who was very attentive and kind, although she showed no special interest in her nephew's message. The second night, however, revealed the harsh reality of traveling without purse or scrip as seven homes abruptly closed their doors to him when he humbly asked for lodging and something to eat. At the eighth home he was reluctantly admitted, although he went to bed without supper and was sent away the next morning without breakfast.

With nothing to rely upon for sustenance except the kind-heartedness and liberality of the people, Lorenzo soon learned about the tenuous and uncertain nature of our existence. Having never before been concerned about the necessities of life, he now came face to face with the specter of hunger and want. Not only was Lorenzo made aware of his dependence upon others, but there came a sudden dawning of his pervasive and constant dependence upon God, for both the physical and spiritual necessities of life.

With this altered perspective, the young missionary prepared to conduct the first meeting of his ministry, held in a private home in a rural area not far from his birthplace. "I had sought by prayer and fasting," he wrote of the experience. "I had humbled myself before the Lord, calling on Him in mighty prayer to impart the power and inspiration of the holy priesthood." The results of this preparation were clearly evident. "When I stood before that congregation," Lorenzo wrote, "although I knew not one word I could say, as soon as I opened my mouth to speak, the Holy Ghost rested mightily upon me, filling my mind with light and communicating ideas and proper language by which to impart them."

Those present at this meeting requested a second one, then a third. Lorenzo spoke of modern revelation through a living prophet, who lived within a two-day walk away. He related the pentecostal outpourings of his previous year at Kirtland and capped his remarks by relating the circumstances of his own conversion.

So widespread was the interest stirred up by Elder Snow's first two meetings in this area that the third meeting was scheduled in the Medina County courthouse to accommodate the large crowd that was anticipated. The fervor of Lorenzo's testimony, the clarity of his logic, and the scriptural soundness of the concepts he elaborated were so compelling that many came forward to receive baptism at his hands.

Among his first converts were an aunt and uncle named Goddard and several cousins, one of whom, Mary Adaline Goddard, was to become his wife eight years later. At the time of Adaline's baptism, however, neither she nor the eloquent young cousin who baptized her had any inkling of their later marital ties.

From Medina, Lorenzo's journey took him through Huron, Summit, Portage, Trumbull, and Geauga counties. In the villages and byways of this picturesque and fertile land, young Lorenzo repeatedly lifted his voice, proclaiming the reality and power of God and his son, Jesus Christ, and the saving effect of their doctrine.

The friendly reception he was given in and near Medina was repeated at Mantua, his birthplace, where he spoke to large and attentive crowds and where he was privileged to baptize several former classmates.

But he did not have unbroken success and satisfaction. Traveling without purse or scrip continued to be a difficulty. Yet Lorenzo knew that asking for food and lodging was necessary to carry out his mission, and that those who refused him, a servant of the Lord, refused the Lord himself.

One evening at dusk Lorenzo and a companion, who had joined him after his mission began, approached an innkeeper asking for supper and a place to sleep. "He very gruffly refused," Elder Snow reported, "saying he kept travelers for their money—not for Gospel pay, and advised us to go home, get employment, earn money, then give him a call, and he would be happy to entertain us." As the two missionaries turned to leave, abashed by this unwarranted rudeness, there welled up in Elder Snow a feeling of righteous indignation. Turning back, he felt impressed to tell the man he had just refused succor to a pair of God's servants. "The future results of what you have done you do not now know," Elder Snow said, "but we know, and a time will come when you also will know." These unexpected, startling words riveted the innkeeper's attention upon the two young men whom he now regarded in an entirely different light. Assured of an attentive audience,

Elder Snow continued by referring to Matthew's account of the last judgment and quoted the significant passage, "Then shall the righteous answer him, saying, Lord, when saw we thee an hungered, and fed thee? or thirsty, and gave thee drink? When saw we thee a stranger, and took thee in? or naked, and clothed thee? . . . And the King shall answer and say unto them, Verily I say unto you, Inasmuch as ye have done it unto one of the least of these my brethren, ye have done it unto me." To make certain that the innkeeper had gotten the point, Elder Snow concluded, "When this event takes place, you will be there with us, and you will then know that we were the servants of God, commissioned to preach His Gospel, and when engaged in this work, we asked you to administer to our necessities, and you turned us away."

As the two young men turned again to leave, "the gentleman," as Elder Snow was later to recall, "seemed struck with amazement and at a loss what to say or do." At length, recovering his composure and his tongue, he called after them, "Stop, gentlemen, hold on—you need not go off *mad*. . . . Turn back gentlemen, walk in—walk in."

In this incident is revealed one of the most prominent qualities in Lorenzo Snow's character, his resolute, even adamant determination to do what the circumstances and his sense of propriety required. And once he had decided his course of action, he was unshakable in pursuing or advocating it. He later declared, "We have to exert ourselves and go from grace to grace, to get the law of action so incorporated in our systems, that it may be natural to do those things that are required of us. It is a great matter to act firm, for one of the main objects that the Saints should accomplish is to be perfectly calm and serene, no matter how sudden accidents may occur."

But if Lorenzo's first mission helped him develop strength, it was equally important in his spiritual development. One night at the home of a Brother Smith in Stark County, Ohio, he had a vivid dream in which he was shown that plans were afoot to mob him. The next evening as he sat visiting with friends, two well-dressed young men, strangers, came knocking to invite him to speak to a gathering at a nearby school. When Lorenzo showed some reluctance to go, the two became quite insistent. When at last he flatly refused, their insistence turned to anger. Lorenzo's clear recollection of his dream had helped him decide what to do. He later learned that while, indeed, a gathering had waited at the schoolhouse, its object was to mob him, not listen to him. This and many similar experiences on his mission taught him that God does communicate with man, and that the wise will listen and obey.

It was a much wiser and more confident man who returned to Kirtland in the fall of 1837 after completing his first mission. As he toted up the results, Lorenzo must have been impressed with what he had accomplished and grateful for the blessings of God that had made it possible. Many converts had joined the Church through his efforts, and he had learned much that would help him in his future ministry.

Chapter Four

A Time of Trial and Change

The environment Lorenzo found in Kirtland upon returning from his first mission was hardly conducive to the growth of a budding testimony. Instead of a spirit of love, forbearance, and humility, which the returned missionary had been teaching his converts and investigators for months, he found a violent spirit of arrogance, hate, and retribution. In the vanguard of those who nourished these harsh and unchristian attitudes were five members of the Quorum of the Twelve Apostles and many other high leaders, all of whom stood in bitter defiance of Joseph Smith.

Lorenzo must have found the change in Kirtland hard to believe.

The cause of this extraordinary change was two-pronged: First, many residents had been caught up in a spirit of wild speculation that had gripped the whole country. In haste and greed, they had made improvident investments that had turned sour, bankrupting many of them. Second, in search of a scapegoat upon whom to heap the blame for their adversity, they pointed the finger at Joseph Smith, who headed a Kirtland financial institution that had gone under, along with hundreds of other banks across the land, during the panic of 1837. So inflamed and distorted were their feelings, that on one terrifying occasion, guns and knives were brandished by the dissidents in the temple in an attempt to wrest its control from the Church leaders.

Had not Lorenzo's convictions about the Church and the Prophet Joseph Smith rested on a spiritual, not intellectual, foundation, he could easily have been misled, as were many others whose spiritual perceptions had been clouded. But Lorenzo weathered this storm relying with confidence upon the things he knew within himself to be true. Indeed, he may well have been strengthened by the incident, being compelled to reappraise his convictions amidst the din of riotous public discord. To compare the measured and dignified response of the Prophet Joseph Smith and his father to the vicious and unruly clamor of their enemies was evidence in itself of the different spirits that moved them.

There is much to suggest, in Lorenzo's later life, that the example of the Smiths, at this trying time, had a profound effect upon the development of one of his most notable traits— deliberate poise and calmness in the face of trouble. In his later years, President Snow's temperament seemed never to vary in its response to outward influences. Whether a messenger brought good, bad, or disastrous news, he might expect the same benign and controlled reaction from the Prophet. It was almost as if Lorenzo had been endowed with a measure of omniscience, so that nothing caught him off guard.

But, it was only the embryo of the mature prophet that experienced the trauma and terror of Kirtland in the autumn of 1837, an embryo that needed protection and proper nourishment. Lorenzo received this from his family, now together in Kirtland, consisting of his parents, two sisters, two brothers, and two nieces, the daughters of his eldest sister, who was then a widow. He received it, too, from the many staunch members of the Church who still remained in Kirtland, and especially from the Smith family.

Even before his conversion, Lorenzo had been profoundly influenced by the Patriarch, Joseph Smith, Sr. Their relationship was further cemented when the Patriarch spent several weeks in the Snow home, during the upheavals in Kirtland, to avoid legal harassments initiated by the apostates. Lorenzo also benefited, during this period, from a continuing close relationship with the Prophet Joseph Smith, made possible chiefly because of the role his sister Eliza played in tutoring the Smith children.

We may infer from later events that even at that early day, when Lorenzo's character and leadership qualities had barely begun to emerge, the Prophet saw in him the high promise that was later to be fulfilled. If this was the case, and there is much to suggest it was, we may also infer that Joseph instructed and encouraged him.

But the unruly spirit that dominated Kirtland decreed an end to the intimate and valuable relationship the young missionary had enjoyed with the Church's leading family. He would later have contact with the Smiths, of course, but never in the degree he enjoyed at Kirtland.

By mid-January, 1838, conditions had become so intolerable that Joseph Smith found it necessary to leave Ohio. He had anticipated this move when, several months before, he had gone to Missouri to search out "places of gathering" to accommodate the Saints who he expected would flock there from Mormon centers elsewhere in the United States and from the fruitful mission fields in Great Britain that had only recently been opened.

In late April, the Snow family followed the Prophet, leaving Kirtland in a horse-and-ox-team caravan that included nine members of the Snow family and members of the Huntington, Moses, and Pearce families. Twenty-four-year-old Lorenzo was in charge of one of the wagons. En route, the party visited Father Snow's sister, Charlotte Granger, and her family, who treated the travelers with the courtesy and love Eliza thought might have been given a "bridal party."

About a hundred miles from Far West, Lorenzo was stricken with a neuralgic ailment identified as "bilious fever," which required that he relinquish his teamster duties. For the remainder of the trip to Far West, he suffered so much discomfort that Eliza often had to hold his head firmly between her hands to minimize the excruciating pain caused by the jolting of the wagon. The patient's condition was so bad that he was left in Far West at the home of Sidney Rigdon to be nursed by

Eliza, while the remainder of the party went on to their destination at Adam-ondi-Ahman.

Lorenzo was delirious from the violent fever that racked
his body most of the time he spent at Elder Rigdon's. When at
last he had recovered sufficiently to travel, Eliza supervised
his move to Adam-ondi-Ahman, placing him on a makeshift
bed in the bottom of a wagon. Free from pain and fever,
Lorenzo was now able to enjoy the sights of his new, but
temporary, home. The rolling, wooded countryside, dotted
with prosperous-looking farms, presented an unusual scene
of domestic tranquillity. One looking at it for the first time,
without knowing the human turmoil that produced it, might
have thought himself to be in the Garden of Eden. Indeed,
Lorenzo had been taught that this area was once inhabited by
the earliest patriarchs of the race, and that here, in the last
days, Adam, the Ancient of Days, would sit down in council
with those who had followed him in the prophetic line.

But Lorenzo was soon to learn that this extraordinary event
would have to await the passage of many years and a radical
change in the Missouri settlers. Although the young convert-
missionary knew of the difficulties that had befallen the Saints
in Missouri, knew of the earlier expulsion from Jackson
County with its mobbings, burnings, and pillaging, and knew
of the continuing pressure that had been exerted upon his
people by the old settlers, he was prepared neither for the
deep and persistent antagonisms, nor the murderous inten-
tions, shown toward the Latter-day Saints by the Missourians.

Moreover, he was not prepared for the dissensions and
turmoil that existed within the Church itself. Only a few
months before his arrival, the Presidency of the Church in
Zion, consisting of old-line Mormons David Whitmer, W. W.
Phelps, and John Whitmer had been "rejected" by the local
membership; later, W. W. Phelps and John Whitmer were sev-
ered from the church "until they learn to blaspheme no more
against the authorities of God, nor fleece the flock of Christ."

The principal authority who supposedly had been "blas-
phemed" was Thomas B. Marsh, then the President of the
Quorum of the Twelve Apostles, who was himself drifting

19

toward apostasy and within a year would be excommunicated. Lorenzo, whose spiritual perceptions were always acute, detected Elder Marsh's disaffection when he met him in Far West about this time. "In our conversation with him," wrote the young missionary, "our spirits and his did not intermingle, and he seemed utterly blind in relation to the condition of things and the spirit of the time."

Lorenzo's inherent poise and self-confidence were clearly evident in the way he regarded, or, more precisely, disregarded, the attacks made upon the Church and its leaders in Missouri, both from without and within. He settled down in his father's home at Adam-ondi-Ahman, purchased as part of a beautiful farm, and began the long process of convalescence from his recent illness.

Unable to perform heavy physical labor, Lorenzo had ample opportunity to meditate and pray during this important period. His introspection stirred up anxiety as he measured his character against the high standards defined in the holy scriptures. Having received impressions that his future lay in the ministry, and being a man of meticulous rectitude, he realized that if his labors were to be fruitful, his conduct had to coincide in every respect with the principles he enjoined upon others.

The transformation this awakening produced is best illustrated by an incident that occurred at the time near Adam-ondi-Ahman: "One day, to while away the slowly passing hours," he wrote later, "I took my gun with the intention of indulging in a little amusement in hunting turkeys, with which that section of the country abounded." Explaining that he had always been fascinated by guns, and that hunting had been one of his favorite pastimes in Ohio, Lorenzo went on to say, "It never occurred to my mind that it was wrong—that indulging in what was sport to me was death to them; that in shooting turkeys, squirrels, etc., I was taking life I could not give; therefore, I indulged in the murderous sport without the least compunction of conscience. But at this time a change came over me. While moving slowly forward in pursuit of something to kill, my mind was arrested with the reflection on the nature of my pursuit—that of amusing myself by giving pain and death to harmless and innocent creatures that perhaps had as much right to life and enjoyment as myself. I realized that such indulgence was without any justification, and feeling condemned, I laid my gun on my shoulder, returned home, and from that time to this have felt no inclination for that murderous amusement."

Although not clothed in the language customarily used to express it, Lorenzo here enunciated one of the fundamental principles of his adopted religion that accounted largely for the phenomenal growth in his character and spirituality over the years—the principle of repentance. He did not look at it as a restraint upon his freedom, as some do, but as an instrument of improvement. Imbued with a desire to become godlike, to be perfect, he constantly strived to narrow the gap between his conduct and character and the ideal life of Jesus Christ, whom he persistently sought to emulate. This upward reach is expressed again and again in his later sermons and writings, as shown clearly in an entry dated October 1, 1890, in the journal of Abraham H. Cannon, who reported that in a prayer offered at a meeting of the Twelve in the Gardo House, Elder Snow said "that if it was the Lord's will, we might be permitted to see [the Lord's] face even as Joseph and Oliver and Moses of old did." It comes as no surprise that one who so fervently prayed for that blessing and who bent his efforts diligently toward developing the character that would make it possible, would, as the crowning event of a long life, be favored by that personal visitation from the Savior.

Chapter Five

The Second Mission

By autumn, Lorenzo had recovered sufficiently from his illness that he felt ready to undertake another mission. Lacking means to purchase a team or to pay the cost of transportation, the eager young man and his companion, Abel Butterfield, who had been with Elder Snow during part of his first mission, left Adam-ondi-Ahman on foot, headed south for an unknown destination and for an indeterminate period of time. Except for some loose change in their pockets, they were without financial resources, and expected to subsist on the blessings of the Lord and the liberality of the people.

Although Elder Snow had recovered somewhat from his recent debilitating illness, he was hardly a well man. Indeed, members of the Snow family were so concerned about his frail health they had argued strenuously against the mission, urging him to wait until he was more fit. But Lorenzo was so imbued with a sense of evangelical responsibility, was so anxious to "build the kingdom," that he ignored the pleas of his family, whose counsel he ordinarily followed, and set out on foot with Elder Butterfield in the chill of a Missouri October. "My trust was in God," confided the faithful young missionary, "and I felt an assurance that He would give me strength and restore me to soundness of health sooner if I went forth depending on Him, than if I remained at home."

If Lorenzo had any twinges of doubt about his ability to

endure the rigors of a walking mission in his weakened condition, they would have occurred the day of his departure. At first, he was able to walk only a short distance before, exhausted, he had to stop and rest. Determined not to yield to physical weakness, however, he pushed on to the limit of his endurance each time after resting, until, at last, he "was perfectly restored." In this incident, we see the perseverance that was typical not only throughout Lorenzo's long and active life, but in the lives of all who have worn the prophetic mantle.

The two missionaries were given a blessing and wise counsel by the Patriarch, Joseph Smith, Sr., at Far West. This helped them bring their objectives into clearer focus. They decided to proselyte first in southern Missouri. Because of the violent anti-Mormon feelings that existed among the gentiles in that area, Lorenzo and his companion decided to conceal their identity and religious affiliation where to reveal them would threaten unnecessary danger and would not increase their ability to teach. "Our main object," Lorenzo wrote, "was, by giving correct information, to disabuse the minds of those we gained access to, and allay the feverish sentiment of bitterness." The methods the elders used in conducting this novel kind of proselyting was explained by Lorenzo in regard to a meeting they held in Jacksonville, Missouri. In answer to an inquiry about his "religious persuasion," Elder Snow said to the woman who had put the question, "I wish, Madam, this evening, to speak to a promiscuous congregation, embracing all classes of people, therefore, I had thought, on this particular occasion, and for this special purpose, I would beg to suppress the name of the religious denomination of which I am a minister." He later wrote, "That evening I had a large, appreciative audience, and spoke with great freedom; in fact, I seldom, if ever enjoyed greater liberty than on that occasion. What my hearers thought of me or whom they imagined I was, or whence I came, or whither I was going, I am left in ignorance to this day, as I was not required to inform any of my audience and of course was entirely reticent on this point."

Such novel proselyting was not always congenial to one with Elder Snow's penchant for candor. Moreover, it prevented the accomplishment of the very purpose of proselyting. If one did not divulge the identity of the church he represented, he could hardly baptize people into it.

The frustrated missionaries left Missouri, traveling into southern Illinois, and ultimately into northern Kentucky. While they labored in new areas without the kind of fear that had haunted them in Missouri, the results in terms of convert baptisms were not as fruitful as they had hoped. And even beyond the borders of Missouri, perhaps foreshadowing what would occur in Illinois a few years later, they now and then encountered mobocracy. While the knowledge they might be beaten, or tarred and feathered, or even killed by an angry mob was always sobering, if not terrifying, the missionaries stayed at their task with unwavering persistence. And, occasionally, a ray of humor shone through to illuminate what otherwise would have been a dreary scene. Lorenzo told of one instance when a party had gathered outside a home where he was preaching with the intention of mobbing him. "It was a very cold night," Lorenzo reported, "and after the close of the service I stood with my back to the chimney fire, with a number of others—some of whom belonged to the mob party. One of the latter persons, amid the jostling of the crowd, accidentally brought his hand in contact with one of the pockets in the shirt of my coat, which struck him with a sudden alarm on his feeling what he supposed to be, a large pistol. He immediately communicated the discovery to his affrighted coadjutors, all of whom directly withdrew, and, to their followers outside, imparted the astounding news that the 'Mormon' Elder was armed with deadly weapons. That was sufficient—the would-be outlaws abandoned their evil designs for fear of signal punishment; but the supposed pistol which caused their alarm and my protection, was my pocket Bible, a precious gift to me from the dearly beloved Patriarch, Father Joseph Smith."

Lorenzo left Kentucky in February 1839, with Northern Ohio as his destination. Ahead was a journey of five hundred miles, to be negotiated entirely on foot during the most inclement season of the year. Encountering all kinds of foul weather, snow, rain, and wind, and alternating freezes and thaws that brought in their train either hard, icy surfaces or sloshing mud, Lorenzo pushed on determinedly toward his destination. In periods of thaw, it was not uncommon to end a day's work with boots, socks, and feet dripping wet. Even if the hapless hiker was fortunate enough to have a warm fire at night, he would awaken the next morning to find his boots still clammy inside, and his stockings as stiff as, and hardly less rough than, boards. "It was a hard pull," Lorenzo recorded laconically, "but I accomplished the feat, and worn out by fatigue and exposure, I arrived among my friends in Ohio."

Elder Snow had gone to Ohio instead of returning to Missouri because he had some "unfinished business" there, and because Eliza had advised him, by letter, of the Missouri expulsion that had occurred during his absence and of the appalling conditions in Illinois. Until final decisions were made by the Church leaders as to new places of settlement, and until unequivocal calls to gather in Illinois were broadcast, Lorenzo thought it prudent to remain in an area where he had friends and relatives and was well known. However, an experience he had shortly after arriving may have caused him to question his notoriety. Calling at the home of a Smith family, with whom he had lived for a while during his first mission, he was met with blank stares of nonrecognition when he appeared at their door. It soon dawned on them, however, that their friend and brother Lorenzo Snow was concealed behind the gaunt, tattered figure who stood before them. Once recognized, however, Lorenzo was given celebrity treatment and made to feel as if the Smith residence were his own home.

Soon after, his body rebelled at the privations it had suffered during the long trek from Kentucky, sending Lorenzo to bed, where he remained for many days afflicted with a burning fever that brought him to the point of delirium. But "through the kind ministrations of my friends," he wrote, "and the blessings of God in the manifestation of his power, I soon recovered, and resumed my missionary labors."

Once recovered, Lorenzo pursued his work with his customary diligence during the summer and autumn of 1839. As he had not yet received instructions to gather with his family in Illinois, the young missionary, now thoroughly seasoned in the practice and theory of proselying, decided to find employment in Ohio to sustain him during the winter months and to enable him to continue his missionary labors during off-hours. Since all farming operations had geared down for the season, Lorenzo naturally turned to the other activity for which he had special qualifications—teaching school. Being an alumnus of Oberlin College, he doubtless had better scholastic credentials than most teachers in the vicinity, and so was welcomed as a bright new luminary in the educational firmament of Shalersville, Ohio, where he settled down for the winter.

Because of Lorenzo Snow's benign appearance and gentlemanly ways, those unacquainted with his character sometimes judge him as being devoid of competitive instincts. One who renders such a judgment will be surprised to learn that this man was endowed with a competitive drive to excel possessed by very few. This quality surfaced dramatically at Shalersville when Lorenzo took over a class of scholastic misfits and nonachievers who had been burdened with a long train of incompetent or disinterested teachers. The perceptive young missionary saw a great opportunity in this situation, where another might have seen only cause for discouragement or complaint. "Here an opportunity [was] presented for me to make a mark," he confided, "and I determined to do it, and set myself to the arduous task of arousing and instilling intellectual life into the mentally dormant brain." The means he used to achieve this end reflects another characteristic that sets Lorenzo Snow apart from most men. Wrote he, "I labored day and night to accomplish my purpose, i.e., to elevate my students to a higher standard of intellectual improvement." The sense of elation and achievement Lorenzo felt at the results of his efforts is clearly revealed in this entry: "I succeeded, and before its close, my school had attained to such a celebrity, that it was everywhere spoken of for its wonderful progress, and as having outstripped all of the neighboring schools."

We shall see this aspect of President Snow's character reflected again and again, under varied and ever-changing circumstances. In whatever context it appears, however, we shall invariably see in it his constant and aggressive reach for perfection. In his earlier years, as was true in this case, he was inclined to test his strength and to sharpen his skills in competition with others. As he matured, however, and as his perceptions and objectives became more refined, his competitiveness turned inward in a constant and intimate battle to excel his own performance.

Chapter Six

Mission to England

The young missionary, who had now added "school-teacher" to his growing list of credentials, left Ohio in the spring of 1840 for Illinois, where he arrived about the first of May. He found his family, who had undergone severe hardships in their flight from Missouri, huddled in makeshift quarters at La Harpe, a small community about thirty miles from Nauvoo. Although the Latter-day Saints were living on the edge of poverty, reeling from the blows inflicted by the mobs around Far West, Lorenzo found them with an optimistic, forward-looking spirit that was exciting and infectious. Their charismatic leader, Joseph Smith, who had survived the squalid jails and violent mobocracy of Missouri, was already projecting a vast new city to be built on a swamp in a bend of the Mississippi River, as well as a dramatic acceleration in the work of proselyting abroad in Great Britain, a work that would reap thousands of converts who would add stability and strength to the burgeoning Mormon population. Shortly after arriving in Illinois, Lorenzo was called by the Prophet to join the many other brethren who had been summoned to proselyte in England; and by May 20, only three weeks after reaching La Harpe, Elder Snow was on the way to his third mission in three years. But in the short time he was in Illinois, he enjoyed one of the most unusual experiences of his life. It occurred at the home of H. G. Sherwood, while his host was explaining the Savior's parable of the husbandman and the hired servants. As Lorenzo listened attentively, the Spirit of the Lord rested "mightily" upon him, producing a spiritual illumination that filled him "with wonder and astonishment." Of the incident he said: "I saw as clear as the sun at noonday . . . the pathway of God and man." Afterward, he formed this couplet, which succinctly expresses the profound idea revealed to him on that occasion:

As man now is, God once was:
As God now is, man may be.

So startling was this revelation and so advanced beyond anything revealed before, that for the moment Lorenzo kept it to himself, the only exception being that he confided in his brilliant sister Eliza, who, at the time, was his only real confidante in such delicate matters. Later, in England, Lorenzo took Brigham Young into his confidence, divulging the incident to him. While the Lion of the Lord showed keen interest in this revolutionary idea, he wisely advised his friend that if it were true, it had been revealed to him for his own personal blessing and use, and that he ought to "lay it upon the shelf" until such time as it might be revealed to the Prophet. After returning from England, Lorenzo mentioned the experience to Joseph Smith, who declared it to be "true gospel doctrine" and that it was a revelation from God to him. As to the ultimate effect of this revealed truth upon Lorenzo's evolving character, we may only speculate. But, judging from the persistence of his habits, from the sincerity of his beliefs, and from the high spirituality later exhibited in his character, it can be fairly assumed that the effect was powerful, profound, and pervasive. It seems clear that Lorenzo believed he was a spiritual son of Deity, and that with the blessings of his eternal parent, joined with his own unwavering obedience to heavenly principles, he might become like him.

But all this was shrouded in the uncertainty of future events as Elder Snow prepared to depart on his third mission. That he had been home only three weeks when he left seemed not to trouble him in the least. Indeed, he appeared to be in a high state of excitement and anticipation at the prospect of joining members of the Twelve, headed by Brigham Young, and scores of other missionaries who were then reaping a bounteous harvest of converts in Great Britain. It apparently made no difference to Lorenzo and the other members of this relentless corps of missionaries that conditions at the heart of the Church were in an extreme state of flux, which created some uncertainty about the precise place to which converts should gather. They pursued their work with a certain assurance that left no room for doubt or speculation. Their faith taught them that patience, diligence, and time would solve their problems. They would prevail, being the servants and agents of God, whose will would ultimately control all things in heaven and earth.

Harboring such convictions about the Church he represented, Elder Snow made the rounds of many families, living along the Mississippi River in the scattered Mormon communities whose husbands, fathers, or sons were filling missions abroad. Being aware of the needs of missionaries, he offered to take messages or correspondence with him, knowing that such direct word from loved ones at home would be appreciated more than anything else.

While doing this, he learned an important lesson about keeping proper attitudes. He asked the wife of one of the members of the Twelve, who obviously was living in grinding poverty, if he could take a message to her husband. "You see my situation," she told Lorenzo, "but tell him not to trouble, or worry in the least about me—I wish him to remain in his field of labor until honorably released." Calling at the home of another member of the Twelve, he put the same question to the wife, who, to Lorenzo's surprise and disappointment, asked him to tell her husband to come home immediately because she needed his help.

Lorenzo's reflections on these two incidents years later, against the background of what had intervened, revealed a striking example of the contrasting results of positive and negative thinking. The first wife, whose husband later became President of the Church, retained her steadfast attitude through all her days. The other wife later apostatized and was excommunicated. Although she ultimately returned to the Church, her erratic conduct and negative attitudes also misled her husband into temporary apostasy, thereby marring his otherwise flawless record and depriving him of the opportunity to render even greater service in the Church.

From La Harpe, Lorenzo traveled directly to Ohio, where he arranged a loan, at heavy interest, to finance his mission. Then followed a two-week journey from Cleveland to New York City, negotiated mostly on the intricate canal system that then served the northeast United States. Equipping himself with a blanket, a buffalo robe, and necessary provisions, Elder Snow booked deck passage on a packet ship destined for Liverpool, which then was the main English port of entry used by the nomadic Mormon missionaries.

Having had no previous exposure to the sea, Lorenzo at first seemed to have highly romantic ideas about ocean travel. All these fled at once when he boarded the cluttered and smelly little vessel that was to be his home for forty-two nauseous days. The ship passed through three violent storms, which Lorenzo described as "fearfully terrific." He marveled at the power of the sea, whose angry waves tossed the ship about as if it were driftwood. The chaos that followed seemed to be beyond his power to describe. However, he did leave this vivid word-picture of the jumbled scene below deck during one of the storms: "Now take a peek into the deck below," he wrote in a letter to an aunt, "where boxes, chests and barrels, having broken loose from their storage, are slipping and tumbling about among the women and children, whose groans and cries for help are in vain, so long as each man has all he can possibly do to take care of himself." But, the most distasteful aspect of the voyage was neither the weather nor the accommodations. It was the constant presence of the "huddled crowd of rough, uncouth people, very filthy in their appearance and habits" that he found most repugnant. Of a highly refined nature and upbringing, Lorenzo found it difficult to tolerate any uncleanliness in body, mind, or speech. And to be placed in a situation where, night and day, for almost six weeks, he was exposed to these conditions, created one of the most unpleasant experiences of his life.

Arriving at Liverpool, Elder Snow was pleased to find a thriving branch of about a hundred members. He remained there several days, during which he had the opportunity to speak at one of their evening meetings.

Taking the train to Manchester, Lorenzo "experienced inexpressible joy" in greeting several members of the Twelve and other missionaries from the United States who were laboring in that city, which then had a population in excess of 300,000. Although he remained there only ten days, Lorenzo spoke often and baptized several converts.

His first permanent field of labor in England was Birmingham, a busy industrial city of over two hundred thousand.

Here, during a three-month period, Elder Snow began to show the qualities of leadership and discipline that, in time, would elevate him to the highest levels of Church authority. His proselyting efforts had previously been conducted on an individual, somewhat unstructured, basis. Of course, he had made periodic written reports to his leaders at Church headquarters, and at the end of his mission had given an overall report and accounting to those in authority over him. But, in the day-to-day conduct of his missionary labors, he had acted independently of all others, except as he was directed by the spiritual promptings that came to him from time to time. Now, however, in England, he began to function in a more formal missionary setting under the direct supervision of mission leaders, who were able to observe in him the skills and aptitudes necessary to direct and motivate others.

In recognition of his superior accomplishments in Birmingham, Lorenzo, at a special meeting held in London in February 1841, was appointed to take the "superintendency" of the Church in London. Presiding at the meeting where these calls were made was Heber C. Kimball, the second-ranking member of the Twelve, who, four years before, had opened the door to the preaching of the gospel in the British Isles. Assisting Elder Kimball was another spiritually attuned apostle, Wilford Woodruff, who was one of the most indefatigable and productive missionaries of any era.

If, in assuming this new role, Lorenzo had recalled the terrifying experiences Joseph Smith and Heber C. Kimball had had with evil powers as they launched new efforts in God's service, he might have been humbled and sobered. When

Joseph kneeled in the grove to seek wisdom from God, an unseen evil power almost overwhelmed him. Heber was assaulted by "legions" of evil spirits the night before the first baptisms in the River Ribble near Preston.

As it was with Joseph and Heber, so it was with Lorenzo. One night in his London apartment, he was abruptly awakened by a strange clamor. To Lorenzo, "it seemed as though every piece of furniture in the room was put in motion, back and forth against each other in such terrible fury that sleep and rest were utter impossibilities." This physical commotion was accompanied by an oppressive spiritual essence that enveloped the room like a pall. The following night, this disturbance occurred again, and it continued during several successive nights. Lorenzo was harassed in this way until he decided that something had to be done. He prepared carefully for the showdown, engaging in a special fast, during the course of which he implored God fervently for spiritual strength. Then, at night, following his fast, he read aloud a chapter from the Bible, kneeled in prayer, and in an authoritative voice rebuked the evil spirits by the power of the holy priesthood and "commanded them to leave the house." Then he went to bed "and had no more disturbance."

During this period, in a letter to Elder George A. Smith of the Twelve, who was three years younger than he, and a special friend, Lorenzo confided, "I want your prayers for the powers of darkness are great in this city; and I shall soon be left alone being assisted only by those who are infants in the kingdom, and at the same time I can scarcely say that I yet have hardly arrived at the state of childhood."

Aside from the afflictions from evil spirits, which spread to others in London after the confrontation in his apartment, Lorenzo saw the main deterrent to the growth of the Church in London to be "pride and folly." Because the arrogance and self-sufficiency of the leading classes, the opinion-makers, in London had filtered down to the artisans, tradesmen, and laborers of the city, Lorenzo and his associates found their proselyting most difficult. Additional opposition came from a hostile press that generated a constant stream of abuse. But Lorenzo had learned to swim against the tide. Indeed, the opposition seemed merely to arouse his competitive instincts and to spur him on to greater proselyting efforts.

Slowly, he began to make progress, until, six months after his appointment as conference president, the membership had more than doubled. Moreover, the members reflected an optimistic, forward-looking attitude they had not had before.

As Lorenzo visited the outlying branches—Bedford, Woolwich, and others that ringed London—he took time both to preach the doctrines of the Church and to train the local leaders and members in proper procedures. Many new members brought with them into the Church false beliefs and ideas that had to be corrected. Elder Snow filled this role of mentor and director with tact and wisdom.

Two months after commencing his duties as head of the London conference, Lorenzo was privileged to attend one of the most historic meetings ever held in the Church, a special conference convened on April 6, 1841, in Manchester under the direction of Brigham Young to commemorate the eleventh anniversary of the organization of the Church. Gathered in Carpenter's hall were several hundred Church leaders and members from different parts of Great Britain. Present also were most of the missionaries then serving in the British Isles, and nine members of the Quorum of the Twelve, three of whom, Brigham Young, John Taylor, and Wilford Woodruff, would later become Presidents of the Church. Never before had a majority of the Twelve been together in one place outside the American Continent. The other members of the Twelve who were present were Parley P. Pratt, editor of the *Millennial Star;* three future counselors in the First Presidency, Heber C. Kimball, Willard Richards, and George A. Smith; Orson Hyde, who was then en route to Palestine to dedicate the Holy Land for the return of the Jews; and Orson Pratt, the brilliant young apostle, then only thirty, who would later distinguish himself as a mathematician, scientist, and gospel theorist.

The meetings held at Manchester during this conference were filled with much earnest preaching and exhortation, but they were also filled with joy and enthusiasm. At one point during the conference a large "richly ornamented cake" was blessed, cut up, and passed to the congregation of about seven hundred, while "several appropriate hymns were sung, and a powerful and general feeling of delight seemed universally to pervade the meeting." While all this was going on, Elder Parley P. Pratt, the author of many ponderous and serious writings, busied himself in composing this wry bit of verse, which was handed up to the clerk and read to the conference with mock solemnity:

When in far distant regions,
As strangers we roam.

Far away from our country,
Our friends and our home.

When sinking in sorrow,
Fresh courage we'll take.

As we think on our friends,
And remember the cake.

Elder Snow returned to his labors in London with renewed enthusiasm and resolve following the Manchester conference. He carried with him a new assignment beyond his usual duties of proselyting and administration—to raise funds for the Nauvoo Temple, the cornerstone of which had been laid that month. Lorenzo brought to this task the initiative and imagination that characterized all his assignments. He originated a series of "tea meetings" held in various homes as entertainment and fund-raisers. By this means he was able to bring his people together in a social setting, which helped to overcome some of the traditional English "reserve," and to prepare the people for the more outgoing life-style they would find in "Zion."

We are left to surmise how much money Lorenzo raised through his tea meetings. It was probably not a lot by today's standards. But, as a measurement of the faith and devotion of the people, we may be sure that the contributions were substantial.

Lorenzo's abilities grew with his authority and responsibility. During this period he wrote a well-reasoned and effective pamphlet, "The Only Way to Be Saved." Published in an edition of 5,000 copies, it was used by his missionaries in their proselyting activities. This tract reflected Lorenzo's intellectual capacity and his solid academic background. Moreover, it revealed a special knack for literary composition like that of his Sister Eliza.

Another talent that emerged during this period was Lorenzo's gift of tongues. The record contains only the barest mention of this phenomenon, a brief statement in the *Millennial Star*, given as part of the report of a conference held in Manchester in May 1842: "Elder Snow concluded his address by singing beautifully in tongues."

Another of Lorenzo's talents that emerged during his mission to Great Britain was his knack for diplomacy. This was reflected in an interview he arranged with Queen Victoria and Prince Albert, during which he presented them with specially bound copies of the Book of Mormon. It does not appear that he was in the least abashed to enter the presence of those with such wealth and cultural upbringing, nor that he manifested any greater respect or deference toward them than toward others whom he met in the course of his missionary labors. Elder Snow had an honest liking and respect for all people, though, as in the case of his steerage companions on the voyage to Liverpool, he sometimes deplored their conduct. Yet he looked upon all human beings as spiritual offspring of God, possessing inherently the seeds of perfection. In that aspect, then, he attached no more importance to the Queen and her consort than to anyone else, although he paid them the honor their royal station deserved.

The superior work Elder Snow performed in England, both as a missionary and a leader, was further recognized before his release by a call to serve as a counselor to Thomas Ward, President of the British Mission, which included England, Scotland, Ireland, and Wales, with a membership of about ten thousand. Here the budding apostle had further opportunity to hone his skills in leadership and diplomacy, being responsible, under the direction of his president, to train and motivate a large corps of missionaries.

At this time, new members were admonished to migrate to the United States and to gather at places designated by the head of the Church. To facilitate the movement of large numbers of Saints, Brigham Young and the Twelve had organized a system of transportation that later evolved into the Perpetual Emigration Fund. In effect, the Church became a vast travel agency, chartering its own ships and other means of transportation as it moved thousands of converts from abroad to the burgeoning Mormon communities in the United States. When it came time for Elder Snow's release, he was placed in charge of one of these chartered ships, the *Swanton*, which left Liverpool in January 1843 with New Orleans as its destination. Aboard were 250 Latter-day Saints, mostly recent converts, who were soon organized into a disciplined, tightly knit group by their leader, who was by now a seasoned administrator. Accustomed to the motley, diverse, and sometimes unruly passengers that usually sailed with him, the *Swanton's* master, Captain Davenport, was almost flabbergasted by the company of Mormons Lorenzo Snow led aboard, who were clean, orderly, and happy, who prayed and sang, who studied and worshiped regularly, and who engaged in well-planned and enjoyable recreations. They must have seemed almost unreal to the worldly crew, whose long experience with sullen and disgruntled passengers had ill-prepared them for what they now saw.

But the surprise of the *Swanton's* captain and crew was heightened by a spiritual occurrence during the voyage. The ship's favorite steward, a young German lad, had contracted an unknown illness that would not respond to medical treatment. It became progressively worse until his friends feared for his life. Convinced the steward was dying, the captain invited the crew to pay their last respects as he began to prepare for a burial at sea. But Sister Martin, a faithful Saint, learned of the steward's condition and urged the captain to allow Elder Snow to administer to him. Unwilling to do so at first because he felt the boy was beyond human help, Mr. Davenport at last gave in and permitted the Mormon leader to bless the patient, though he had no confidence it would help. "Mr. Snow, it is too late," said the captain in tears as Lorenzo entered the cabin where the boy lay. "He is breathing his last." Hardly acknowledging the presence of anyone except the young steward, Elder Snow walked directly to his bed, looked at him meditatively for a while, as if engaged in silent prayer, and then, after laying hands upon his head, prayed in a clear authoritative voice, rebuking the disease and, in the name of Jesus Christ, commanding the boy to be made whole. Not long after, the steward stirred, arose, and was up and about, expressing amazement and gratitude for his sudden and miraculous recovery.

The effect of this incident upon the officers and crew was immediate and profound. From that moment, they began to give a more attentive ear to the message these unusual passengers were anxious to share, and watched their conduct to see if it measured up to their professions of faith. Becoming convinced of the truthfulness of the gospel, several of the officers and crew, including the first mate, were baptized on February 26, 1843, after the *Swanton* docked at New Orleans.

At this famous Louisiana port, the voyagers transferred to a river steamer, the *Amaranth*, which chugged its way slowly up the Mississippi, arriving at the Nauvoo dock on April 12, 1843. Being the first boat of the year to bring a company of convert-immigrants, the *Amaranth* drew a large crowd of spectators who thronged the landing as the cumbersome paddle-wheel craft maneuvered into its berth. Among these were the Prophet Joseph Smith and other leading brethren, who went out of their way to greet the newcomers and bid them welcome to "Zion." Also present were members of Lorenzo's family, including his sister Eliza, who carried a secret deep in her heart that she must have wanted to divulge to her admired brother, but did not feel at liberty to reveal.

Chapter Seven

The Nauvoo Enigma

Three years abroad had worked mighty changes in Lorenzo Snow. Dressed neatly in his British clothes, the young elder, who had celebrated his twenty-ninth birthday aboard the steamer as it wended its way up the river, stepped off the gangplank amidst a flurry of greetings from family and friends and assisted the members of his company as they disembarked from the *Amaranth*. He had cast out evil spirits, healed the sick, and baptized many new members of the Church. He had learned the principles of administration, and had become a giant spiritually, in spite of his small stature (he stood only five feet six inches tall and weighed one hundred and forty pounds). Elder Snow was now a man to be reckoned with in any society, and especially the Mormon society he found in Nauvoo.

To say he must have been surprised at what he found in the "City of Joseph" would be a gross understatement. The drab little community, once named Commerce, had evolved into the magnificent city "Nauvoo the Beautiful." Instead of the few scruffy cabins that had comprised Commerce, Lorenzo found hundreds of modern homes, either completed or in various stages of construction, featuring most of the popular architectural styles of the day. Through intelligent drainage, the marsh lands near the river had been largely reclaimed, and with their disappearance, the rate of illness in the city had dropped significantly. Business and industry had grown with the influx of newcomers. The city also boasted a university, a military legion second to none in what was then the western United States, and a charter from the Illinois legislature so broad in its scope as to make Nauvoo an almost autonomous political entity. And, crowning the hill above the bottomlands rose the gleaming shell of the great temple that ultimately would be the city's most distinctive edifice.

But these changes were less significant than the subtle change that had taken place in the lives of the people. This could be traced, in part, to a new spiritual dimension that had been added to the Church with the introduction of the doctrine of vicarious work for the dead. But there was something else astir in the city's religious and social life, never spoken of openly in Church gatherings, although whispered about furtively in private conversations and shouted loudly and distortedly by enemies and apostates. Lorenzo had received hints of this in correspondence or in conversations with missionaries newly arrived in England from the United States, where veiled references were made to apostate charges that the leading elders of the Church had begun to take "spiritual wives." More important to him, however, Elder Snow had received inner impressions that the order of domestic life lived by the ancient patriarchs was to be reinstituted in his day. But, having received no official word about the matter from those in authority, he had filed it away in memory in much the same way that he had laid aside, for the time being, his amazing revelation about man's potentialities for godhood.

Once the hellos had been said, the reports of his missionary service had been given, and arrangements for housing had been made, Lorenzo began to adjust to the less hectic life in Nauvoo. In doing so, he encountered a secretive, noncommittal attitude among the members that was annoying and quite baffling. He sensed that this was related to the "spiritual wife" rumors. He began to make oblique inquiries, which were met either with stony silence or adroit evasions. To his surprise, he received the same arms-length treatment from Eliza, for whom he had always had a special affinity, and who, up until the time of his departure for England, had always been his most trusted mentor and confidante. Meeting with such an unexpected rebuff, Lorenzo began to withdraw into his own shell of secrecy. A memoir written by Eliza provides insight into the tensions between her and her brother: "I was forced, by his cool and distant manner," she wrote, "to feel that he was growing jealous of my sisterly confidence—that I could not confide in his brotherly integrity. I could not endure this—something must be done." The remedy was to ask her husband, Joseph Smith, to whom she had been secretly married as a plural wife, "to open the subject" to her brother. Not long afterward, Joseph took Lorenzo to an isolated spot on the bank of the Mississippi River and explained to him the doctrine of plural wives. Reporting the results of that meeting to Eliza, Joseph told her that Lorenzo's mind "had been previously enlightened on the subject."

Despite the spiritual impressions Lorenzo had previously received, when this doctrine was presented to him he experienced the same reticence that others had shown when it was first revealed to them. Indeed, Joseph Smith himself had resisted the doctrine with as much stubbornness as anyone. On the occasion of their riverside chat, he confided to Lorenzo his initial repugnance when the doctrine was first revealed to him in the early 1830s as he and Sidney Rigdon prayed about the ancient patriarchs who lived in polygamy. The Prophet carried the revelation in memory for a decade before it was finally reduced to writing in July 1843, just a few weeks after his visit with Lorenzo.

It is not surprising that Joseph, Lorenzo, and the other leading brethren at first reacted negatively to the doctrine. Most of them had been raised under the strict discipline of puritan morality. The idea of having more than one wife had never even occurred to them; and had it occurred, they doubtless would have repented the thought at once. But Joseph "knew the voice of God," Eliza recorded of his intimate visit with her brother, "knew the commandment of the Almighty to him was to go forward—to set the example, and establish Celestial plural marriage." Continuing, Eliza recorded the testimony Joseph Smith bore to Lorenzo by the river: "He knew that he had not only his own prejudices and pre-possessions to combat and to overcome, but those of the whole Christian world stared him in the face; but God, who is above all, had given the commandment, and He must be obeyed. Yet the Prophet hesitated and deferred from time to time, until an angel of God stood by him with a drawn sword, and told him that, unless he moved forward and established plural marriage, his Priesthood would be taken from him and he should be destroyed."

Lorenzo's hesitancy in embracing the new doctrine is shown in the fact that he did not marry for almost two years after Joseph explained it to him. But, as we shall see, when at last he took the step, he did so with a dramatic flourish that removed any doubt about his whole-hearted acceptance of it.

In the meantime, Elder Snow took his place in the new Mormon society, rendering the service he was able to perform with his customary diligence and flair. He was appointed as a captain in the Nauvoo Legion, reviving momentarily the dormant spirit that had once fired his ambition for a military career. He raised and trained his own company, for which he was complimented by the Prophet Joseph Smith (lieutenant general of the Nauvoo Legion) for its "fine martial appearance and good military maneuvering." He also contracted to teach school at Lima, a small community lying thirty miles south of Nauvoo, inhabited mostly by a claque of unfriendly gentiles. The school was made up of a motley collection of "rough, ungovernable and rowdy boys," most of whom were larger than their new teacher and took special pride in a reputation for insubordination. Being apprised beforehand that this group of incorrigibles had whipped and demoralized several of his predecessors, Lorenzo knew, as Eliza put it, that he "was taking an elephant by the bitts" in accepting this employment. But he needed the money and was prepared to face up to the challenge. Realizing he could not control his new charges by physical force, even had he been of a mind to do so, Lorenzo relied upon his superior mental and spiritual powers to dominate them. With keen psychological insight, he appealed to their vanity by the use of lavish, though honest, praise; to their manhood by subtly indicating the cowardice in gang intimidation; and to their aspirations by adroitly feeding them the Mormon doctrine of their high status as spiritual offspring of God. The changes in the attitudes and accomplishments of his students were not, of course, instantaneous. But slowly and inexorably Lorenzo changed them from roughnecks into genuine students whose intellectual curiosity had been kindled for the first time. The parents could not fail to see the transformation, and, despite their reluctance to acknowledge such ability and achievement in a Mormon, expressed thanks to Lorenzo for having "civilized, moralized and mentalized" their children.

These employments did not occupy all of Elder Snow's time, and so, during his off-hours, he continued to pursue what, to him, was his most important task—to teach others the principles of the gospel and to inspire them toward perfection. We are indebted to Eliza for providing us with a window into Lorenzo's teaching methods and into his intellectual and spiritual development during this period. The following excerpt, from detailed notes made of a talk he delivered as 1843 drew to a close, has special significance: "He forcibly suggested the utility of suppressing all anxiety with respect to the future, saying 'How illy were we qualified one year ago to pass through the scenes through which we have been led with success. From which, let us realize the folly of an over-anxiety to pry into scenes that are lying before us, inasmuch as God will prepare the way by a gradual process, step by step, and leading us forward in a manner that will prove easy, as we pass along, but which, if presented to our view at once, would seem insurmountable.' "

These words typify Lorenzo's faith and patience. He learned early that it is fruitless to worry about or to fear anything. He seemed to take everything in stride, to be poised and deliberate in his approach to any task, to accept with equanimity the outcome of any enterprise. Results appeared to be a matter of indifference to him, the critical thing being whether his performance measured up to the spiritual standards that guided his actions. We may read or infer all this from his correspondence and sermons. The following excerpt from a letter written to his cousin Edwin in January 1844, is revealing: "It is still, and always has been, my grand aim to do right, to keep a clear conscience, enjoy myself, fearing nothing. When a course of duty presents itself, to enter upon it, regardless of consequences or dangers."

Chapter Eight

Campaign and Martyrdom

Although his habitual faith would not entertain feelings of fear or worry, Lorenzo faced the year 1844 with anticipation, an alloy of excitement and foreboding. The rumblings touched off by the secret introduction of polygamy had become progressively more violent and ominous. The Prophet's enemies and detractors were ever more shrill and unreasoning in their harassments and more determined in their efforts to silence him, by legal or illegal means. Amid the fury of these condemnations, the voice of the Mormons pleading for understanding and redress for the wrongs that had been heaped upon them was either muffled by the attacks of their enemies or fell upon deaf ears. A direct appeal for help to President Martin Van Buren, for example, had been rejected with callous indifference, and Congress agreed that any relief must come from the hands of those who had driven and persecuted them. Finding every other avenue of relief barred, and faced with the loss of his sanctuary in Nauvoo through the threatened revocation of its charter, Joseph Smith took tentative steps toward a migration to the Rocky Mountains, where, as he confided to friends, the Mormons could "build a city in a day, and have a government of [their] own." Seeking this objective, the Prophet directed that an exploratory party be sent west to search out a place of settlement. Lorenzo was called as a member of this party, but the call was frustrated by more urgent events. In 1843, Joseph

Smith had written to all of the presidential candidates, posing stiff questions to learn whether the Mormons could expect help were the candidates to be elected. Receiving either non-committal responses, or no responses at all, Joseph decided on a course of action that surprised friend and foe alike—he announced himself as a candidate for the presidency of the United States! With typical vigor and precision, the Prophet and his aides organized a campaign that was to see Mormon elders sent into every state in the union. Lorenzo headed the campaign in his native Ohio. There he prepared a pamphlet setting out Joseph's novel platform and arranged for the printing and distribution of several thousand copies. While Elder Snow, like most of his coworkers, did not entertain a serious belief that his candidate could be elected, he nevertheless campaigned vigorously. The objective was actually three-pronged: to plant ideas about government that would later grow into beneficial policies, to put the plight of the Mormons before the public in a favorable light, and to expound the principles of Mormonism.

While campaigning, Lorenzo received the shattering news of the martyrdom of the Prophet and his brother Hyrum. At the time, he was working near Cincinnati. He immediately traveled there and found Amasa Lyman, a member of the Twelve, who had recently been in Nauvoo and who briefed him on the details of the tragedy. In addition to a momentary concern about the effect of this incident upon the Church, Lorenzo suffered a great personal loss in the murder of Joseph and Hyrum, who had been his exemplars and teachers. He also realized the devastating effect the martyrdom would have upon Eliza, who wrote afterward:

> But, two so wise, so virtuous and so good,
> Before on earth, at once, never stood.

However, Elder Snow was too well-grounded in the spiritual roots and the doctrines of the Church to entertain permanent doubts about the capacity or right of others to carry on the work. He disdained the superficial predictions of critics that Joseph's martydom sounded the death knell of Mormonism.

So, once the initial shock had subsided, Elder Snow's thoughts turned toward Nauvoo, where he would be needed to help the Twelve and to console his sister. After winding down his affairs in Cincinnati, he traveled to Nauvoo by horse and buggy, stopping briefly in Kirtland to transact some business.

Lorenzo's route also took him through Carthage, where the bloody martyrdom had occurred. There he fell under a temporary mood of gloom and despondency as he reflected upon the tragic event that had robbed the Church of its two most powerful and able leaders. He commented later on the spirit of "destruction, mobocracy and murder" that seemed to pervade not only Carthage, but the entire area surrounding it. Since he carried several hundred dollars with him and by now was well known as a leading member of the Mormon community, he also became apprehensive about his own safety, so he hurried toward Nauvoo where he expected to find safety among his family and friends.

Not long after leaving Carthage, as he approached the summit of a long hill, he saw in the early dawn about a dozen mounted men, whose rough appearance was accentuated by the guns and bowie knives they openly carried. Alone and unarmed, Lorenzo's only weapons of defense were faith and his unflappable poise and resourcefulness. Suppressing his fear, the traveler did not alter the pace of his team nor make any sign of recognition of the horsemen until he had drawn near to them. At that moment, his buggy lurched violently as its wheels struck a large stone in the roadway. Without premeditation, Lorenzo angrily turned to the horsemen and uttered a sentence whose tone and content would have stunned anyone who ever knew Lorenzo Snow: "Boys," he said loudly, "why the hell don't you repair this road?" This was sufficient to convince the horsemen that the lone traveler was not one of the despised Mormons. "He is all right," growled one of them, "let him pass."

This unusual incident says as much for the Mormon reputation for gentility as it does for Elder Snow's poise under pressure.

Chapter Nine

Marriage and Exodus

T he scene that greeted Lorenzo upon his arrival in
Nauvoo was not as chaotic or stressful as one might
have imagined. Although the city was still tinged
with tragedy and mourning, there was also an optimistic expectancy that would have surprised a stranger. Once
the martyrs had been laid to rest and once the sensitive issue
of succession had been resolved in favor of the Twelve, with
the powerful Brigham Young at their head, the work Joseph
had commenced was resumed.

One important concern was the completion of the temple.
Lorenzo joined enthusiastically to contribute his slender
means and his labor to complete this beautiful building. He
was acutely aware that a principal ordinance to be performed
in the temple was the sealing of husbands to wives in an eternal union. Given his total commitment to the Church and its
doctrines, the counsel he had received from the Prophet
Joseph Smith about polygamy, and his advancing age, we
may be sure that as the temple neared completion Lorenzo became increasingly conscious of the need to marry. The depth
of his feelings may be gauged by the fact that in 1845, at age
thirty-one, he was sealed to four women in the Nauvoo temple: Mary Adaline Goddard (his cousin, who had three sons
by a former marriage, Hyrum, Orville, and Jacob); Charlotte
Squires; Sarah Ann Prichard; and Harriet Amelia Squires.
When the new husband accompanied his wives to the altar,

one of the temple officiators, impressed by the dignified appearance of this unusual quintet, was heard to comment: "And his train filled the temple."

On the face of things, Lorenzo seems to have bridged the gulf between celibacy and family life with hardly a break in his stride. Much of the credit for this must be given to his wives, whom Eliza described as "stately appearing ladies." These able women were fired with the same convictions and zeal that burned with such intensity in the heart of their husband. And they shared with him the goal of exaltation, the door to which had been opened for them by the sacred ordinances performed in the temple.

If either Lorenzo or his wives thought that the road leading to their objective would suddenly become smooth and straight, they were jolted out of that misconception within a few months after receiving their blessings in the temple. As winter descended upon Nauvoo at the close of 1845, it became increasingly apparent that the Mormon exodus, originally planned for the spring of 1846, would have to be accelerated. Spurious charges of counterfeiting brought against Brigham Young and other leaders of the Church, and disturbing reports that the government was sending a military force up the Mississippi to confront the Latter-day Saints, caused the change in plans. So, instead of an orderly and more leisurely departure in the spring, the Saints were forced to cross the Mississippi in the dead of winter and to plunge westward toward the mountains in search of a haven from persecution.

When the Twelve sounded the call for the exodus, Lorenzo and his family responded promptly. This was not done, however, without some misgivings, especially on the part of the wives, who had to leave their comfortable homes. All the clothes and furnishings it was feasible to take, together with a tent and foodstuffs, were stowed in two wagons Lorenzo had acquired. With pots and pans and other miscellaneous gear hanging on the exterior of the wagons, and with the family cow tethered behind, the Snows set out on the great adventure that would ultimately take them to the high mountain country in Utah.

They crossed the Mississippi on February 12, 1846, and

traveled first to Sugar Creek, several miles west of the river. Here Brigham Young organized the Saints along military lines into units of 100 families each, with subdivisions of "fiftys" and "tens." Lorenzo was made captain of ten families, including the families of Parley P. Pratt and Orson Pratt, members of the Twelve.

By the latter part of April, the struggling Saints, who through trial and adversity were earning the title "Pioneers," had reached a point about 145 miles west of Nauvoo. There a community, a way station, named Garden Grove, was established. The Saints erected temporary buildings and planted over seven hundred acres in grain and other crops for the use of the few families who remained there and for the thousands of others who were behind them on the trail.

By mid-May, the Mormons reached the middle fork of the Grand River, some twenty-seven miles west of Garden Grove, where another temporary community, Mount Pisgah, was established.

Soon after his company arrived at Pisgah, Elder Snow became gravely ill from a combination of fatigue, malnutrition, and poor hygiene. His high fever produced a delirium that lasted for several days, during which the patient was oblivious to everything around him. Almost despairing of his life, Lorenzo's family consented to a remedy which, though effective, our modern medical skills would surely deplore. "Elder Phineas Richards, the father of apostle F. D. Richards," Lorenzo wrote, "assisted by other kind brethren, took me from my bed, wrapped in a sheet—placed me in a carriage, drove to a stream of water, and baptized me in the name of the Lord, for my recovery." The blessing of the priesthood and the invigorating effect of the cold water produced a miraculous result. "The fever immediately abated," Elder Snow confided, "and through kind, unwearied nursing and attention, by my faithful, loving wives, and my dear sister, E.R.S. Smith, aided and sanctified through the power and blessing of God, I was delivered from suffering and returned to health." This almost fatal illness seems to have built up an immunity in Elder Snow that was to carry him unaffected through a veritable epidemic of disease that was to plague Mount Pisgah during the months ahead.

The first presiding officer at Pisgah was Elder William Huntington, whose counselors were Ezra T. Benson and Charles C. Rich. These energetic men supervised the establishment of a large temporary community and the cultivation of several thousand acres of land. Within a few months, however, Elder Benson was called to the Twelve by President Brigham Young, and Elder Huntington was taken in death, a victim of overwork and disease. After his death, Elder Rich succeeded him for a short time and, in turn, was succeeded by Lorenzo Snow.

He had not been in office long before Pisgah began to hum with an industrious purposefulness it had not known before. Committees organized for every imaginable purpose began to proliferate—committees to repair broken wagons and farming implements, committees to manufacture furniture and household accessories for sale in the nearby Gentile communities, and committees to solicit temporary employment for the residents of Pisgah. Moreover, the new leader looked beyond the horizons of opportunities in Iowa and sent two brethren back to his native Ohio to seek financial aid from non-Mormon friends and sympathizers. This resourceful effort garnered a fund of $600, a significant amount for that time and place.

Wisely assessing that the Saints required periodic relief from the pressures that weighed heavily upon them, Elder Snow encouraged frequent religious gatherings and devised a host of recreational activities for his people. One of the most novel and creative of these was a theatrical, staged in Elder Snow's "humble family mansion" (a fifteen-by-thirty-foot log cabin with dirt roof and floor) that included "appropriate songs, recitations, toasts, conundrums [riddles], exhortations, etc." To add a touch of elegance to the rustic surroundings, the unfinished walls of the cabin were draped with sheets and the dirt floor was strewn with clean straw. Special lighting from candles placed in hollowed-out turnips cast a mellow glow over the happy proceedings.

The Saints at Pisgah needed these and other diversions to

help mask the specters of sickness, poverty, and death that constantly hovered over the community. Here on the cutting edge of civilization, life was arduous and raw. The unpredictable fluctuations in the weather; malnutrition; drafty, makeshift buildings; and poor hygiene produced a whole compendium of illnesses. Respiratory ailments were the most common and the most deadly, taking off scores of Latter-day Saints. Pisgah's cemetery began to fill rapidly as young and old alike fell prey to the grim reaper, who was relentless and impartial in targeting his victims.

Even the family of the presiding officer at Mount Pisgah did not escape. At first elevated to heights of joy when his wives Charlotte, Adaline, and Sarah Ann gave birth to baby daughters, Lorenzo was plunged into despair when little Leonora, Charlotte's baby, died. This deceased infant was named after Elder Snow's eldest sister, Leonora, while the two surviving daughters born at Pisgah were named Rosetta and Eliza, after his mother and another sister.

With four wives and five children to provide for, in an economy that never rose above the poverty level, Lorenzo's meager resources were never sufficient to fill the needs of his growing family. In these circumstances, we can understand why, during the winter of 1847-48, the death of the Snow's cow was mourned as if she were human. This tragedy was compounded not long after when one of Lorenzo's oxen strayed away while grazing and drowned in the river.

The travail and woe of the preceding winter were muted somewhat when, in the early spring of 1848, Elder Snow was called by Brigham Young to move on to the Salt Lake Valley. Assembling his family and belongings, he traveled along the well-marked trail to Council Bluffs, forded the Missouri, and moved thence to the Mormon staging area at the crossing of the Elkhorn River, familiarly referred to by the Saints as "the Horn." There Lorenzo was appointed the captain of a hundred families, whom he was to lead to the Promised Land. Little time was lost in making final preparations for the strenuous journey that lay ahead, the hazards of which had been greatly minimized by the pioneering companies that had blazed the trail in the preceding year.

In the midst of his busy preparations, overseeing not only the organization and loading of his own gear, but assisting, where necessary, the 321 people under his charge, Elder Snow married still another wife, Eleanor Houtz, who was once re- ferred to as "the belle of Pisgah." The addition of this fifth wife to his household raised its number to ten.

The departure of Elder Snow's company from the Horn can hardly be imagined today. His company included a train of ninety-nine wagons laden with food, clothing, furniture, and utensils, each with three or more passengers. They took 388 oxen, 188 cows, 158 chickens, 139 sheep, 38 loose cattle, 25 pigs, 20 horses, 3 mules, 26 dogs, 10 cats, and 2 doves. One can picture this massive conglomeration of humans, beasts, fowl, and wagonry making its tortuous way along the Mormon trail north of the Platte River in a cloud of dust from which comes the creaking of the wagons, the rattling of the pots and pans, the lowing of the cattle, the grunting of the pigs, the gee-haws of the teamsters, the barking of the dogs, the cackling of the chickens, and the excited voices of the children, all an- nouncing the commencement of a great adventure.

Armed with maps and instructions, the travelers watched intently for each new landmark to determine how far they had progressed and the distance remaining to their destination. Chimney Rock, Fort John (later Fort Laramie), the last cross- ing of the Platte, Independence Rock, the Green River, and Jim Bridger's Fort were some of the interesting signposts that broke the monotony of their journey, providing interesting topics of conversation for days before and after the company passed them. In between, the travelers were fascinated by the mileage and time markers William Clayton had thoughtfully left along the way as he accompanied the Pioneer Company in 1847.

All in all, the journey to the Salt Lake Valley was a pleasant interlude for Lorenzo and his family. They had ample food; the weather was good; the trail was well-marked and in satisfac- tory condition, judged by the standards of the day; the Indians were friendly; and, for the most part, the numerous other travelers they encountered were agreeable and helpful. These favorable conditions removed much of the tension Elder

Snow had labored under since his stressful departure from Nauvoo. And the long peaceful days on the trail, unburdened by any cares except the occasional fording of a swift stream, the momentary alarm at the approach of a band of Indians, or news of strayed children or animals, afforded a welcome opportunity to visit unhurriedly with family and friends, to reflect on the past and ponder the future.

At the successful conclusion of his trip to the mountains, he wrote, "I managed to discharge my obligations as captain of my hundred very satisfactorily, for which I felt truly grateful to the Lord."

Chapter Ten

Member of the Twelve

L orenzo's company emerged from the narrow confines of Emigration Canyon, east of the Salt Lake Valley, to gaze upon an awesome sight that others who had seen it had vainly tried to describe in conversations at the Horn. The floor of the valley, marked at irregular intervals by the many streams that flowed from the surrounding canyons, was still covered by the lush grasses, now turning brown in the late September sun, that had so amazed the Pioneer Company, grasses that stood well above a horse's belly. Shimmering in the sun, far to the northwest, lay the fabled Great Salt Lake, whose buoyant waters caused swimmers to float, corklike, on its briny surface. Sandwiching the open expanse were the towering peaks of the Oquirrh Mountains to the west and the Wasatch Mountains to the east, whose rugged canyons Lorenzo's hundred had just negotiated. And, off to the right, protruding like a round turret high above the valley floor, stood the peak where, the preceding summer, Brigham Young, and his brethren, had symbolically raised an ensign to the nations, an ensign that summoned the world to join the Saints where they intended to fulfill Isaiah's ancient prediction about establishing "the mountain of the Lord's house . . . in the top of the mountains."

Lorenzo and his family temporarily settled into the "old fort," which was the first building project undertaken by the 1847 pioneers. Later, they occupied a separate cabin near the fort, and still later, Elder Snow built a new cabin similar in style and size to the one his family occupied at Mount Pisgah. Ultimately, his main residence in Salt Lake City was a gracious two-story home located at South Temple and Third East streets.

By the time of his arrival in Salt Lake Valley, Lorenzo Snow was an experienced, skilled, and dependable leader. His loyalty was unquestioned, as were the depth and sincerity of his commitment to the teachings of his Church. All these qualities in his character, and many more, had been observed over the years by those who presided over him, which had caused some of his family and friends to speculate privately about the possibility of his being called to the leading councils of the Church.

After December 27, 1847, the First Presidency was reorganized, thereby creating three vacancies in the Quorum of the Twelve Apostles. Still a fourth vacancy occurred with the excommunication of Lyman Wight on December 3, 1848. That the well-meaning, but thoughtless, predictions of those close to Lorenzo had not aroused his aspirations is shown by the fact that when he was invited to meet with the First Presidency on February 12, 1849, he had no idea what was afoot. Indeed, as he walked to the home of George B. Wallace in the old fort where the meeting was being held, he wondered whether he was being summoned "to answer some unsuspected charge or other." At the Wallace residence, he found not only the First Presidency, Brigham Young, Heber C. Kimball, and Willard Richards, but also Parley P. Pratt and John Taylor of the Twelve. To his "great surprise," instead of being chastised or admonished, he was called to fill one of the vacancies in the Quorum of the Twelve, and was promptly ordained and set apart by these brethren. On the same day, Charles C. Rich, Erastus Snow, and Franklin D. Richards were called to fill the other vacancies in the Twelve.

Lorenzo Snow had progressed one step at a time to the eminence of his new calling. The following excerpt from a talk delivered early in his role as an apostle provides this revealing glimpse into how he built his character: "We have to do what is required," he declared to an audience assembled in the old tabernacle. "But it is a warfare, and we have to live so that we can be approbated in our doings. We have to look at things calmly, cooly, seriously, and firmly, and to live in a way to get righteousness incorporated in our systems. We are placed under certain regulations, certain restrictions, that we may get the notion of acting from practice."

The order and discipline in Lorenzo Snow's life, the meticulous attention to detail the above statement suggests, equipped him admirably for the first major assignment he received as a new member of the Twelve. Ever conscious of the value of pageantry to motivate and to instruct his people, Brigham Young sought to dramatize the accomplishments and challenges of the Saints by staging a spectacular celebration to commemorate the second anniversary of their arrival in the Salt Lake Valley. Perhaps knowing of the imaginative theatricals and socials Lorenzo had organized at Mount Pisgah, Brigham appointed him to supervise the second Pioneer Day celebration.

President Young must have been impressed with the young apostle's arrangements. The Saints in Salt Lake City were aroused from slumber early on the morning of July 24, 1849, by the firing of a cannon manned by a proud corps from the Nauvoo Legion. Following this attention-getter, the Pitts Brass Band paraded through the principal streets of the city, "playing martial airs." According to the elegant prose of Eliza R. Snow's account of the affair, the band rode in "a gaily decorated omnibus, with prancing steeds, and with banners flying." Confident that everyone was now awake, the band and its escort proceeded to the bowery, where an enormous American flag was hoisted to a 104-foot liberty pole. This ceremony was accompanied by the firing of a rifle salute, the ringing of the Nauvoo bell, and more "stirring" renditions by the band.

By now it was 8:00 A.M., and time for the Saints to take their places in the Bowery, where they were seated by wards, each having banners with distinctive inscriptions.

All this, however, was mere prelude to the formation of an escort to summon President Young and accompany him to the Bowery. At its head was the grand marshal on horseback, attired in full military uniform, followed by the brass band; twelve bishops carrying their ward banners; twenty-four young men (one of whom carried a banner inscribed, "The Lion of the Lord") dressed alike in white pants and black coats, with white scarves on their right shoulders, sheathed swords at their sides, and coronets on their heads, carrying copies of the Declaration of Independence and the Constitution of the United States; and twenty-four young women (one of whom carried a banner inscribed, "Hail to our Captain") in white dresses with blue scarves on their right shoulders and wreaths of white roses on their heads, carrying copies of the Book of Mormon and the Bible. Then came members of the Twelve and twenty-four men carrying staffs painted red, mounted by white ribbons. One these men carried an American flag inscribed, "Liberty or Death."

After adding President Young to its entourage, the escort returned to the Bowery for a program featuring speeches and poems with a patriotic theme, lively music, public devotions, and laudatory remarks about the prophet, Brigham Young. Afterward, thousands were served at a banquet, including a number of "gentile emigrants" and "threescore of Indians."

Aside from the enjoyment this celebration gave the Saints, as well as the concepts of duty to God, loyalty to country, and appreciation for the fortitude of the pioneers it inculcated, this pageantry, devised by Lorenzo Snow, taught a vital lesson—that joy comes from the pursuit of excellence, a lesson Lorenzo was to teach throughout his apostolic career.

Only a few months after staging this celebration, Lorenzo was called by the First Presidency to perform another service for which he was specially qualified through experience and temperament—to establish a formal organization to generate funds with which to transport indigent Mormons to their new home in the mountains. Before the exodus, at a special meeting in the Nauvoo Temple, the Saints had entered into a solemn covenant that they would not "cease [their] exertions" until they had "brought the poor to the Salt Lake Valley." So, at the general conference in October 1849, Heber C. Kimball, acting for the First Presidency, presented this proposition to the conference: "Shall we fulfill this covenant, or shall we not?" When the vote was unanimous in the affirmative, a committee was appointed for that purpose. Lorenzo Snow was the key member of this group that included only one other member of the Twelve, Franklin D. Richards, who, significantly, had assisted Lorenzo in planning the July 24 extravaganza. These two aggressive young apostles, assisted by John S. Fullmer, Willard Snow, and John D. Lee, immediately undertook a fund-raising campaign.

Barely two years in the valley, and under the pressures of building a whole new community, the pioneers seemed already taxed to the limit of their endurance and resources. But Lorenzo and the brethren associated with him were to find that people of faith often perform beyond the limits of normal human capacity, and, in doing so, achieve results and reap benefits that border on the miraculous.

Of the stories of faith and sacrifice Elder Snow gleaned from his rather brief experience with the Perpetual Emigration Fund, none was more touching to him than that of a poverty-stricken convert from abroad who insisted on giving his only cow to the cause. To him it was a sign of appreciation for the incalculable blessings that had resulted from his membership in the Church.

The committee raised five thousand dollars during its first year. And its foundations were greatly strengthened in 1850 when the fund was incorporated under the laws of the provincial government of the State of Deseret. From this small and tentative beginning, the Perpetual Emigration Fund generated funds of about three-and-a-half million dollars during the next thirty years, providing assistance to approximately forty thousand people to emigrate to Utah.

Chapter Eleven

Mission to Italy

A t the same general conference in which the Perpetual Emigration Fund was created, President Brigham Young called three members of the Twelve to open new missions abroad. Elder John Taylor was called to France, Elder Erastus Snow to Scandinavia, and Lorenzo Snow to Italy. At the same time, Elder Franklin D. Richards was called to preside over the already-established European Mission. That President Young was willing to part with four men of such ability, whose leadership skills were much needed, attests to the predominant emphasis of the Church leaders upon proselyting.

Joseph Toronto, whose ancestral roots extended into Italy, was assigned as Lorenzo's companion. The pair left Salt Lake City in the latter part of October 1849 with a large group of missionaries who were either accompanying the other three apostles or were headed for other fields of labor in the United States.

Traveling light, without furniture, freight, flocks, or family to impede them, Lorenzo and his companions made good time in negotiating the plains and badlands of Wyoming and Nebraska. The only stressful incident that occurred was a threatened attack by a band of two hundred mounted Indians, daubed with war paint and heavily armed, who thundered toward the elders' train as if to attack it, and who, as if moved by an unseen hand, dispersed moments before reaching it.

Lorenzo saw in this incident clear evidence of the Lord's protection of his servants, particularly over his special witnesses.

Finding the Missouri River frozen over, the missionaries crossed it on the ice and were ushered into the Mormon community of Kanesville to the accompaniment of singing and shouting, punctuated by the intermittent roar of a cannon fired in their honor.

The frigid and uncomfortable journey across the prairies of Iowa was enlivened for Lorenzo by the nostalgic, and not always pleasant, memories evoked as he renewed acquaintances at Pisgah and Garden Grove and encountered familiar landmarks along the trail.

The sight of Nauvoo must have made Lorenzo heartsick. The burned-out temple, the deteriorating homes, and the cluttered yards and gardens stood in sharp contrast to the clean, thriving young metropolis the Mormons had created through their intelligence and industry. At Carthage, he was overwhelmed by feelings of "horror and indignation" as he reflected upon the bloody martyrdom of Joseph and Hyrum. "Who were those Martyred Ones?" he asked rhetorically in a letter written to Eliza from England on June 14, 1850. "Ask the ministering angels from on high. Ask the mighty throng whom they have guided to peace, knowledge, wisdom and power! And who are they? My friends—the friends of millions, the friends of Universal Man."

Traveling through Saint Louis, Lorenzo was pleasantly surprised to find a thriving branch of four hundred members who met in a "spacious and beautiful hall." From there, by river or canal boats and stages, he and his companion traveled to New York, where they were treated hospitably by the members of the branches in the Manhattan area.

After making arrangements for funds, food, and other necessities for their voyage, Elders Snow and Toronto booked passage on the packet ship *Shannon*, which weighed anchor and sailed for England on March 25, 1850. Twenty-four days later, the pair arrived at Liverpool after a customarily rough Atlantic crossing that tested their will, endurance, and immunity to seasickness. Any unpleasant memories Lorenzo may have had about the voyage were swallowed up in his excitement at once again seeing England, a land he had learned to love, and which he sometimes referred to by its poetic name, "Albion." A poetic impulse seized him as the *Shannon* glided toward the dock at Liverpool. "I never beheld a more lovely morning," he wrote to Eliza. "Everything wore an enchanting appearance. A calm serenity rested upon the broad bosom of the water. Old England lay before me, besprinkled with farms and multitudes of human dwellings with beautiful hawthorn hedges and newly plowed grounds. Around, about on the water, in full view, were ships of all nations—some passing in one direction and some in another."

Lorenzo spent almost two nostalgic months in England before departing for Italy. During that time, he renewed acquaintances in many of the places where he had labored eight years before, including Manchester, Birmingham, and London. At each of these places, he was happy to find those whom he fondly referred to as "my children in the gospel" occupying positions of high responsibility and authority.

Elders Snow and Toronto ended their tour of England at the port of Southampton, from where they intended to cross the channel and travel across the continent toward Italy. Lorenzo announced at a gathering of the Saints there that Elder T. B. H. Stenhouse, president of the Southampton Conference, would join him and Elder Toronto. When this announcement was made, the Saints in Southampton "were astounded for a time," wrote Elder Thomas Margetts, a missionary who was present, "and the only way they could give vent to their feelings was by tears."

Elder Snow and his companions crossed the channel and made their leisurely way over the continent, through Paris and Lyon to Marseilles. There they embarked by ship to Nice, just west of the famous gambling resort of Monaco, and thence to their first Italian headquarters at Genoa on the northwest coast of Italy.

This ancient portal city was to present an insuperable obstacle to Elder Snow and his proselyting companions. Unlike the communities in Piedmont to the north, where the missionaries would later find success, Genoa was dominated by the Catholic Church, whose iron discipline and pervasive influence made it almost impossible for the elders to make any headway. Another powerful deterrent in Genoa was the ominous presence of armed troops, who filled the city's crowded streets, intimidating evidence of the bloody French Revolution, which had ended two years before but whose shock waves had continued to wash over most of Europe. In its wake had followed economic and social chaos, which required a powerful armed presence to maintain order, a presence Lorenzo had observed with some uneasiness in every major continental and port city he visited after leaving England. "Little money is circulating," he wrote from Genoa on July 20, 1850, "and commerce languishes on every side. The country is not yet sufficiently settled to induce the enterprise of the capitalist. Since the revolution, the working classes have suffered severely from the depression of business. Wages are, of course, very low; upon an average, not more than twenty cents for a day's work, for a laborer; which is commonly made to consist of about sixteen hours."

Learning through study and inquiry about the proud and stubborn independence of the Waldenses, a protestant sect that inhabited the valleys of the Piedmont, Lorenzo decided soon after his arrival in Genoa that this would be his main field of labor in Italy. He confided in a letter to Elder Franklin D. Richards that the Spirit had revealed that the Lord had "hidden up a people amid the Alpine Mountains" and that he would "commence something of importance in that part of this dark nation." Acting upon this impression, he first sent Elders Stenhouse and Toronto there to survey the situation and lay the groundwork for proselyting. Later he joined them, at which time the Italian missionary force was augmented by the arrival of Elder Jabez Woodward from the London conference.

While the deterring effects of Catholic dominance were not present in the Piedmont (the Waldenses outnumbering the Catholics four to one), Elder Snow still faced great obstacles in establishing the work there. Barriers of language, social customs, and cultural background seriously impeded the missionaries. Lorenzo first attempted to bridge these by "cultivating friendly feelings" with the people. He then wrote a tract titled "The Voice of Joseph," which he had translated into French, the predominant language in the area. But, by the early part of September, there had been no visible fruits from their labors. The course of events that turned things around for them and brought about the results predicted in the letter to Franklin D. Richards began on September 6, 1850. On that day, Lorenzo saw for the first time a three-year-old boy named Joseph Guy (or Grey) who was critically ill and seemed to be on the verge of death. With his eyeballs turned upward, his face and body emaciated, his complexion ashen with a "pale marble hue," and his body covered with cold perspiration, the boy seemed to be beyond earthly help. Indeed, his grieving family and friends had given him up for dead, the father whispering "Il meurt! Il meurt!" (He dies! He dies!) Lorenzo recognized an opportunity both to heal the boy and to breathe new life and success into his work. That night he spent "some hours" imploring God for direction, and the following day he and Elder Stenhouse fasted and retired to a nearby mountain, where they "called upon the Lord in solemn earnest prayer, to spare the life of the child." Returning to the city that afternoon, the elders administered to the boy, "silently [offering] up the desires of [their] hearts for his restoration." They left immediately, learning afterward that the boy slept peacefully that night for the first time in many days. He was so much improved the following day that the parents were able to return to their usual work.

Word of this miraculous healing spread rapidly through the valleys of Piedmont. Some doors that had been closed to the missionaries were suddenly opened. An intense interest in their message supplanted the cold indifference or hostility previously shown toward the Mormon elders, and many people joined the Church.

Even so, the work in Italy did not run a smooth, untroubled course. Lorenzo reported to Brigham Young in November that slanderous tales about the missionaries were being widely circulated, and that all the principal facts about the Church were being distorted and misrepresented. "Our course is often dark and difficult," he wrote gloomily, but then he added, ". . . but I believe that, however slow it may be for a while, it will ultimately brighten with complete success."

The formal act of organizing the Church in Italy was directed by Elder Snow in the autumn of 1850 atop a mountain near LaTour. With him were Elders Stenhouse and Woodward, Elder Toronto having been allowed to go to Sicily to try to locate some of his relatives. The mountain was designated "Mount Brigham" by the brethren, and the rock upon which they stood they named "The Rock of Prophecy." Although there were only the three elders present, the meeting went forward with all the formalities of a general conference, with singing, prayers, preaching, and the sustaining of officers. On motion, duly seconded, Lorenzo was sustained as "President of the Church in Italy" and Elder Stenhouse as secretary. Significantly, all three elders prophesied during the meeting, presumably while standing on the rock of prophecy, that while the work there would move slowly and obscurely, it would ultimately succeed, and that the opposition raised against them and the Church would ultimately inure to their benefit. On returning to their rooms, Lorenzo put up pictures of Joseph and Hyrum. "From that day," he wrote, "opportunities began to occur for proclaiming our message."

Once the work was making good progress in the Piedmont, Lorenzo assigned Elder Stenhouse to labor to the north in Switzerland. And when Elder Toronto returned from Sicily, he was assigned to work with Elder Woodward. This left Elder Snow free to return to England to arrange for the translation and printing of the Book of Mormon in Italian. He crossed the Alps in February 1851 during a heavy winter storm and spent a month in Switzerland working with Elder Stenhouse. His pamphlets "The Ancient Gospel Restored" and "The Voice of Joseph" were used there, not only to acquaint investigators with basic gospel themes, but to open doors for interviews with men of education and influence. We may gauge the effect of these writings from a report submitted to the *Millennial Star* by Elder Stenhouse, who wrote: "There is not a minister,

Protestant, Catholic, or Methodist of any shade or colour in Geneva but is more or less acquainted with Mormonism and Lorenzo Snow."

Lorenzo spent over nine months in the British Isles during the tedious work of translating and publishing the Book of Mormon. Because of the inevitable delays in the work and his supervisory role, he had a great deal of leisure time, which he put to good use in proselyting and building up the Saints.

April found him in London, where he addressed two hundred and fifty brethren assembled in a priesthood meeting. "It would have done your soul good to have been present and have witnessed the deep stillness that pervaded the assembly," reported London Conference President Eli Kelsey. So caught up were both speaker and audience in the inspiration of the occasion that the meeting did not end until near midnight, "and even then many seemed loth to part."

Later, the itinerant apostle extended his interim ministry into Scotland, Ireland, and Wales. Almost invariably his sermons included a personal testimony of the reality and power of God, a testimony that had burned brightly and with ever-increasing intensity since his conversion in Kirtland years before. Since then, many experiences had confirmed this testimony, the bearing of which was the most effective proselyting tool Lorenzo possessed, and which always struck a responsive chord with those who were sympathetic to his message.

But the deferential attitude the Saints and interested investigators showed toward Lorenzo was counterbalanced by the callous, sometimes brutal conduct of his enemies and detractors. This malignant spirit manifested itself again in early November 1851, as he toured in Wales with an Elder Phillips. Following a meeting in Tredagar, the missionaries were taken to a hotel where, following supper, they were shown to a room whose lock, Elder Snow noticed, was defective. Thinking nothing of it at the moment, they retired, only to be aroused by the alarming presence of three powerful intruders, whose leader profanely ordered them from bed. When, in a scuffle, the light carried by one of the trio was extinguished, leaving the room in total darkness, the men left hurriedly to get another light. The elders immediately barricaded the door and, with the added weight of their bodies, prevented the intruders from reentering the room when they returned. Later evidence revealed that the three, in collusion with the innkeeper, had been engaged by a mob to kidnap the missionaries. Years afterward, Elder Snow saw a providential retribution in the fact that the hotel had been converted to a horse stable, and the innkeeper, reduced to poverty, had become "a vagabond upon the earth."

Lorenzo's feeling that he enjoyed heavenly protection and guidance was constant, confirmed by frequent spiritual manifestations and objective evidence of the kind noted above. These manifestations were predominantly "whisperings," "impressions," or "promptings." "Lately my mind has been much impressed with the idea of introducing the gospel to India," he wrote in a letter to Elder Franklin D. Richards. Accustomed through long discipline to acting upon such impressions and having received authority from the Brethren to broaden the scope of his mission, he sent Elders William Willes and Joseph Richards to India to labor in Simla. Also, he sent Elder Hugh Findlay from the British Mission to labor in Bombay. Elder Snow opened Malta for proselyting by sending Elder Obray there.

By January 1852, when Lorenzo had been away from Italy for eleven months, he became anxious to return to his appointed field of labor. So, although a hundred pages of the Book of Mormon remained to be translated into Italian and printed, he prepared to leave. In doing so, he was prompted to write to the Saints in Great Britain an extensive letter that was published in the *Millennial Star*. It defined the priesthood as an instrumentality that would "give you character, renown, wisdom, power, and authority, and build you up here below among the children of men; and above, exalt you to peace and happiness, to thrones and dominions, even through countless eternities." It admonished leaders to preside "in the spirit of humility, wisdom and goodness" and not by "authoritative rule." It declared that "Purity, virtue, fidelity and godliness must be sought ambitiously" to make one "a fountain of truth, of equity, justice, and mercy." Then, in a more philosophical vein, he observed that in one's present acts and conduct lie the seeds of "a life to be continued through the eternities," and noted that "it is necessary that we suffer in all things, that we may be qualified and worthy to rule, and govern all things, even as our Father in Heaven, and His eldest Son, Jesus." Before commending his associates and the Saints for their faithfulness, and outlining his projected travels, he offered this final counsel as a rule of conduct for all those who would take the Savior as their exemplar: "Be honest, be virtuous, be honorable, be meek and lowly, courageous and bold. Cultivate simplicity, be like the Lord; hold to the truth through fire and sword—torture and death. Act honorably towards all men, for they are our brethren—a part of the family of God, but are ignorant and blind, having forgotten their God and their covenants with him in eternity."

Having bid farewell to the missionaries and Saints in Britain, this modern apostle crossed the channel in early January 1852 in what he characterized as a "boisterous and stormy passage." Traveling directly to Paris, he was pleased to find a small but active branch established through the efforts of Elder John Taylor and Elder Bolten. "Elder Taylor may comfort his heart," Lorenzo wrote, "with the assurance of having laid a lasting foundation for the spread of the Gospel in the French dominions."

Leaving Paris on January 27, Elder Snow traveled through the midlands of France in a "diligence," or stagecoach, arriving at Geneva, Switzerland, at midnight on January 28. In two days of strenuous travel, he had passed through some of the most fertile and pleasant farmland in all of France. The sights, sounds, and odors of the countryside seemed to evoke memories of his boyhood years on his father's Ohio farm. "The country over which I passed," he wrote, ". . . seemed, though in the midst of winter, to wear the appearance of an American spring. . . . Everywhere people were seen in pasture and ploughed fields, meadows and vineyards, busily occupied preparing for approaching spring." The only "dark spot" to him in this idyllic scene was the sight of "poor women slavishly engaged in manual labor, and exposed to all the hardships of out-door occupations."

Lorenzo spent two pleasant weeks in Switzerland as the guest of Elder Stenhouse, whose wife had by now joined him in the mission field. "I had the gratification of setting down to an excellent supper, prepared by Sister Stenhouse," he wrote appreciatively about the day of his arrival in Geneva. Although his record does not say so directly, this brief exposure to the comforts and joys of domestic life was probably a bittersweet experience for him, both relieving the rigors and loneliness of itinerant living and poignantly reminding him of the long separation from his loved ones at home.

Whatever memories the incident evoked were soon submerged in a sea of activities. Lorenzo conducted meetings and interviews in the growing branch in Geneva. Visits with investigators and influential nonmembers were also on the busy agenda Elder Stenhouse had arranged for his visiting leader. One of these was with Professor Reta, an "Italian gentleman of literary talent" to whom were submitted for review the four hundred pages of the Book of Mormon Lorenzo had with him that had been translated into Italian. According to Lorenzo, the professor pronounced it to be a correct translation, with a good literary style.

Interspersed with the activities in Geneva were trips to surrounding areas where the visitor exhorted and instructed members and nonmembers alike. One of the most significant of these was a trip to Lausanne, reached by a pleasant trip across Lake Geneva. Almost waxing poetic, Lorenzo conveyed his impressions of this scenic Alpine retreat in a letter written to his fellow apostle Franklin D. Richards: "We were much pleased with the general beauty of the country. The many fine villas and chateaux, surrounded with gardens and vineyards, that besprinkle the gently rising banks on one side of the lake, formed a beautiful contrast with Mont Blanc and the lofty, snow-capped mountains on the other." But as if to allay any concern by the dedicated young president of the British Mission that his associate in the Twelve had turned sightseer, Elder Snow hastened to add: "Though the works, wonders and beauties of nature prompted our minds to contemplation, and raised their springs of gratitude to the good and wise Preserver of all, yet there was a still higher theme for contemplation, a still greater incentive to gratitude—the work of the Lord."

Lorenzo could hardly have picked a worse time of the year to cross the Alps. Leaving Geneva on February 9, his conveyance, a mail coach drawn by ten horses, approached the narrow, precipitous trail over Mount Cenis as dark fell and a winter storm struck. Accompanied by high winds, the storm deposited a blanket of snow that drifted to a depth of four feet. The ascent was made even more perilous by the hairpin turns the team had to negotiate in the black of night. "One stumble," Lorenzo wrote, "or the least unlucky toss of our vehicle would, at very many points of our path, have plunged us a thousand feet down rocky precipices." The single aspect of this harrowing trip Elder Snow found laudatory was the comforting presence of "Houses of Recovery" that had been constructed at intervals along the trail to provide refuge for winter travelers.

After reaching Turin, Lorenzo followed the same routine as at Geneva, visiting and instructing the missionaries and members and traveling to outlying areas. At Angrogna, Lorenzo was satisfied to learn that the gifts of the Spirit had begun to appear among the new members. One brother testified of several gifts of healing, another told of seeing an open vision, and a sister excitedly told the visiting apostle, "Mr. Snow, it is the first time I see you with my bodily eyes, but the Lord gave me a manifestation a few weeks ago, in which I saw you as plain as I see you now."

Moreover, Lorenzo found that the harvest of new converts included men with administrative skills. Chief among these was John D. Malan, who had been appointed a branch president, and whose leadership competence was such that Elder Snow decided to leave him in charge of the work in the Piedmont and to transfer Elder Woodward to Nice. However, that plan was changed when, at Geneva, Lorenzo decided to take Elder Woodward with him to Malta.

Embarking on the French steamer *Telemaque* on February 20, 1852, the pair reached Malta six days later after intermediate stops at Leghorn, Civitta Vecchia, Naples, and Messina.

At Malta, Lorenzo visited the bay where the Apostle Paul was shipwrecked, and probably tried to visualize the hazards that confronted his fellow apostle centuries before as he traveled to Rome. He must have been sobered by the large building that housed the ancient court of the Inquisition, whose walls still bristled with the rings and hooks to which prisoners of the court had been tethered. And, he was bemused by a huge painting in the Church of the Inquisition that pictured Martin Luther in hell, engulfed by flames of burning torment. "Whether the artist, when [painting] the picture, was on the spot, we are not informed," Elder Snow observed, tongue in cheek.

Lorenzo's original intention was to remain at Malta only briefly, and then to leave for India. He was unavoidably detained, however, because of the breakdown of one of the Oriental Steam Company's ships, which threw its schedule into turmoil and caused a lengthy delay in booking passage. This delay finally prompted Elder Snow to decide against going to India. He was concerned there would be insufficient time to go there as well as comply with instructions from the First Presidency for the members of the Twelve to return to Salt Lake City for the April 1853 general conference.

This decision having been made, Lorenzo began to wind down his affairs in the Mediterranean before leaving for home. He arranged with a businessman in Malta to print Church publications that would then be distributed to Italy, Spain, Switzerland, Bombay, and Calcutta. Before his departure, Lorenzo also supervised the publication of another edition of "The Voice of Joseph," revised from the Italian, and also French and Italian editions of the tract "The Ancient Gospel Restored." He then assigned Elder Woodward to return to the Piedmont and placed Elder Obray in charge of the work in Malta.

Booking passage for Portsmouth, England, Lorenzo made a brief stop at Gibraltar, later recommending that missionaries be sent there. Back in England, he visited the branches in London, traveled through the midlands to Liverpool, and embarked from there on the packet ship *Niagara* on June 12, 1852. Forty-eight days later, on July 30, Lorenzo entered the Salt Lake Valley to a tearful and joyous reunion with his family.

Chapter Twelve

Settling in the Mountains

An absence of almost three years had brought about pervasive changes at Salt Lake City. Those that affected Elder Snow most profoundly had occurred within the close circle of his immediate family. Missing from that circle was his wife, Charlotte, who had died suddenly on September 25, 1850, while Lorenzo was in Italy. The great distances involved, the demands of his apostolic calling, and the delayed notice of her passing had ruled out the possibility of returning home at the time. His bereavement and sense of loss were softened when, soon after Charlotte's death, the wife of Jabez Woodward told him of an open vision she had seen, in which appeared a beautiful woman, "the most lovely being she ever beheld, clothed in white robes" who said she was a wife of Lorenzo Snow. After returning home, he learned that his wife, Sarah Ann, had had a similar experience when, shortly after Charlotte's death, she appeared to Sarah Ann in a vivid dream or vision, saying she was very happy and dwelt in a beautiful place. These spiritual manifestations brought great solace and comfort to Elder Snow, softening the feelings of regret he had at not being present when she passed away.

But, there was a new face in that circle, too, in the person of a "little prattler, named Sylvia," who was born shortly after Elder Snow left home. Reluctant at first to even acknowledge his presence, the baby at length planted herself in front of him to ask imperiously: "Is you my favvy?" Assured that he was, she then deigned to give him a hug and a kiss.

As his family was still living in a rough-hewn cabin whose roof leaked like a sieve, Lorenzo soon set about to build a more substantial home. With only limited means, he had to do most of the work himself and to practice the most strict economy. His sister Eliza wrote, "He frequently knelt within its foundations and prayed that the small means he could command, might be blest and multiplied in its use." The results, a large two-story adobe home with nine rooms, attest to the efficacy of those prayers and the industry of the builder.

But Lorenzo's herculean efforts at home-building comprised only one piece in the elaborate mosaic that made up his busy life. Immediately upon returning home, he took up the reins of his duties as a member of the Twelve, attending the regular meetings of his quorum, filling numerous speaking assignments at the various wards in the city, and traveling to nearby communities for conferences. Soon after his arrival, he was elected to the territorial legislature, thus beginning a career of public service that was to extend over a period of thirty years. And, about the same time, he was appointed as one of the regents of the newly formed University of Deseret.

Not content, however, merely to do the things he was obligated to do, Lorenzo, during this exceedingly busy period of his life, initiated one of those extra-mile projects with which his career is liberally studded. It was given the tongue-twisting name of "The Polysophical Society," a name created by the founder to express his object of fostering personal development in all fields of thought and endeavor. The society met weekly in Lorenzo's home, where the members were treated to wide-ranging intellectual fare that included commentaries on scientific and philosophical subjects interspersed with instrumental and vocal music selections, readings, poems, and essays. Nor was it unusual for parts of the programs to be presented in languages other than English. And, occasionally, the members were given instructions in the Deseret alphabet, the Latter-day Saints' new and distinctive written language.

To keep the meetings fast-paced and interesting, Lorenzo insisted that each part, assigned well in advance, be no longer than fifteen minutes. And, to rivet the attention of all, the order of the presentations was not announced in advance, the performers being notified during the program in notes scribbled by the master of ceremonies and delivered by one of his children designated as a messenger.

We see in this creation of Elder Snow's a broad extension of the ideas that underlay the socials and entertainments he sponsored at Mount Pisgah, as well as some of the ideas that ultimately found their way into the mutual improvement organizations of the Church.

Lorenzo's beautiful home and the intellectual and spiritual atmosphere he created in it were only reflections of the special house that would be raised later in the heart of Salt Lake City. This, of course, was the house of the Lord, the holy temple, whose site had been designated by President Young shortly after the pioneer company arrived in the valley in the summer of 1847. Now, almost six years later, Elder Snow learned that the First Presidency had summoned him and the other members of the Twelve home for the April 1853 general conference to help lay the cornerstone of this sacred building. The event was scheduled for April 6, the twenty-third anniversary of the organization of the Church. It began with a procession that formed on South Temple Street, where Elder Snow took his place with the other leaders of the Church, who then marched solemnly to the temple site to the accompaniment of a brass band. After the southeast, southwest, and northwest cornerstones had been laid by the First Presidency, the Presiding Bishopric, and the leaders of the Salt Lake Stake, respectively, Lorenzo joined with his brethren of the Twelve to lay the northeast cornerstone.

We can only speculate about Lorenzo's thoughts on this occasion. Given his highly developed historic sense, however, he could hardly have failed to think of the Kirtland Temple, where he had been inspired and blessed by Joseph Smith, Sr., and the Nauvoo Temple, where he had been endowed and sealed. Nor could the words of Brigham Young on this occasion have failed to evoke memories of his travails in Missouri and images of the magnificent temple that would later crown the center stake at Independence. "Protect us until we have finished this temple," implored the Lion of the Lord, "receive the fullness of our endowments there, and then build many more; and I pray, also, that we may live to see a great temple in Jackson County, Missouri."

Only six months after the cornerstones of the Salt Lake Temple were laid, Elder Snow was called by Brigham Young to preside at Brigham City. The severe demands of building a new civilization in the wilderness had prompted the First Presidency to appoint the apostles as permanent leaders in outlying areas. Lorenzo, at Brigham City, was sandwiched between Ezra T. Benson and Franklin D. Richards who presided, respectively, at Cache Valley and Ogden. Charles C. Rich and Amasa Lyman directed the Saints at San Bernardino, California; Orson Hyde was sent to Carson City, Nevada, and later was transferred to San Pete County, Utah; and Erastus Snow and George A. Smith directed affairs in Utah's Dixie.

Lorenzo was authorized to select fifty families to accompany him to Brigham City. By the spring of 1854, many of them had joined him at their new home. As seen through even the most optimistic eyes, the Brigham City of that day was a most forbidding place. Adorned only with the colorless and scruffy vegetation indigenous to the area, it presented a scene of dreary ugliness. Its main building complex was a rough, insect-infested fort, constructed by the first settlers in 1851 as protection against the unfriendly Indians who roamed the area. Elder Snow took up his first Brigham City residence with part of his family in a "small and incommodious adobe hut" within the fort. The rest would join him later when he had prepared adequate accommodations for them.

Lorenzo was repulsed by the insects that plagued the fort. "Even the big meeting house," he wrote later, "with its ground floor and earth roof was more extensively patronized as a receptacle for bed bugs than for the assemblage of Saints." Spurred on by this annoyance and by the desire to unite his family under one roof, he concentrated on building a new, insect-free home, which was ready for occupancy by autumn. Although very modest by today's standards, it was the largest dwelling in the community at the time, being "one story and a half in height, thirty by forty."

Lorenzo Snow's new Brigham City home

Elder Snow had barely settled into his new home before he began to raise the cultural level of the community with socials, theatricals, lectures, and debates staged in the large "hall" in his home. Later, these were moved to the basement of a new courthouse, at which time Elder Snow helped organize the Dramatic Association of Brigham City, of which he became the first president.

Several months after the new theater was put into use, a heavy wind, roaring out of the canyons to the east, demolished the walls of the courthouse. The resulting debris and dust ruined the scenery, costumes, and staging in the building's basement. As Lorenzo inspected the damage with his friend, Joseph Young, he said despondently, "I cannot see how we can ever rebuild these walls." Without hesitation, Brother Young answered, "Brother Lorenzo, the Lord will soon open up your way to build, and you shall have a much better house than the first." Then, to give substance to his statement, he took a coin from his pocket and, handing it to Lorenzo, said, "Take this for that purpose as a commencement."

Brother Young's statement proved prophetic. By degrees the way was opened, so that with donated material and labor and some tax revenue, the structure was rebuilt. Later, the theater was moved to the second floor, where better and more permanent staging and fixtures were installed. Here, many young people in the community, including some of President Snow's children, developed their dramatic skills, to the enjoyment of their families and friends.

In tandem with his initiatives to foster the cultural development of his people, Lorenzo led out in the establishment of a public school system. At a meeting held on March 10, 1856, he, Samuel Smith, and Joseph Grover were elected trustees of the Box Elder school district. To finance the school system, a 1-percent tax was assessed against all taxable property in the district. Lorenzo's rich background as a college student, teacher, and university regent prompted him to take special interest in the Box Elder schools. Not only did he provide good leadership, but he was the most effective and active recruiter in the district, using his influence and contacts to induce competent teachers to accept employment there.

Nor was the new stake president's influence restricted to civic, cultural, and ecclesiastical matters. Indeed, there were few things in which the members did not look to Elder Snow for guidance and instruction.

A grievance the new stake president began to hear from his people soon after arriving in Brigham City was that most of the irrigable land and the water were owned by a very few. Not only did this create inequities and dissension among those who had already settled in the area, but it was a powerful deterrent in persuading others to cast their lot with the Box Elder Saints.

Lorenzo could have solved the problem by administrative fiat, but chose a more diplomatic way. Convening a meeting in the enclosed bowery of the old fort, with its dirt roof and floor and rough, backless benches, the new stake president explained the principles of consecration, emphasizing the brotherly spirit that must actuate those who aspire to dwell in the presence of the Father and the Son. He did not suggest that those who possessed the water and the land should merely donate it to others, but only that they share on some equitable basis. Then, to avoid any hint of compulsion that might arise from a public vote at the meeting, he urged those present to consider the matter prayerfully for two weeks and then decide. He was gratified to learn, at a subsequent meeting, that many of those with large landholdings had heeded his counsel and were arranging for transfers under mutually acceptable conditions.

While this brought a temporary solution to a critical problem, Elder Snow foresaw that with an expanding population and a limited water supply from the mountain streams to the east, squabbles over water would agitate the Box Elder Saints indefinitely. Seeking a long-range answer to this troubling issue, he invited the territorial surveyor, Jesse W. Fox, to study the possibility of diverting the waters of the Bear River, to the north, to the land around Brigham City. Reporting at a public meeting of the Saints, the surveyor concluded that such a diversion was feasible but impractical because of the large capital outlays it would require. Looking beyond the poverty that held his people in its grip at the moment, Elder Snow, moved by prophetic impulse, arose to predict that the waters of the Bear River would ultimately be diverted for this purpose and that lands that were then barren would yield crops in abundance. This prophecy saw its fulfillment years later when the West Side Bear River Canal was completed.

But something had to be done immediately to fill the temporal needs of the many converts in the community who lived constantly on the raw edge of poverty. In addressing this need, Lorenzo relied upon a device that had been used elsewhere, but perhaps never with the consistency nor the success it enjoyed at Brigham City. This was the monthly fast, which was presented by Elder Snow at a conference and adopted by the stake membership. Under it, the Saints committed themselves to refrain from two meals on the first

Thursday of each month and to contribute the amount saved to the fast-offering fund, which was administered by the bishops to alleviate the suffering of the poor.

Lorenzo relied heavily upon the Lord to help him solve such problems and fulfill his civic, church, and family duties. "I have no time to get away from public business," he wrote from Fillmore, Utah, to his friend Porter Squires, "except in the evening, when I go out in the fields alone by myself, to call upon the Lord to bless me and my family. I never enjoy myself so well as I do on these occasions. Men change and circumstances alter, but the Lord is always the same kind, indulgent and affectionate Father, and will bless those that will, in childish simplicity, humble themselves before him, and ask for what they want."

Chapter Thirteen

The Squire of Brigham City

L orenzo did not spend all of his time in Brigham City. He frequently attended to Church and legislative matters either in Salt Lake City or Fillmore (then the state capital). In addition, he filled speaking and counseling assignments given to him by the First Presidency or the President of the Quorum of the Twelve, and occasionally accompanied other leading brethren in making extended trips to outlying areas, where they instructed and encouraged the people.

In the autumn of 1854, following the October general conference, Lorenzo was invited by President Young to join a few of the Brethren on a trip to some of the Mormon settlements south of Salt Lake City. They visited Palmyra, Provo, Nephi, Manti, and Ephraim, as well as other villages, where the Saints, troubled by inclement weather and Indians, listened avidly to the admonitions and counsel of the visitors. In a gesture toward improved relations with the Indians, the Brethren counseled with Chief Aropeen who, despite some past depredations of his braves, received the Mormon leaders in a spirit of conciliation.

Later, in the spring of 1857, Lorenzo made another trip with President Young and an official party, this time into the Salmon River country of Idaho. Unlike the earlier trip south, this one had a recreational as well as ecclesiastical purpose, the official party of almost one hundred and fifty including a sprinkling of women and young boys. The itinerary, which followed a rather circuitous route, took the party up through the Malad Valley to Fort Lemhi, where there was a Mormon outpost. During this thirty-three day trip, Lorenzo had his eyes opened to the beauty and grandeur of this large area that would be colonized extensively by the Latter-day Saints in the years ahead.

But Lorenzo's main concern was to build Brigham City into a prosperous, righteous community, one that even the First Presidency could be proud of. When he learned that the First Presidency was coming to town, he began planning for the event weeks before their scheduled arrival. Lorenzo's home, where the visitors always stayed, would be specially cleaned and decorated for the occasion, while the other residents would be admonished to tidy up their yards, corral their animals, and leash their dogs. A crew would then be assigned to repair the road entering town by removing stones from its surface, filling holes, and repairing bridges and causeways. After these mundane affairs had been arranged, Lorenzo would turn his attention to more aesthetic matters. He attired "forty or fifty intelligent, interesting looking young gentlemen" in gray uniforms, mounted them on the finest horses to be found in the community, and armed them with lances tipped with shining paint and decorated with "gay ribbons." Also, sixteen young ladies dressed in white were seated in wagons drawn by two span of horses "properly caparisoned." These young people, who comprised the formal escort for the visitors, carried flags and banners bearing "appropriate mottoes." Ahead of the escort in the procession were carriages "occupied by the authorities and leading men of the city," and, leading all, was a martial band. Having met the visitors on the outskirts of town, this colorful procession then accompanied them to Lorenzo's house along streets lined with Latter-day Saints and their children amidst "loud cheers, the ringing of bells and waving of banners."

We can imagine the surprise of President Young and his party on first witnessing this pageant staged by the remote and struggling pioneer community. But it was a sight with which the guests became familiar, since it always greeted them whenever they visited Brigham City. Later, most other Mormon communities throughout the territory copied Lorenzo's idea to welcome distinguished visitors. This practice continued until after the coming of the railroad, which removed the special conditions and atmosphere in which Elder Snow's pageantry had flourished.

Lorenzo even influenced the names of many Utah towns and sites. The picturesque town of Mantua, five miles east of Brigham City in Little Valley, was named by President Snow after the small Ohio town where he was born. Later, he attached the name of Mount Hope to a knoll in Little Valley, which did become a pleasant and secluded place. Elder Snow later conferred the name Portage upon a small community near the Utah-Idaho border, thus memorializing the Ohio county in which he was born.

It was inevitable that a town in Box Elder County would ultimately be named after Elder Snow himself; Snowville is located in the Curlew Valley, in the northwest part of the county. Although it can't be verified, legend has it that Lorenzo made a prophecy about Deep Creek, a stream that bisects Curlew Valley, calling it "one of the everlasting streams whose waters should never diminish." Many years after the founding of Snowville, an old-time resident, Esther Arbon Goodliffe, reported that this prediction had been fulfilled, and that "in very dry seasons its water[s] never decrease."

Whether or not Lorenzo ever made such a prediction, it is clear that he had a deep and pervasive influence upon the area and people over which he presided. Elder Snow's friends often called upon him for priesthood administrations. Joseph Smith, Sr., had even promised Lorenzo in his patriarchal blessing that the sick would send handkerchiefs for Lorenzo's blessing, by which they would be made whole.

During his service as a missionary in England, while visiting in Wibersom, Lorenzo permitted a convert sister to read his patriarchal blessing. Years later, after migrating to the United States, this sister, who had married William Smith and was living in Kaysville, Utah, was distraught over her husband's grave illness, which had not yielded to frequent priesthood administrations. In her anguish, after having exhausted all other means for her husband's recovery, she remembered the unusual promise contained in Elder Snow's patriarchal blessing. Sister Smith sent a new silk handkerchief to Lorenzo in Brigham City, a distance of about forty miles, with a note that explained her husband's condition and requested a blessing upon him through the handkerchief. Elder Snow later wrote, "I took the handkerchief and a bottle of perfumery, and on retiring to my closet, I prayed, and then I consecrated the perfumery and sprinkled it on the handkerchief. I then again bowed before the Lord, and in earnest supplication besought him to remember the promise he made through his servant, the Patriarch, whom he had now taken to himself, and let the healing and life-inspiring virtues of his Holy Spirit be imparted to this handkerchief, and from thence to Brother Smith when it shall be placed upon him, speedily restoring him to life, health and vigor."

It is reported that when the handkerchief was placed over the patient's face, his recovery was almost "instantaneous," which produced a sense of "surprise and astonishment" in those who witnessed it.

This miraculous healing typifies the influence Lorenzo had through his faith in the Lord upon Brigham City and the surrounding communities and the members of the Church who lived there.

Chapter Fourteen

Difficulties from Within and Without

Not all of Lorenzo's Latter-day Saint contemporaries were able to reach his level of spiritual and mental discipline. Indeed, most of them fell far short, mainly because of the harsh requirements for survival in the wilderness. The physical needs and wants of the Saints were so overwhelming during the first few years after the exodus that they monopolized their thoughts and aspirations. A proportionate decline in the attention devoted to spiritual matters followed. The result was a general relaxation among the people of their adherence to the standards of the Church. Many became negligent in attending their meetings, in paying their tithes and offerings, and in cultivating spirituality through study, fasting, and prayer. Alarmed by this general retrogression, the First Presidency, aided by the Twelve, took steps to reverse it through an initiative known as "the Reformation."

Without hesitancy, Elder Snow threw the full weight of his energies and influence behind this movement. "Brethren, is it not strange, and should we not be ashamed of ourselves," he said accusingly to a Salt Lake Tabernacle audience, "that after receiving the words of life, and coming to a knowledge of glory and immortality and eternal lives, instead of pressing forward and preparing ourselves for these blessings, we slacken our pace, close our eyes, and sink into a state of drowsiness? . . . The men who are sitting here this day ought to be, when in the presence of their families, filled with the Holy Ghost, to administer the word of life to them as it is administered in this stand from sabbath to sabbath. . . . It becomes the duties of fathers in Israel to wake up and become saviors of men, that they may walk before the Lord in that strength of faith, and that determined energy, that will insure them the inspection of the Almighty to teach the words of life to their families, as well as to teach them when they are called into this stand. Then all our words will savor of life and salvation wherever we go, and wherever we are. . . . Let us remember that we have all got to show by our works that we are worthy of this life and of this salvation which is now offered. . . . I say . . . you must learn to govern yourself, or you will never be saved in the kingdom of God."

But Elder Snow was a realist. He knew that many backsliders, inspired by an eloquent speech or a motivating example, might be moved to repent, but then, overcome by competing interests or weighed down by the burden of habit, would sink back into their slothful ways. To such as these he held out the hope of ultimate victory through the accumulation of strength and skill from diligent practice. He assured another Salt Lake Tabernacle audience, "An individual undertaking to learn to play upon a flute at first finds a difficulty in making the notes, and in order to play a tune correctly there is a great deal of diligence and patience required. He has to go on, to pause, to turn back and commence afresh, but after a time he is enabled, through a great deal of exertions, to master that tune. When called upon to play that tune afterwards, there is no necessity for remembering where to place the fingers, but he plays it naturally. It was not natural at the first; there had to be a great deal of patience and labor before it became natural to go through with the tune. It is just so in regard to matters that pertain to the things of God. We have to exert ourselves and go from grace to grace, to get the law of action so incorporated in our systems, that it may be natural to do these things that are required of us."

Given the eloquence, spirituality, and persistence of Elder Snow and the other Mormon leaders and the basic loyalty of the Saints, it was expected that the unity and recommitment sought by the reformation would be achieved. The Reformation was greatly accelerated a few months later, however, by a threat of invasion by a division of the United States Army sent by President James Buchanan, who had been misled by the stories of a claque of federal officials who had run afoul of President Brigham Young. The startling report of the approach of this army was received at Brighton, in the Wasatch Mountains east of Salt Lake City, where Lorenzo, his family, and hundreds of other Latter-day Saint leaders and members had gone to celebrate the tenth anniversary of the arrival of the Saints in the Salt Lake Valley. The electric shock this announcement produced surged rapidly through the Mormon communities, welding the Saints into a unity of purpose seldom achieved before or since.

The First Presidency and the Twelve began immediately to prepare the minds of the people for what lay ahead. They shifted from talk about reformation to plans for their defense, realizing, perhaps, that the threat from without had instantly produced the unity and cohesion they had sought so diligently through their oratory and example.

On October 7, 1857, Lorenzo Snow added his persuasive voice to those of his brethren in directing and motivating the Saints to prepare for possible armed conflict. Hardly concealing his early bent toward military tactics and discipline, the well-seasoned young apostle addressed the Saints assembled in the Bowery in Salt Lake City with poise and self-confidence: "I presume to say that the people before me today feel that all is well," he declared, "that all is right, notwithstanding an armed force is only about 147 miles distant from us, full of their hellish designs for our destruction and have formed their schemes for the purpose of entering into our settlement for the destruction of the principles of righteousness and to gratify their hellish lusts. . . . The least idea never entered their hearts that the people would be found here that would dare to oppose them. The power of the Almighty bears record in every heart that the position for us to take is not to suffer them to come in here, and this is the universal feeling in the community, and it is the power of the Holy Ghost which testifies to every man and to every woman that this is our position."

The lessons Lorenzo and his followers in Box Elder County learned from the so-called Utah War will not be found in any textbook. They were distilled from the hard reality of preparing to defend against a well-trained army while trying to build a new community from scratch, wrest a living from the thirsty soil, and conciliate the nearby Indian tribes, who were becoming progressively more belligerent as they watched the Mormons appropriate more and more of what they considered to be their lands and resources.

Although Lorenzo did not directly command the battalion of the Nauvoo Legion that had been organized in Box Elder County, he exerted a strong influence upon it because of his ecclesiastical positon; his key role in the territorial legislature, under whose mandates the Legion existed and functioned; and his interest and skill in military affairs. The actual commander of the Box Elder Battalion was Colonel Chester Loveland, whose unit later merged with the Weber County Battalion of the Legion to form a regiment commanded by General Chauncy West.

General West, with Elder Snow and Elder Franklin D. Richards (who presided at Ogden), led his regiment into the Bear Lake country to intercept a cavalry unit of Johnston's Army that was reported to be moving down the Bear River from Ham's Fork in Wyoming. Before reaching Soda Springs, however, a messenger intercepted the regiment with orders to return home, as the cavalry had gone back to Ham's Fork, where the bulk of Johnston's Army was bivouacked. Later, the regiment moved to Echo Canyon where, with other military units, it helped dig trenches and throw up breastworks in anticipation of an assault by the invaders, an assault that never materialized because of the frigid weather and Lot Smith's attack force that operated behind the lines, constantly harassing the enemy.

This ended the involvement of the Box Elder Battalion of the Nauvoo Legion in the Utah War. By spring, the decision had been made to rob the invading army of the spoils of war by adopting a scorched-earth policy. Lorenzo was ordered to evacuate Brigham City, leaving only a token force of fifty men to protect the buildings from Indian depredations, or to incinerate them on the approach of the army. Lorenzo led his people to Utah County, settling some of them around what was then called Pond Town, later Salem, where many lived in crude dugouts.

When at last an uneasy truce was reached with the army, Elder Snow led his people back to their homes in Brigham City. What greeted the eyes of the returning refugees was more heartrending and difficult to bear than anything experienced during their brief flight and return. The rear guard that had remained in the city had, for some unexplained reason, departed, leaving it exposed to the Indians. "We found every home broken open and its contents strewn about," wrote one disheartened resident.

By degrees, Lorenzo and his people accommodated themselves to their altered circumstances and began again to weave the fabric of their lives as pioneer Latter-day Saints, committed to principles of sacrifice and service.

Chapter Fifteen

Mission to the Isles of the Pacific

In 1864, the First Presidency called Lorenzo and apostle Ezra T. Benson to fill a special mission to the Sandwich (now the Hawaiian) Islands. The main object of the mission was to discipline an unruly elder, Walter M. Gibson, and to try to repair the damage caused by his insubordination. They left Salt Lake City on March 1, 1864, with San Francisco as their intermediate destination. Accompanying the two apostles were three other brethren, William W. Cluff, Alma Smith, and an aggressive young elder, Joseph F. Smith, son of Hyrum Smith and nephew of the Prophet whose name he bore. He had filled a mission in Hawaii several years before when he was only a boy of fifteen.

The transcontinental railroad then being only an unfulfilled dream, the party traveled to the coast by stage, crossing the western Utah salt flats, the dreary and seemingly endless Nevada valleys, and the rugged Sierras in a teeth-rattling, dusty, never-to-be-forgotten ride. "It is true, so far as the tremendous jolting was concerned," Lorenzo later confided, "we had decidedly the advantage of Horace Greeley in his ludicrous lone stage ride over the same road, inasmuch as five of us could maintain a better balance than a lone man. At any rate, on the roughest portions of the route, we partially succeeded in keeping our heads from the top of the stage, which, as per report, he failed in doing."

The rugged trail had ready partners in the human specimens the travelers encountered along the way. Early one Sunday morning, for instance, at a remote Nevada mining camp, while waiting for their driver to exchange mail bags, Lorenzo and his companions witnessed a shooting. It hardly corresponded with the usual western scenario of two weather-beaten, intimidating gunslingers, holsters riding low on their hips, facing each other menacingly and waiting for each other to make a move toward his gun. A terrified black man, bursting wildly from a nearby saloon, ran a zigzag course across the street. Following him was a white man, who drew a gun and deliberately fired several shots at the fleeing black man, who fell to the ground. Hurrying to the fallen man, probably an emancipated slave, the travelers found him writhing and moaning in pain and pointing helplessly at his wounds. Before they could render aid, the elders were ordered back into the stage by their driver, who had a schedule to keep, and who obviously had no intention of worrying about the cold-blooded shooting of a black man.

With relief, Lorenzo found a new driver, who took over the stage later, to have the "air and appearance of an intelligent gentleman." That impression was strengthened by the discovery that he had a beautiful, cultured singing voice. "It really seemed to me," Lorenzo recorded after hearing the man sing, "that a sweeter, a more pathetic or melodious voice I had never heard. It is quite possible that the stillness of night and the wild scenery of nature around us had a tendency to enhance the effect and increase our appreciation of melodious accents; whatever it might be, I was charmed, delighted, and felt that I could embrace that man and call him brother."

However, when the coach suddenly lurched, the serenade turned into an outburst of profanity. The driver, having drunk too much before the trip, lashed the team with his bullwhip, and the stage began a long downhill descent as the driver continued to whip his team violently. "Our coach swayed fearfully," wrote Lorenzo, "the wheels ... striking fire as they whirled over the rocks, with a double span of horses upon a keen run, tossing us up and down, giving us a few hard strokes of the head against the cover of the coach." Foreseeing a serious accident unless the speed were reduced, Elder Benson rediscovered his tongue and "in a tremulous yet powerful voice, demanded of the driver to moderate his speed." Heedless of this demand, seemingly angered by it, the driver responded "by an increased and more furious lashing of the foaming, panting steeds." The panic-stricken passengers were relieved of their terror only when they arrived at the next station, where another driver took over. Elder Snow later learned that the drunken driver had been discharged.

But Lorenzo's relief was soon dispelled as the stage coach made its perilous way over the Sierras. He wrote, "Many portions of the road were covered with snow and ice, and ran a long way close beside fearful ravines, hundreds of feet in depth. One sitting in the coach, by inclining the head a little to one side, could gaze down into the vast depths below, conscious that the wheels of the vehicle were often within a few inches of the terrible gulf; consequently, the slipping of the wheels, the least blunder of a horse, or a strap or buckle giving way, or the least carelessness of the driver would plunge the whole outfit over the rocky crags into the abyss below. The danger was increased by the ice and snow, and the sudden, abrupt turns in the road. When we approached very slippery places, where the road frequently was barely of a sufficient width for the coach to pass between the high sharp rocks on one side and the frightful chasm on the other, the driver, in guarding against catastrophes, would put his two spans on their utmost speed."

The tension this hazardous passage created was hardly eased by the running dialogue of the driver, who took pains to call attention to the places along the trail where other coaches had fallen into the depths below, carrying all passengers and the drivers to their deaths. "These nerve-stirring recitals," Lorenzo noted, "caused us more seriously to realize the gravity of our situation, and our dependence on God for the preservation of our lives." On reaching the western base of the Sierras, Lorenzo expressed gratitude for his "deliverance" from the perils of the journey. "[We] felt our pulses restored to their normal state as we dismounted," he wrote.

At San Francisco, the elders were the guests of Brother Eveleth, whose home had practically been turned into a private hotel for the missionaries traveling to and from Salt Lake City and the Sandwich Islands. Booking passage on a steamer, Elder Snow and his companions departed from San Francisco a few days later. Passing through the Golden Gate, their ship breasted the powerful ground swells beyond and, at last, struggled its way on to the broad highway of the Pacific. The record is devoid of Lorenzo's impressions of this voyage, but we can assume that he would have been impressed, as other sea voyagers have been, by the customary smoothness of the Pacific when compared with the turbulent Atlantic; by the "mariner's fire," caused by the luminescent organisms that abound in the Pacific; by the spectacular sunrises and sunsets as the sun seemingly emerges from the ocean in the morning and disappears into its watery depths at day's end; and by the spectacular flying fish whose impromptu and brief forays out of their watery home never fail to intrigue and amaze the watcher. Lorenzo must have enjoyed his first sight of Diamond Head on Oahu, rising up out of the sea, the dead remnant of one of the mighty volcanos to which the islands largely owe their being. And, on closer approach to the welcome harbor, he would have been fascinated by the pearl-like underwater formations that adorn the entrance to it, and from which it takes its famous name, Pearl Harbor.

The travelers remained at Honolulu on Oahu for two days, sailing March 29, 1864, on the schooner *Nettie Merrill* for Lahaina on the island of Maui, ninety miles away. After a two-day voyage, the *Nettie Merrill* anchored on the morning of March 31 a mile from the mouth of Lahaina harbor. There was a stiff wind that morning. Indeed, it was of such force that one commentator later referred to it as a typhoon. Moreover, the sea was running high, with huge breakers clearly visible as they rolled spectacularly and broke upon the coral reefs that guarded the narrow mouth of the harbor. But at the point where the *Nettie Merrill* was anchored, the only turbulence of the water came from the ground swells, and since, at the distance of a mile, the breakers did not appear to be too intimidating, Elders Snow and Benson, anxious to begin their apostolic labors, decided to transfer to a small boat and make a landing. Accordingly, the elders' gear was stowed on the small craft that was manned by a native crew and which, in addition to the elders, had as passengers the captain, another white man, and two or three natives. At the last minute, however, Elder Joseph F. Smith balked at boarding the small craft. His earlier experiences in the islands, the force of the wind, and the size of the breakers convinced him it was unsafe to try to land. Yet he was amenable to the direction of those in authority. He said to Elder Snow: "If you by the authority of the priesthood of God, which you hold, tell me to get into that boat and attempt to land, I will do so, but unless you command me in the authority of the priesthood, I will not do so, because it is not safe to attempt to land."

Not desiring to impose his will on the young man by dictation, Lorenzo did not force the issue, but allowed Joseph to remain aboard the ship. It is a credit to both men that Elder Smith's obstinacy on this occasion did not mar their relationship. On the contrary, it seemed to enhance Elder Snow's opinion of his young companion because of a spiritual impression that came to him at the time. "It was revealed to him then and there," President Heber J. Grant later said, "that the boy, with the courage of his convictions, . . . who stayed on that vessel, would yet be the Prophet of God."

This spiritual impression would have been powerfully confirmed in Lorenzo's mind by the near-fatal accident that befell him as the small boat carried its passengers toward Lahaina's beach. Within a quarter-mile of its destination, the boat reached a point where the ground swells began to take the form of huge waves that would soon crash upon the coral reefs off shore, creating a roaring, foaming, chaotic turbulence. The first inkling Lorenzo had that the boat was in peril came when the captain shouted to the oarsmen, "Hurry up! Hurry up!" in an apparent attempt to catch the crest of a wave and ride it to the safety of the beach. Glancing backward, Lorenzo saw what had provoked the captain's urgent command: "I saw an immense surf, thirty or forty feet high," he later reported, "rushing toward us swifter than a race horse." This gigantic wave hurtled the boat violently forward as if it were a piece of driftwood, but the boat remained afloat and under control. However, a second mountainous wave, following close behind the first, "raised the stern of the boat so high that the steersman's oar was out of the water and control of the boat was lost." The rudderless craft was then swept along on the crest for a short distance until the wave began to break up. At that instant, the boat capsized, and its passengers and their gear were thrown into the churning surf. In the short interval between his first apprehension of danger and the capsizing of his boat, Lorenzo experienced the kind of tightly compressed replay of major incidents in his life that seems to be characteristic of those who face the threat of imminent death. "In such extreme cases of excitement," he reflected later, "we seem to live hours in a minute, and a volume of thoughts crowd themselves into one single moment. It was so with me in that perilous scene."

Despite the extreme hazards this emergency presented, Elder Snow remained calm and composed up to the moment he lost consciousness in the water. "I felt confident," he wrote later, "there would be some way of escape; that the Lord would provide the means, for it was not possible that my life and mission were thus to terminate. This reliance on the Lord banished fear, and inspired me."

Because of a tendency to faint, Lorenzo lost consciousness shortly after he was hurled into the sea amidst a jumbled conglomeration of barrels, valises, oars, hats, umbrellas, and human beings.

Elder Cluff, an experienced and powerful swimmer, who had mastered the treacheries of the Polynesian surf when he served his first mission in the islands years before, was the first of the elders to surface after the boat capsized. Soon after, Elder Benson bobbed up near him on the same side of the overturned craft and, in an instant, Elder Alma Smith appeared on the opposite side, gasping for breath while trying to cough up the seawater he had unwillingly swallowed. As the three clung to the bobbing craft, they looked intently for Elder Snow, who had not yet surfaced. In the meantime, the native crew, who were expert swimmers and accustomed to the wild waters of the islands, had begun to dive for the missing "haole," the natives' disparaging name for white strangers. As they did so, two boats were launched from shore, manned by native oarsmen who had witnessed the accident and who hurried to lend assistance. One boat picked up the captain, who had finally surfaced and appeared to be drowned, and the remaining passengers. The other remained near the capsized boat as the native crew continued to dive repeatedly in search of Elder Snow. At length one of them felt him with a foot and raised him immediately to the surface. According to Elder Cluff, "his body was stiff, and life apparently extinct" when they pulled him into the rescue craft.

While they were being rowed to shore, a distance of over a thousand feet through the boisterous surf, Elders Cluff and Smith laid Lorenzo's apparently lifeless body across their laps and quietly administered to him, imploring God "to spare his life, that he might return to his family and home."

On reaching the shore, the two young elders hurriedly carried Lorenzo to an empty barrel lying on the sandy beach and, laying him face down, "rolled him back and forth" until they had "succeeded in getting the water he had swallowed out of him."

The elders worked feverishly over Brother Snow. When their efforts at artificial respiration had failed, they tried washing his face with camphor, a remedy prescribed by Mr. E. P. Adams, a merchant who, with a group of curious onlookers, had walked down to the beach from the village when word spread that a man had been drowned in the surf. The merits of this curious remedy were never explained, although the theory likely was that the acrid odor of the camphor would seep into the subconscious awareness of the victim and cause him to try to avoid it, thereby setting his breathing apparatus in motion.

After the lapse of a considerable period of time, with no visible sign of success, the spectators, who doubtless were not unfamiliar with drownings, gave up on Elder Snow and advised the missionaries "that nothing more could be done for him."

Elder Cluff wrote, "But we did not feel like giving him up, and still prayed and worked over him, with an assurance that the Lord would hear and answer our prayers." As they struggled in this way, the brethren were led to do not only what was "customary" in such cases, "but also what the Spirit seemed to whisper" to them. "Finally," Elder Cluff recorded, "we were impressed to place our mouth over his and make an effort to inflate his lungs, alternately blowing in and drawing out the air, imitating, as far as possible, the natural process of breathing." Persevering in this procedure, which the spectators thought useless, the elders were at last rewarded with "faint indications" of life. "A slight wink of the eye," Elder Cluff reported, "which, until then, had been open and death-like, and a very faint rattle in the throat, were the first symptoms of returning vitality. These grew more and more distinct, until consciousness was fully restored."

According to the best computations Elder Cluff could make, almost an hour intervened between the time the boat capsized and the time Elder Snow was revived. During that entire period, he was either underwater or was lying stiff and immobile as if dead. Despite this, however, he suffered no apparent ill effects from the ordeal.

After he was able to move about, Lorenzo was taken to the home of a Portuguese alien who lived in Lahaina and who had been most helpful during the rescue and revival efforts. There Elder Snow recuperated for two days, following which, on April 2, his party traveled across the channel, sixteen miles, to Lanai, where the object of their mission, Walter M. Gibson, lived and ruled as a virtual monarch.

Chapter Sixteen

The Censure of an Apostate

D isturbing rumors began to circulate about Walter M. Gibson soon after he went to Hawaii. This able and devious man was baptized in Salt Lake City in 1860 by Heber C. Kimball and was confirmed the same day by Brigham Young. Because of his desire to proselyte in Japan, he was later called as a missionary by President Young and was given the commission, frequently given in those days, to proclaim the gospel "to all nations upon the earth." In a public meeting held in the tabernacle, Brigham also said of Elder Gibson that "he should go with [my] good will and blessing."

This ambitious new convert never reached Japan. En route there, he stopped in the Hawaiian Islands while other elders from the mainland were absent. Enlarging the scope of his authority by a gross misinterpretation of his calling, he assumed the presidency of the Hawaiian Mission, took control of the Church lands there, and worked at enlarging his land holdings on Lanai. He generated funds to do this by organizing a new church that included apostolic and other priesthood offices, and by selling rights to these offices to gullible natives. Needing money to feed his land speculations, Elder Gibson extended the priesthood to women, selling them positions as priestesses. To provide the labor necessary to cultivate his plantations, he accelerated missionary work on the other islands and ordered new converts to migrate to Lanai, where they were employed in building up his burgeoning empire. At last, some of the native members who had been converted by the earlier missionaries wrote to Salt Lake City, outlining Elder Gibson's unorthodox doings and asking if they had the sanction of the presiding brethren. These inquiries had prompted the call of Elders Benson and Snow to go to Hawaii.

Any doubt of the apostles concerning the accuracy of the incredible reports about Walter Gibson evaporated on reaching Lanai. They found that all the real and personal property of the members had ended up in the hands of Elder Gibson, presumably under a perverted doctrine of consecration. He had also designed a new flag, which, by his decree, floated above every chapel in the islands. He had inducted all male members into a militia and had ordered an end to family and personal prayer and scripture reading on the grounds that stress upon temporal affairs was overdue and that spiritual matters had been overemphasized. Moreover, he played upon the superstitious traditions of the people, insisting that they approach him on their hands and knees in the way their ancestors had been required to approach the ancient Polynesian kings. He had also designated a certain rock as a "holy place," in which a Book of Mormon and other objects had been deposited, and had surrounded it with an air of mystery, warning that any unauthorized touching of the stone would bring death.

Knowing the strong hold Elder Gibson had upon the minds of the people, the visiting brethren spent three days preparing for a conference scheduled for April 6. During this time, the apostles, in addition to scouting around and interrogating some of the members, vainly attempted to persuade Elder Gibson to abandon his unorthodox views and conduct. The only result of this effort was to provide them with confirming evidence of his complete apostasy. They learned, for example, that his object in raising and training a militia was to bring the neighboring Pacific islands under his subjugation, and to organize them into a vast oceanic empire.

The village in which Elder Gibson resided consisted of about fifty families, who lived in neat grass huts and worshiped in a large open-air bowery covered with a grass canopy. At the appointed hour of 10:00 A.M., the entire village assembled in the bowery for the conference, eager to hear from their exalted leader, to whom they attributed supernatural powers, and only incidentally to hear from the visiting brethren. Elder Gibson endeavored to set the meeting in a perspective that would support his claims and discredit the apostles. He excused himself on some false pretext just before the elders entered the bowery, explaining that he would join them soon. The visitors took seats on the stand and patiently awaited Elder Gibson's return. At his appearance a few minutes later, the congregation, except for the visiting brethren, arose as a body and remained standing in respectful silence until he was seated.

After the audience had settled comfortably into their seats, he announced the opening hymn, following which he called on Elder Cluff to pray (who responded only after obtaining Elder Benson's approval). He then proceeded to announce a second hymn and to speak, again without obtaining the consent of the apostles or without acknowledging them. His earlier conversations with the visiting brethren obviously had alerted him to the reason for their visit. Knowing, therefore, that his membership was in jeopardy, and being unwilling to abandon his apostate views and practices or his ambitious designs of empire, he immediately launched into a harangue extolling his own virtues and accomplishments while demeaning and deriding the party from Salt Lake City. "These strangers may say they are your friends," he shouted to the audience, "but let me remind you how, when they lived here, years ago, they lived upon your scanty substance. Did they make any such improvements as you see I have made? Did not I come here and find you without a father, poor and discouraged? Did I not gather you together here, and make all these improvements that you today enjoy? Now you, my red-skinned friends, must decide who your friend and father is, whether it is these strangers or I who have done so much for you."

The following day a meeting was called by the apostles to try Walter Gibson for apostasy and insubordination. They read the letters of complaint against Elder Gibson and then invited him to respond. He did so, treating the visiting brethren and the audience to the same kind of harangue he had inflicted upon them the day before. He exhibited his letter of appointment to serve as a missionary as evidence of his authority to preside. The visitors hardly recognized this document, duplicates of which were to be found in the hands of hundreds of Mormon missionaries, because of the elaborate and colorful array of ribbons and seals with which Elder Gibson had adorned it to impress the natives and lend credence to his claim. "Here is my authority," he announced unabashedly, "which I received direct from President Brigham Young." Then, pointing at the two apostles, he declared scornfully, "I don't hold myself accountable to these men."

Despite the clear evidence of his fraudulent intent and the earnest pleas of the visiting brethren to reject him, the natives continued to support their self-appointed leader. When, toward the end of the meeting, Elder Benson moved that the conduct of Elder Gibson be "disapproved" and the motion was put to a vote, all but one of the native elders opposed it. Then Elder Snow arose to prophesy that in time Gibson would be rejected by all those who then supported him. Although it was more than two decades before this prophecy reached fruition, it was at last fulfilled in 1887, when Elder Gibson was driven from the islands to San Francisco, where he died a few months later.

Following the unsatisfactory meeting on April 7, the two apostles appointed Joseph F. Smith as the president of the mission and departed soon thereafter for Maui where, on April 8, they formally excommunicated Walter M. Gibson from the Church. With that act, the two apostles had completed their mission in Hawaii. Since there was no further duty to detain them in the islands, they were anxious to leave for home.

The first leg of the return trip took them back to Honolulu on Oahu, from which they departed on April 18. During the voyage to San Francisco, Lorenzo had the opportunity to preach to the passengers and crew of the steamship on which he and Elder Benson traveled, whose captain, moved by curiosity, had invited the Mormon elders to speak. Elder Benson, electing not to accept the invitation, instructed Elder Snow to represent them. "I ... had great liberty in explaining our faith," Elder Snow wrote later, "and the principles of the everlasting gospel." Although Lorenzo doubted he had convinced them of the truth of his message, it was satisfying that all present listened attentively and respectfully, with the exception of a certain clergyman who showed "great uneasiness and displeasure by dark expressions of countenance and various contortions of his features and body."

The returning apostles spent several days in San Francisco, where Lorenzo was impressed, and not a little intimidated, by the gigantic and elaborate restaurants where they dined. One in particular, that had a "miniature indoor railway" to carry food and dishes to the hundreds of diners, was distressing to him. He found that the "noise and clatter" of the place was hardly "soothing and musical to a delicate ear" and to one with the kind of "sensitive nervous organization" he possessed.

While eating at one of San Francisco's famous restaurants, Elder Snow detected "a heaving or rocking motion of the floor, as if the foundation was giving away." While failing to understand the reason for it, he was soon caught up by the sense of fear and urgency that had seized the other diners, who had bolted for the exits without bothering to claim their wraps or pay for their meals. Paying as he left, Lorenzo "begged" the cashier to explain the abrupt departure of the others. "An earthquake," he shouted. Since Elder Snow was the last one to leave, he attributed the cashier's "vexation" to the fact that the other guests had left without paying. "Much [damage] was done," he recorded afterward, "not only to the restaurant so suddenly vacated, but to many other buildings."

The growing stature and prominence of the Church was illustrated to Elder Snow when, before leaving San Francisco, the president of Western Telegraph Company, on his own initiative, furnished the two apostles with a free pass to Salt Lake City.

At a public meeting held in the "Old Tabernacle" on May 29, 1864, Elder Snow and his companion reported their mission to the islands and their excommunication of Walter M. Gibson. On motion of President Brigham Young, this judgment was ratified by the unanimous vote of the congregation.

Later, in private counsel with the two apostles, President Young expressed doubt about the wisdom of continuing to spend time and effort proselyting in Hawaii in view of the difficulties involving Elder Gibson. "I plead with him," Lorenzo said of the incident, "by the deepest and strongest feelings of my heart, not to slacken his interest, nor withhold from continuing his former . . . plans in relation to that field of missionary labor. I told him that if I were twenty years younger, and should the Presidency think proper to invest me with the privilege of selecting the field for my missionary work to continue for twenty years, I would prefer to spend those years among the good, simple, warm-hearted natives of those islands."

Chapter Seventeen

The Box Elder Cooperatives

fter the Hawaiian interlude, Lorenzo returned to his
family and leadership duties in Brigham City. There
he was to devise an ambitious and successful plan
for cooperative communal enterprise based
upon the principles of the united order.

In the mid 1860s, at the time of Lorenzo's return from
Hawaii, there was added reason for the Mormon leaders to re-
emphasize these principles. They expected that within a few
years a railway would cross the nation, thereby opening up
the intermountain area to large numbers of non-Mormons,
diluting the influence of the Church and weakening the cohe-
sive forces that welded together the Saints and their leaders.

Typical of Lorenzo's views on the united order is this excerpt from a talk delivered at a meeting in Saint George:
"Many years have transpired since we received the revelation
of the United Order, and in one sense that long period of time
bespeaks negligence on our part in not more fully obeying it.
The very principles of that order, in my estimation, were given
for our temporal and spiritual salvation. In order to derive the
benefit that God designed should flow from them, they must
be established and systematized on the principle of righteousness, each person learning to love his neighbor as himself.
Then will they enter into the spirit of the two great commands
upon which, said the Savior, 'hang the law and the Prophets,'
namely, loving the Lord with all our might, mind and strength,

and our neighbors as ourselves. This, in my opinion, is the foundation of our future success, temporally and spiritually, in this United Order."

These high objectives, enforced by urgent directions from Brigham Young, moved Elder Snow to begin the development of an extraordinary group of Brigham City cooperatives. Eventually totaling from thirty to forty separate projects, these cooperatives had their genesis in a conventional business corporation, whose name ultimately evolved into the Brigham City Mercantile and Manufacturing Association. It began with four stockholders, including Lorenzo Snow, and a capitalization of three thousand dollars. In the beginning all earnings were plowed back into the operation by paying dividends only in commodities sold by the store. As the business prospered and expanded, other investment capital was attracted to the mercantile company which, at last, became firmly established in the community with a substantial capital surplus. At this point Elder Snow proposed an expansion into what he called "home industries." Following the pattern set at the inception of the parent organization, he also proposed that any dividends realized from their operation would be paid only in the products they manufactured. Moreover, he proposed that one-fourth of the value of the labor performed by those establishing or operating new home industries would be paid in merchandise from the parent or subsidiary organizations, and the remaining three-fourths would be paid with capital stock. In this way the artisan who lacked financial resources would be able to capitalize his labor into an investment that would have a continuing and, hopefully, ever-growing value. As important as anything else, however, an artisan with no management skills would be the beneficiary of the administrative talents and experience of those who managed the mercantile company.

At the outset, the stockholders of the parent company were reluctant to accept Lorenzo's proposals. They were concerned about the risks involved in investing hard-earned surpluses in unproven enterprises and about the dilution of their interests through the issuance of stock for labors performed by the workers. Through his persuasive eloquence and exam-

Lorenzo Snow as he appeared about the time of the Box Elder co-operatives

ple, Elder Snow was able to convince his associates to go forward with the plan to promote home industries. Lorenzo wrote to Bishop Lunt in Cedar City, who was interested in the cooperative movement, "It required some effort on the part of our stockholders to reconcile their feelings with a knowledge of their duty and obligations as Elders of Israel and servants of

God. A good spirit, however, prevailed, and a desire to build up the Kingdom of God, and work for the interests of the people, outweighed all selfish considerations; hence, consent was granted by all the stockholders to establish home industries and draw dividends in the kinds produced."

The first major project was to build a two-story tannery "with modern improvements and conveniences." The cost of this building was ten thousand dollars, exclusive of materials and masonry and carpentry work, which were furnished by those involved in the enterprise in exchange for capital stock. Later, as this project became established and began to thrive, satellite businesses were created, consisting of a boot-and-shoe shop and a saddle-and-harness shop.

After gaining valuable experience in founding and operating the tannery and its related businesses, Lorenzo and his associates undertook what proved to be their most intricate and fateful project, a water-powered woolen factory. With this new enterprise, a sheep herd was built up as a reliable source of wool to satisfy the hungry demands of the factory. Beginning with fifteen hundred head of sheep, contributed by livestock owners in exchange for capital stock in the cooperatives, this herd ultimately enlarged to ten thousand head. At the height of its operations, the woolen factory employed thirty-two workers and generated forty thousand dollars annually through the production of men's and women's wear, blankets, and yarns.

Beginning with the development and operation of the tannery and the woolen mill, Elder Snow's fertile mind conceived and his iron will saw to fruition an almost bewildering cluster of other industries, including a millinery shop and a tailor shop. Branching out to satisfy the demands of the community for more variety and elegance in its apparel, silk and cotton divisions of the clothing industry were organized. Thousands of mulberry trees provided food for the silkworms from which the silk was manufactured, and the cotton came from a 125-acre farm the cooperatives acquired in Utah's Dixie, over three hundred miles away. It was operated by young men from Brigham City who were called to serve two-year "cotton missions." These missionaries also produced raisins and sugar. Elder Snow helped acquire several farms to produce vegetables and grains. A horticultural department supervised the cultivation of orchards, vineyards, flowers, and shrubs. The machinery necessary to operate these agricultural enterprises was manufactured and repaired by a machine and maintenance department that included a blacksmith shop. A dairy at Collinston, reputed to be the "best and most commodious" of any dairy in the territory, produced quality milk, butter, and cheese. Pigs that ate the refuse from the dairy, a horn herd of cattle, and sheep furnished meat for the table.

To provide housing for his people, Lorenzo directed the formation of a dizzying variety of guilds, or departments, devoted to the construction of private and public buildings, including sawmills; a brick-and-adobe department; a lime kiln; carpentry, masonry, and architect departments; and a woodworking factory. A furniture-and-cabinet department manufactured furnishings for these buildings. Elder Snow also spearheaded the formation of tin and pottery shops; rope, broom and brush factories; a greenhouse and nursery; a public works department to supervise the construction of roads, bridges, and irrigation projects; an education department to administer the school and seminary; and even a "tramp department," which gave handouts to itinerant hobos in exchange for menial labor.

Lorenzo was frequently invited to explain the intricacies of his system to audiences outside Brigham City. And his correspondence on the subject, written in answer to inquiries about how to organize and operate cooperatives, provides the most detailed explanation of what he did and how he did it. Moreover, Brigham Young, Elder Snow's mentor and presiding officer, recognized his significant achievement with this accolade: "Why, up there in Brigham City Brother Snow has led the people along, and got them into the United Order without their knowing it."

President Young's statement takes on added meaning when it is realized that the first united order community established at Saint George in 1874 used the Brigham City cooperatives as its model, and other such communities organized afterward followed closely the pattern set at Saint George. One might even say that Lorenzo Snow's cooperatives were the foundation of the whole united order movement commenced on a large scale in the mid 1870s and pursued so tenaciously for many years thereafter.

Chapter Eighteen

Disaster Strikes the Cooperatives

The major administrative change made when the Brigham City Cooperatives were converted to the united order in 1874 was the creation of a "United Order Council" comprised of sixty influential citizens of Box Elder County, which acted as a policy-making body under the direction of Elder Snow. Moreover, the interests of the people in their cooperatives, or home industries, were then looked upon as "stewardships" for which they were ultimately accountable to the Lord acting through his earthly priesthood leaders. In the main, however, the work went on as before.

To assume that life in Brigham City in those days ran a smooth, untroubled course would be an error. Inequalities and personal conflicts, while minimized by the system, were not wholly eliminated. And the burgeoning enterprises of the united order began to impose heavy administrative burdens upon Lorenzo, burdens he had not quite anticipated when he first began to promote home industries. "When Israel left their leeks and onions," he wrote in a letter to President Brigham Young shortly before the latter's death, "they looked to [Moses] for their supplies, and became very quarrelsome and troublesome whenever they failed. This is a feature in the United Order which I contemplate with no small degree of anxiety, viz. concentrating a multitude of individual responsibilities upon one man or a few men. One may assume the responsibility of looking after the general interests of a community but to be required to provide for their daily wants, their food and clothing, one might do very well in prosperous times, but not very desireable in a financial crisis unless abounding in resources."

As the weight of Lorenzo's responsibilities steadily increased, he was intermittently seized with feelings of doubt and uncertainty. "I confess," he wrote to President Young, "[that] in the silence of the night...I have sometimes inquired of myself, where are we drifting, in following this untrodden path for many generations, and in sailing upon a sea so little known and unexplored? Is there not a danger of getting an elephant on our hands (to use a common phrase) that our wisdom and ability cannot manage or support? In other words, may we not drift into responsibilities that would be difficult or even impossible to discharge?"

The doubts that assailed Elder Snow never materialized. But, on November 1, 1877, only a few weeks after Lorenzo had written his letter to President Young, he was startled from sleep by the clangor of bells and the excited cries of voices shouting, "Fire! Fire!" At that early day, when fire-fighting equipment and procedures were primitive, a fire that had gained headway before being discovered invariably spelled disaster. Hurriedly pulling on his clothes and running into the crisp autumn night, Elder Snow was dismayed to find that the blaze was at the woolen factory, a key fixture in the intricate structure of his cooperative empire.

It took only thirty minutes for the fire to consume the results of the thousands of hours of rugged toil performed by the Brigham City Saints. And as they gazed at the dying embers of the fire, we may be assured that there were many tears shed and many fearful apprehensions aroused as to what the future held for them.

The destruction of the woolen factory resulted in a thirty-thousand-dollar loss, not to mention the incidental losses suffered by the satellite operations. But Elder Snow and his associates began to build anew. And within six months, another factory was erected, phoenix-like, upon the ashes of the old one, and was pronounced by Lorenzo to be "superior to the one destroyed."

But the Saints had incurred heavy debt to rebuild the woolen factory. Since the cooperatives were founded chiefly upon a system of barter, they generated little cash revenue. This required that Elder Snow look afield for the money with which to pay the mortgage on the new factory. He contracted with the Utah & Northern Railroad to furnish ties and other wood products to construct and maintain its line. This, in turn, required further borrowing to finance the construction of a sawmill in Marsh Valley, Idaho, near the stand of timber from which the wood products were to come. Once the mill was constructed (which included an auxiliary steam sawmill transported to Idaho from Brigham City), a hundred brethren from the Box Elder Stake were called to Idaho to conduct the logging and milling operations necessary to fulfill the railroad contract.

The mill had hardly begun to produce when its operations were stopped by an injunction obtained by enemies of the Church on the ground that the timber being fed to the mill had been removed from government land without authorization. Moreover, thirty to forty of the workmen were arrested and imprisoned for the alleged violation of certain criminal statutes. Enmeshed in a complicated legal snarl, and harassed by determined enemies, this abortive enterprise was shot down almost before it became airborne. It gave Elder Snow and the imprisoned workmen little comfort when their legal position was later vindicated through the influence of the President of the United States, who intervened in the matter at the urging of the powerful railroad executive and financier Jay Gould. By then it was too late to enable Lorenzo to fulfill his contract with the Utah Northern. So the sawmill was sold for a pittance, and the steam mill and related equipment were moved back to Brigham City, the whole fiasco entailing an out-of-pocket loss of six thousand dollars, not to mention the loss of time, the agony of the legal skirmishing, and, for the workmen, the degradation of being imprisoned.

Only a few months elapsed before another calamity descended—an assessment for $10,200 levied by the collector of Internal Revenue on the scrip used by the cooperatives as a medium of exchange. Again, it was little consolation to Lorenzo when, several years later, the collector's decision was reversed and the assessment returned, especially since the reversal came as the government was commencing its preparations to indict him for unlawful cohabitation under the Edmunds Act.

Reeling from these three massive setbacks, Elder Snow continued to struggle to protect his cooperative enterprises from the ruin that now threatened so ominously, but he was confronted by two final adversities. The first was a drought that shriveled the crops on his cooperative farms; the second was a grasshopper invasion that all but destroyed the vegetation that had managed to fight its way upward through the parched soil.

The Squire of Brigham City clinically analyzed his precarious situation in a letter written in 1879 to his friend and fellow-apostle Franklin D. Richards: "There appeared now but one course left for us to pursue—curtail our business, close several of our departments, lessen the business of others, and dispose of such property as will assist in discharging our cash obligations." He estimated that these obligations totaled over fifty-three thousand dollars, all of which had been incurred in a period of nine months.

The disintegration of the once-powerful system of cooperatives continued unabated until, by 1880, only the general store remained. This keystone establishment, the proud ancestor of the numerous enterprises that were spawned during a fifteen-year period, continued to operate until 1895, when it went bankrupt as the result of the severe depression of the 1890s.

The most fitting epitaph for the marvelous Brigham City Cooperatives was penned by Lorenzo Snow in the united order minutes on July 20, 1880: "Because of many losses and disasters, we have discontinued some of our enterprises and curtailed others. Yet for a period of fifteen years, our union has prevented division in mercantile business; to say nothing about many other things which have been done by our union, and I have nothing to regret of all we have accomplished. We have kept out our enemies, and in all these matters we did them by common consent."

Chapter Nineteen

The Burgh on the Bear

The enemies Elder Snow referred to in his epitaph of the Brigham City Cooperatives had begun to proliferate in Box Elder County in the late 1860s coincident with his aggressive promotion of home industries. These were the apostates and gentiles who, looking toward the completion of the transcontinental railroad, were determined to neutralize the influence of the Church on the economic lives of the Latter-day Saints. The key to their plan was the town of Corinne, located a few miles northwest of Brigham City, whose foundations were laid in March of 1869, two months before the driving of the golden spike at Promontory Summit. Referred to by Stenhouse in his book *The Rocky Mountain Saints* as the only "Gentile commercial city in the territory," Corinne was named after the daughter of General J. A. Williams, one of its early settlers. Because of its location near the mouth of the Bear River as it flows into Willard Bay, and because of irritation at the pretentious claims the gentiles made for it, the Mormons soon began to refer to Corinne disparagingly as "The Burgh on the Bear."

The gentiles seemed justified in their optimism for Corinne. Lying on the Central Pacific Railroad only a short distance below the junction of the Malad and Bear Rivers, it was a logical gateway to the Malad and Bear River Valleys and thence to points in Northern Idaho, Montana, and Oregon. Moreover, it was expected that Corinne would become the terminus of the Central Pacific and Union Pacific lines.

It was with high expectations, therefore, that the promoters of Corinne gathered at Promontory Summit on May 10, 1869, to officially link the two lines that had been extended feverishly from the east and the west. The only two high leaders of the Church who deigned to attend these ceremonies were Elder Franklin D. Richards, who was duty-bound to be there because of his role as a principal figure in Ogden, through which the line passed; and Elder Ezra T. Benson who, with two others, was a contractor for the construction of a portion of the Central Pacific line from Humboldt, Nevada, into Utah. But, none of the Salt Lake brethren attended, nor did Elder Snow see fit to be there representing Brigham City. The main reason these leaders absented themselves from such a historic event lay in the political jockeying that had resulted in both Salt Lake City and Brigham City being bypassed by the line, a decision the promoters of Corinne believed would cause the economic withering, if not the death, of both communities.

If Elder Snow was conspicuous by his absence on this occasion, T. B. H. Stenhouse, Lorenzo's old friend and co-worker from the days of his Italian mission, was conspicuous by his presence. During the intervening years, the paths of these two brilliant, highly literate men had diverged sharply from the parallel course they had once followed. Lorenzo had concentrated on the development of his spiritual qualities, while Elder Stenhouse had devoted himself almost exclusively to the nurturing of his intellect. And he had achieved some success. He had worked with distinction on the staff of one of New York City's most prestigious newspapers. Later, moving to Salt Lake City, he became the editor and proprietor of the *Salt Lake Telegram*, which soon gained the respect of all for its literary qualities. At this point, however, his views and objectives collided with those of the Mormon hierarchy, including Elder Snow, his former presiding officer in Europe. Feeling, perhaps, that his experience in Britain, Europe, and New York City, coupled with his unquestioned literary talent, gave him

115

skills and insights not possessed by men raised in rural, un-tamed America, and obviously lacking deep knowledge or convictions about the prophetic role of the Church leaders, it was easy for him to begin to criticize the Brethren in a field where he considered his knowledge and understanding to be superior to theirs—economics.

He and a small clique of intellectuals loudly rejected the idea of home industries and cooperatives, contending that the flood of manufactured goods to be available through rail transport would fully satisfy local needs and would be less expensive and of better quality than those produced in Utah. Their voices on this issue became even more loud and strident when the Mormon leaders asked those working on coopera-tive projects to accept a reduction in pay to enable the local manufacturies to compete with the less expensive goods from outside the territory.

On the positive side, it was the view of these dissidents that more of the energies of the Saints should be channeled into the development of the area's vast mineral resources, a contention that made them even more odious to the apostles, who could see only degradation for their people in pursuing such a course. As the issue became more clearly defined, and as the controversy heated up, Elder Stenhouse and his friends began to deal more in personalities, thereby shifting their focus from the policies of the Mormon hierarchy to the hierar-chy itself. Their writings, vented in the columns of the *Telegram*, or in the *Utah Magazine*, which they also controlled, painted unflattering caricatures of the Mormon leaders, portraying them as venal, dictatorial men more interested in feathering their own nests than in caring for the needs of their flock.

Against this background, T. B. H. Stenhouse must have known, as he sat with the press corps watching the golden spike ceremony, that the schism opened up between him and his former associates was irreparable. And had he been en-dowed with foresight, he would have seen that in less than six months his rebellion would be rewarded with excommunica-tion from the Church. Still further ahead, he would have seen his final and absolute rejection of Mormonism, ostensibly be-cause he had "outgrown" it.

It was when his apostasy had ripened to this point that Mr. Stenhouse published what he considered to be his most significant literary creation, *The Rocky Mountain Saints*, whose preface, while acknowledging he "had fellowship of the church for over a quarter of a century" and "enjoyed familiar intimacy with the apostles and leading elders," declared that he "utterly" disbelieved "the assumption that the Mormon Church is the exclusive and only true Church of Christ upon the earth." Through more than seven hundred pages, the author, a former converted, dedicated, and testimony-bearing mission president, then painted a highly deprecatory portrait of the Latter-day Saints and their leaders that embarrassed and saddened his former friends and associates. Chief among them was his former leader and advocate, Lorenzo Snow, who probably mourned over this apostate more than any other he knew over the long years of his ministry because of their parallel interests and affinities in the intellectual realm. We may infer a continued feeling of respect for Elder Snow by Mr. Stenhouse from the fact that the author fails to make any mention of him in the entire course of his lengthy and well-researched book.

Having been exposed to a quarter-century of Mormon tenacity and resourcefulness, it is doubtful that T. B. H. Stenhouse or any other intelligent observer would have believed the Mormons would concede the economic supremacy of the Burgh on the Bear that some observers at the golden spike ceremony were anxious to claim for it. Indeed, there was already afoot a project intended to minimize the economic advantages that would inure to Corinne by reason of its favored location on the main line of the transcontinental railroad. This project was set in motion only a week after the golden spike was driven. The occasion was a groundbreaking ceremony held on May 17, 1869, near the Weber River just below Ogden. Brigham Young was in charge in his role as the president of the Utah Central Railway, a company organized to construct a spur line connecting Salt Lake City and Ogden. Present were most of the leading brethren who had deliberately refrained from attending the event held just a week before at Promontory Summit, including Lorenzo Snow. This line was completed in just eight months, and, unlike the Union Pacific and Central Pacific lines, was constructed without government subsidies.

On a cold wintry day in January 1870, Elder Snow joined a group of dignitaries from Box Elder, Cache, and Weber Counties to ride to Salt Lake City on the new line to participate in ceremonies celebrating its completion. Providing another sharp contrast with the event held at Promontory Summit eight months before, Lorenzo and nine other members of the Quorum of the Twelve, and two members of the First Presidency were on the stand to witness the ceremonies.

President Young symbolically pounded home the last spike, which was moulded from iron manufactured in southern Utah, using an "elegantly chased steel mallet" made at the Church blacksmith shop in Salt Lake City. An emblematical beehive had been engraved on the top of the mallet, along with the inscription "Holiness to the Lord" and the letters U.C.R.R. The program included several talks and a dedicatory prayer offered by Elder Wilford Woodruff of the Quorum of the Twelve, all of which were interspersed with the firing of gun salutes and numbers rendered by the four bands. Numerous banners festooned the stand and buildings in the city bearing mottoes like "Hail to the Utah Central" and "Utah Stretches her Arms to the Two Oceans"; that night, there was a great bonfire and a fireworks display on Arsenal Hill, north of the city.

One of the talks delivered at the spike ceremony was especially pleasing to the large partisan Mormon crowd, estimated at 15,000. This was given by the chief engineer of the western division of the Union Pacific Railroad, who said in part, "I have been fifteen years engaged in railroad business; but I have never seen a single road made to which capitalists did not contribute their money, or the responsibility of which did not fall upon the government, or the state in which said road was made. But here nearly forty miles of railroad have been built, every shovelful of dirt of which has been removed by the workingmen of Utah, and every bar of the iron on the road has been placed in position by their labor. [At this point loud cheers arose from the crowd.] You can publish to the world that the workingmen of Utah built and own this road."

Here the speaker paused, and then, half in jest and half seriously, he added these words of admonition: "I have said one thing, and I want to say one thing more. Do not stop where you are. When you laid the last two rails today, they stuck out a little. That means—'Go On!' "

As if he were acting upon that command, Elder Snow soon became a supporter of the Utah Northern Railway, a narrow-gauge line that would connect Ogden, Utah, with Franklin, Idaho. It was a signal event when, in August, 1871, ground was broken for this new line in Lorenzo's own Brigham City; and when, on the twenty-fifth of March of the following year, the first rail was laid there, the community's enthusiasm boiled over.

The completion of the Utah Central and the Utah Northern railroads effectively neutralized the commercial advantages of Corinne, sealing its doom as an insignificant challenge to the predominant influence of Salt Lake City and the Church in the economic lives of the Latter-day Saints. For a short time, it was a temptation for the Brigham City Saints to travel the short distance to Corinne to purchase the plentiful and inexpensive goods that crowded the shelves of its merchants.

But, with his ecclesiastical authority and personal influence, Lorenzo was able to slow the traffic of his people with the merchants of Corinne to a mere trickle. And the completion of the railroad to Salt Lake City and eventually to Ogden and to Franklin, Idaho, finally strangled the Burgh on the Bear, leaving only a cluster of unimpressive, nondescript buildings and the ruined expectations of the ring that had planned and built it.

Chapter Twenty

Pilgrimage to the Holy Land

Having served as a special witness of the mission and divinity of Jesus Christ for nearly a quarter of a century, Elder Snow found meaning and satisfaction in a call that came to him in 1872 to accompany a party in a pilgrimage to Palestine, the land of the Savior's birth. Heading the group was President George A. Smith, who, four years before, had been called as the first counselor to Brigham Young, replacing Heber C. Kimball.

The appointment of President Smith to lead this pilgrimage came in the form of a letter from Brigham Young and Daniel H. Wells. It directed him to look for missionary openings as he conferred with men "of position and influence" during his travels in Europe and the Middle East. It also instructed him to dedicate and consecrate the land of Palestine "that it may be blessed with fruitfulness, preparatory to the return of the Jews."

Having been given authority to select his traveling companions, he chose, in addition to Elder Snow, Feramorz Little, Paul A. Schettler, George Dunford, Eliza R. Snow, and Clara Little.

Leaving Salt Lake City in late October 1872, Eliza traveled to Ogden on the Utah Central. Meeting her brother there, the couple traveled eastward on the Union Pacific Railroad toward a rendezvous with the other members of the party in New York City. Observant and literate, this pair, so alike in their interests and outlook, wrote lengthy and descriptive letters along the way that were published afterward in a booklet entitled "Correspondence of Palestine Tourists."

This being his first transcontinental trip in a railway luxury car, it was inevitable that Lorenzo, the veteran of Garden Grove, Pisgah, and the Horn, would draw this comparison: "We now felicitate in palace cars magnificently arranged, sitting at our ease, sleeping at our pleasure, all in happy security. Then it was driving oxen, watching for savages, building camp fires with buffalo chips, sitting and sleeping upon the ground under the enchantment of the hiss of the serpent, and thought of the scorpion, the wolf and the painted warrior."

The travelers, appalled by the devastation inflicted upon Chicago by the great fire the previous year and enthralled by the mighty power of Niagara Falls, arrived in New York City on November 3. During their three days there, they made the necessary arrangements for their passage and obtained helpful letters of introduction from the German consul general, Mr. Roesing, whom President Smith had met in Salt Lake City when the consul general was touring America.

The traveling party, all assembled now, boarded the *Minnesota* on November 6.

Lorenzo wrote of the voyage, "The sea a long distance around in the direction of the land seems to be playing at hide-and-seek, that appeared almost ludicrous yet of course highly diverting, having formed itself into innumerable living shapes tossing themselves up, covered their caps with frothy white, instantly dissolving into sea, then up again with their pretty caps covered with silvery spray. We have now been to sea many days and seen nothing but sun, moon, stars, sky and sea; no whales, no serpents, no mermaids. We have seen waves in countless numbers rolling up and down, tumbling around, then quietly falling off into calm peaceful slumbers. Then on a sudden roused as if stirred by some demon of the deep, gather up into monstrous billows driving madly one upon the other, like mountain chasing mountain."

Perhaps nowhere in his writings does Elder Snow reveal more clearly his poetic nature than in these entries. If he had possessed the leisure and the means necessary for major literary achievement, this sensitive and perceptive man possibly would have left to succeeding generations significant works of prose or poetry, but thirty-six years of work in the Church had channeled his interests and energies away from a life of literature. The entry that followed his poetic description of scenes at sea implies Lorenzo's desire to get on with his work: "This is all quite splendid and magnificent, but to the fearless soon becomes tiresome, and monotonous, and to the nervous, unfascinating."

When Lorenzo disembarked at Liverpool, a port he knew well by this time, he was greeted by a group from the European Mission Office, headed by President Albert Carrington, who, two years before, had joined Lorenzo as a member of the Twelve.

During their short stay in Liverpool, the visitors counseled with the local leaders and addressed congregations of the Saints who avidly listened to firsthand accounts of what was going on at Church headquarters. The visitors toured the city, and were shown the places and objects of special historical and cultural interest. Then the visitors departed for London, traveling through the Midlands, rich in English history and lore. The wooded hills, the fields enclosed with stone fences, the quaint villages with cobbled streets and picturesque buildings, and the ancient castles and baronial mansions filled them with wonder. Of special interest to Lorenzo and Eliza was Stratford-upon-Avon, the birthplace of William Shakespeare, whose literary masterpieces had afforded them many hours of reading enjoyment.

Although he was well acquainted with London, Elder Snow saw this exciting metropolis through different eyes than he had seen it on the occasions of his previous assignments there. Now he had time to visit and write about the places of historic and cultural interest that ordinarily attract tourists. The travelers visited the older landmarks—the houses of Parliament, Westminster Abbey, Westminster Bridge, and Trafalgar Square. Of equal interest was a new underground railway. However, judging from the amount of space he devoted to them in his letters to the *Deseret News*, the object in London that drew Elder Snow's attention most powerfully was the Tower of London. "If one wishes to indulge in melancholy or the sympathetic," he wrote gloomily, "he should visit the Tower of London and devote an hour or two in examining its mouldering records and crumbling inscriptions, pointing to heart-rending scenes enacted in past ages within its dark and gloomy walls." This apostle of love was appalled by the instruments of torture and death displayed for the enlightenment of visitors: "We were shown the executioner's axe, the beheading block, thumb-screws, iron collars and other horrid instruments for human torture. We were conducted to a small enclosure, surrounded with iron palings, where many illustrious men and women of distinction and royalty had been privately executed. . . . The strange scenes enacted in past ages, beneath these frowning battlements, form a dark and bloody page in English history."

From London, the party traveled to Amsterdam via Haarlem. While at Haarlem, Elder Snow's mind was called up to deep reflection about the siege of that city during the Spanish War when, according to reports he had read, "The commandant and the Protestant clergy, together with two thousand townspeople, were barbarously executed, after having surrendered." Also, Saint Bovan, Haarlem's three-hundred-and-seventy-year-old church drew Lorenzo's attention: "This is a magnificent structure," he wrote to the *Deseret News*, "four hundred and twenty-five feet in length, its nave is supported by twenty-eight massive columns, eighteen feet in circumference." He was also impressed by the magnificent organ in Saint Bovan's, then reputed to be "the largest and most powerful in the world." It was pleasing to the travelers to have "the organist and three or four blowers . . . exhibit its merits."

The feature of Amsterdam that most interested Elder Snow was its unusual assortment of charitable institutions "designed for the benefit of the sick, aged and indigent, lunatics, foundlings and widows." It was a source of amazement to the visitors that some of these facilities "appeared more like palaces for the rich than dwellings for the destitute." Lorenzo was also impressed by the voluntary arrangements the Dutch had made for the education of the poorer classes of people. He mentioned especially the "Society of Public Welfare," whose object was to educate teachers, publish schoolbooks and works of literature, and establish Sunday schools, reading rooms, and libraries.

The party's first major stop in Belgium, before proceeding into France, was at Antwerp, where they visited the cathedral of Notre Dame, the royal palace, the theatre, the zoological gardens, and a famous museum that included an extensive art gallery. The painting there that most caught Lorenzo's eye was Ruben's masterpeice portraying Christ's crucifixion. The stunning detail of this painting made Lorenzo feel that he was "witnessing the reality of this shocking scene."

Traveling on to Brussels, Elder Snow was most impressed by a Catholic wedding, whose symbolisms and elaborate rituals greatly intrigued him. Lorenzo's well-developed proselyting instincts were evident too in his observation that of Brussel's population of one hundred and seventy thousand, only six thousand were Protestants.

Lorenzo exulted in his return to Paris, a city whose cosmopolitan air he had learned to appreciate during his previous visits. "Too much cannot be said of the beauty and magnificence of this wonderful city," he wrote approvingly on December 18, 1872. "I will not attempt, at present, to describe all that we have seen of its beauty and grandeur. I have just returned from promenading some of its principal streets, viewing it in its evening splendor, lit up with thirty-two thousand gas burners."

Traveling through the verdure of the forest of Boulogne to Versailles, the visiting Mormons were granted the recognition usually reserved for high government dignitaries. When visiting the National Assembly, Elder Snow reported to the *Deseret News* that they were "accorded seats appointed to foreign diplomats and ambassadors." Later, Monsieur Thiers, the President of the French Republic, granted them a lengthy, personal interview, during which the visitors described the efforts made by the Mormons to tame the western deserts of the United States. They also told him that aside from their pilgrimage to Palestine, a chief object of their tour was "to gather information and statistics of the progress of older nations, that through their experience we might more successfully benefit and improve the people we represented." Lorenzo was intrigued, and probably amused, by a report of their interview with Monsieur Thiers that appeared in a prominent Paris newspaper: "Although the Mormon party at present in France disclaims any other motive than that of pleasure and instruction for their proposed visit to Palestine, it is asserted by some who profess to be well informed, that they are going there to explore the ground for the foundation of a new Jerusalem. We see nothing improbable in this assumption. The people who created a paradise in Salt Lake may well aim at founding an Eden in the land of Prophets."

From Paris, the travelers followed a route familiar to Lorenzo, who had traversed it more than two decades before with Elders Toronto and Stenhouse. It took them through Lyon to Marseille on the Mediterranean.

From Marseille, the party traveled to Nice and thence to Genoa, the scene of Elder Snow's first, and unsuccessful, missionary labors in Italy. Lorenzo was intrigued by the magnificent Catholic cathedral of Saint Lorenzo. He wrote approvingly of a tour conducted through this historic cathedral by a uniformed guide, and amusingly of the fact that Eliza was prevented from visiting the small chapel of Saint John, within the cathedral, because of a rule that women could not enter it except on a certain day in the year. "My sister," he wrote, "who happened to be the only lady of the party present, bore this interdiction with her characteristic grace and fortitude."

From Genoa, the party traveled north to Turin, the capital of Piedmont, where Lorenzo had performed his most effective work during his Italian mission.

A trip into Lombardy was next on the itinerary, with a visit to Milan being the most significant attraction. There Lorenzo marveled at the scope and opulence of the famed cathedral built in honor of "Our Blessed Lady," which, at that time, had been under construction for nearly five hundred years and had cost a hundred and ten million dollars to build. It was estimated that another century would be required for its completion. In the presence of such architectural magnificence and longevity, Elder Snow, accustomed to the new and comparatively simple structures of the American west, stood in reverential awe. He commenced the year 1873 by attending high mass in this famous church on New Year's Day, the Archbishop of Milan presiding.

The travelers were to spend another month in pleasant Italy, dividing their time chiefly among Venice, the city of waters; Naples, the city of volcanoes; and the Eternal City of Rome. Lorenzo reported that the famous "seven hills" of Rome, which once "astounded the world with marble edifices, palaces and magnificent temples" were then occupied by only "a few churches, monastaries, nunneries, old farm-houses, gardens and vineyards." He noted that at its zenith, Rome supported a population of nearly two million, which had dwindled to about two hundred fifteen thousand at the time of his visit. Illustrating the overpowering predominance of the Catholic faith, Lorenzo wrote that in all of Rome, there were only "four hundred and fifty protestants."

Lorenzo and his party saw the remnants of the Temple of Venus; the Tarpeian Rock, from which criminals were anciently thrown to their deaths; the celebrated Colosseum; the Vatican; and Saint Peter's Cathedral. Of all the architectural and artistic wonders he found on every hand in the Vatican, the one that drew Lorenzo's attention most powerfully was Michelangelo's "The Last Judgment."

A natural phenomenon attracted Lorenzo's notice at Naples. "There has been a slight eruption of Vesuvius in the last twenty-four hours," he reported apprehensively. "Flames and red-hot stones were projected to a great height all day yesterday, and windows at Castellamare were shaken out by the earth's vibratory motion. There is an unusual volume of smoke issuing from the mouth of the crater, and the instruments at the observatory indicate the presence of strong electrical currents."

But, buoyed up by the confidence of their guides and by their own inquisitiveness, the travelers decided to see the volcano at close range. "The ascent was difficult and fatiguing," Lorenzo reported, "in places very steep, with ashes and sand nearly one foot and a half deep. . . . The crater was partially clear of smoke, affording a fine opportunity for examining the wonderful abyss. We tumbled a few rocks over the rim, which were more than thirty seconds reaching the bottom. Some of the party tried their strength of nerve by standing upon a craggy point, which appeared to hang over the burning chasm, and thrusting sticks into the smoking apertures, which inflamed in a moment. One of the party also sought to acquire fame in boiling and eating an egg in the midst of the burning heat and sulphurous smoke."

The travelers' last excursion in Italy was a train ride from Naples to Brindisi, a bustling Adriatic port. Boarding a steamer there, they sailed through the Strait of Otranto to Corfu (now called Kerkira), an island of Greece in the Ionian Sea. Remaining only long enough to inspect the extensive olive groves and grape vineyards that flourished there, to worship in the "magnificent" Greek cathedral, and to observe the "gaily and richly dressed" promenades that filled the city square Sunday afternoon, they embarked on a steamer for Alexandria, Egypt, where they arrived on February 6, 1873.

Elder Snow reported, "In Egypt, the practice of raising offspring is the general rule and is fashionable and popular. . . . While in this country I have not witnessed a single case of intoxication, though I have been in many places of large gatherings for general amusement. On every occasion the people were remarkably orderly—no boisterous speeches, loud talking or laughter. In their large crowds, and at hotels where only Egyptian servants and Arabs were employed, I considered my little effects more secure than at American or European establishments." Lorenzo was also impressed with the attitude of worshipful reverence he found among the people, who looked upon Adam, Noah, Abraham, Moses, and Jesus Christ as God's servants, although they regarded Muhammed as "the greatest and best."

As impressive to Lorenzo as the character of the Egyptian people was the history and tradition of their land. He and his party visited the sphinx, the pyramids, Pompey's Pillar, Cleopatra's Needle, and the Catacombs. An excursion along the rich delta of the Nile, with its luxuriant and diverse crops, recalled the wise husbandry of Joseph of old, which had brought temporal salvation to the house of Israel. A side trip to the Red Sea evoked memories of the centuries of Israelitish slavery that had followed Joseph's administration and the miraculous drama of the exodus, dominated by the towering figure of father Moses.

These trips to biblical sites set the stage for the culmination of Lorenzo's historic tour, which began when the steamer the travelers had taken from Port Said dropped anchor at Jaffa, the ancient Palestinian port on the eastern edge of the Mediterranean.

Chapter Twenty-one

Palestine

At Jaffa, there being no taxi facilities, the party had to walk through the city and its suburbs, dotted with citrus groves and tall cypress trees, to an encampment down the coast where their touring equipment had been assembled. The lack of adequate roads or hotels in Palestine made it necessary for the travelers to provide for all their own transportation, housing, and food during the two weeks they would tour the Holy Land. Lorenzo was pleased at the elaborate arrangements the tour guide had made. At the staging area he took an inventory that included three large circular wall tents that were to serve as sleeping quarters, two for the brethren and one for Eliza and Sister Little. The sleeping tent occupied by President Smith and Elder Schettler also doubled as a dining room. These tents were carpeted and were furnished with tables, camp stools, washbowls, iron bedsteads, and "excellent bedding," including mattresses and "clean white sheets." A fourth less elaborate tent was equipped with a range that burned charcoal made from the trimmings of olive trees. A chef, hired by the tour guide, prepared "three substantial meals a day, very well cooked and served." In addition to these amenities, the travelers were provided with "good horses, saddles, an efficient dragoman [interpreter] [and] plenty of servants."

After arrangements had been made for their departure, the three modern apostles (Albert Carrington having joined

President Smith and Elder Snow in England) and their party "struck their tents" at Jaffa and moved in caravan across the Plains of Sharon toward the Holy City of Jerusalem. Lorenzo wrote, "We felt that we were passing over the land once occupied by the children of Abraham, the plains once trod by the Kings of Israel with their marshalled hosts, the land of the Apostles and Prophets. We were in Palestine! The Holy Land!"

Angling in a southeasterly direction, the Mormon caravan slowly made its way across the plains toward the mountains of Judea. After four hours of pleasant travel, it reached the City of Ramleh, where Elder Snow mounted "the Martyrs' Tower," from which he had a panoramic view of the surrounding area—"the Plains of Sharon, Arab villages here and there upon rising mounds, gigantic prickly pear hedges, olive orchards, and now and then a palm tree rising majestically above the whole, and the mountains of Judea appearing in the distance."

Onward the caravan moved toward its destination, passing through the valleys of Ajalon and Elah, the latter having been the scene, centuries before, of the fateful battle between Goliath and the shepherd boy, David. At this season, the valley of Elah was "richly ornamented" with the Rose of Sharon, whose deep red color and velvety texture added a touch of elegance to a picnic lunch the party had there shortly before coming in view of Jerusalem.

Within an hour, the tourists reached the heights from which the city became visible. Seeing, for the first time, the main object of his lengthy pilgrimage, Lorenzo was moved to record this eloquent description of the scene: "Away to the right is Mount Zion, the City of David. Off to our left, that lofty eminence, with an aspect so barren, is the Mount of Olives, once the favorite resort of our Savior, and the spot last pressed by his sacred feet before he ascended into the presence of his Father. These interesting historic scenes, with all their sacred associations, inspire thoughts and reflections impressive and solemn. Yes, there is Jerusalem! Where Jesus lived and taught, and was crucified, where He cried, 'It is finished,' and bowed His head and died! We slowly and thoughtfully wind our way down the hill, passing the Russian buildings and other prominent establishments, until we reach the city and enter our encampment."

As Elder Snow visited various places of historic interest, both inside and outside the walls of the Old City, such as the temple site, the Church of the Holy Sepulchre, the House of Pilate, the Garden of Gethsemane, and the Mount of Olives, he became aware that time had obscured or obliterated the actual location of these sacred places, and that the fabrications of men had given them a mystical, fictitious quality. He gave voice to his concern about these distortions in a dispatch to the *Deseret News* on March 8, 1873: "Religious enthusiasts of opposite sects vied with each other in searching out relics, and places to be reverenced and adored by the people of their respective persuasions, performing pilgrimages to the Holy Land, their zeal, in some instances, carrying them beyond the bounds of honesty, to practicing deceit and imposition. Many of these places had been remaining for centuries beneath the gradual accumulations of debris, and could not be identified, either by history or tradition, consequently, divine intimations were sought, miraculous tests applied, and other methods resorted to in order to establish their claims to genuineness."

After describing in some detail the extreme, almost paganistic rituals performed by one of the Christian sects in the Church of the Holy Sepulchre to celebrate Easter, Elder Snow recorded, "These contradictions, contentions and impositions by the rival Christian sects, in Jerusalem, render the Christian religion a subject of scorn and contempt, both to the Jews and Mohemmedans, and it is certainly a matter of serious regret that, in this enlightened age of Christianity, such things should exist in this sacred locality where our holy religion was established, and our Savior martyred."

In marked contrast to the showy rituals that Elder Snow condemned was the simple yet impressive ceremony at the Mount of Olives on March 2, 1873. The three modern apostles George A. Smith, Lorenzo Snow, and Albert Carrington led a party to the summit. While their tent was being set up and furnished with a carpet, table, and chairs, the travelers visited the Church of the Ascension, which was reported to stand on the spot from which the Savior ascended into heaven after charging his apostles to carry the gospel message to the entire world. When everything was ready, the party entered the tent for the ceremony that had brought them halfway around the world, and which Lorenzo's sister characterized as "the crowning point of the whole tour." The opening prayer was offered by Elder Carrington. Testimonies were borne and a special service was conducted "in the order of the Holy Priesthood," in the course of which President Smith offered his prayer of dedication. In it he dedicated the whole land of Palestine for the gathering of the Jews, invoked divine assistance in the rebuilding of Jerusalem, implored God that he would restore "the early and latter rains" and "fruitfulness to the soil," and expressed gratitude for the restoration of the gospel and for the numerous blessings bestowed upon the Latter-day Saints.

While the dedicatory service conducted by President Smith on the Mount of Olives was the crowning event of the entire pilgrimage, there were other important things for the travelers to see both in Palestine and on the return trip. A three-day tour that held special interest for Elder Snow was a counter-clockwise circular journey that began at Jerusalem and took the party in a southwesterly direction to Bethlehem; then east to the Dead Sea; then northeast past Qumran to the Jordan; then northwest to Jericho; then southwest to Bethany; and then the short distance westward over Mount Olivet and through the Kidron Valley to Jerusalem. Within and along the irregular line of the circle marked by this trip lie some of the most significant sites connected with the Judeo-Christian religion. And having a highly developed historic sense, Lorenzo Snow undoubtedly appreciated and savored everything he saw. En route to Bethlehem, Rachel's Tomb (reverenced by Christians, Jews, and Mohammedans alike) and the Pools of Solomon drew the special attention of the *Deseret News* correspondent. He noted that the latter reportedly were built by King Solomon as storage facilities for water that was conveyed to Jerusalem by aqueduct.

At Bethlehem, a city "pleasantly situated upon a mountain ridge, the slopes of which are terraced with rows of fig and olive trees, rising one above another in regular gradation," the main object of interest was the Church of the Nativity, which presumably was built upon the spot where the Savior was born. As was true with many of the historic places in Jerusalem, Lorenzo was dubious whether this church was indeed standing upon the site of the famous stable where Mary gave birth to her baby. Despite his skepticism, there were aroused in Elder Snow "impressions never to be forgotten" when he saw in the Grotto of the Nativity the inscription "Hic de Virgine Maria Jesus Christus Natus est." Although he was a special witness of the Savior's reality and divinity, and had often felt his presence or influence, when Lorenzo visited this place and read the simple inscription, he was filled with a combined sense of awe and commitment that was never to abate during the remainder of his apostolic ministry. And although there is nothing to confirm it in a direct way, the inference is almost irresistible that from this moment, Elder Snow's yearning to see the face of the Savior while in mortality grew apace with his advancing years.

In making the difficult trek from Bethlehem to the Jordan via the Dead Sea, Elder Snow and his party unknowingly passed near the concealed caves from which were to be removed, almost a century later, the ancient scrolls that would cast an entirely new light upon many aspects of biblical history. Anyone who views a picture of the barren and forbidding area will appreciate the accuracy of Lorenzo Snow's word portrait of it: "Our path [extended] over high, barren, rocky ridges, through a wild, desolate region, skirting fearful ravines, and passing along the brink of frightful chasms and precipices, occasionally catching a glimpse of the Dead Sea, through breaks in the distant cliffs."

After stopping at the Dead Sea and marveling at the unusual buoyancy of its waters, so reminiscent of the waters of the Great Salt Lake, the party moved northward to a point on the bank of the Jordan River. There Lorenzo reflected upon important incidents that had occurred in the area centuries before, reflections about the ancient Israelites crossing the river on dry ground as the priests, bearing the sacred ark, stepped into the flowing stream; about Elijah, who was taken up into heaven by a whirlwind after he divided the waters and passed over on dry ground; about Elisha who, after taking up the mantle of Elijah that fell from him, smote the water of this famous old river saying, "Where is the Lord God of Elijah?"; and about the baptism of the Savior in the waters of Jordan at the hands of John the Baptist. Nor could the probing mind of Lorenzo Snow have failed to reflect upon the physical analogies between this ancient stream and the freshwater and saline bodies it connected and the Latter-day Saints' own Jordan River that connected Utah Lake and the Great Salt Lake.

Leaving the Jordan, the party moved across the Plain of Jericho, once noted for its fertility and verdure but now sustaining only what Lorenzo identified as "small fields of grain intermixed with thorny bush." And, upon reaching the city, he was appalled but not surprised to find that Joshua's curse still rested upon Jericho. (See Joshua 6:26.) "In riding through this disgustingly filthy town," Elder Snow reported to the *Deseret News*, "we were lustily cheered by some dozen dirty, half-naked children, collected for this purpose, but more particularly for backsheesh [money]. Sheep, children, goats, women and men, all indiscriminately huddled together, and no doubt this people deserved the profligate character given them, I.E. similar to that of Sodom and Gomorrah."

On the final lap of this memorable tour through the heartland of ancient Israel, so rich in historical lore, Elder Snow traveled through Bethany, over Mount Olivet, and through the Kidron Valley back to Jerusalem. At Bethany, the home of Mary and Martha and their brother, he recalled with a thrill the incident that occurred there when the Savior, after the stone had been removed from the tomb of Lazarus, who had been dead for four days, cried, "Lazarus come forth." One might imagine that while at Bethany, Elder Snow, inspired by the results of Jesus' command to Lazarus would have recalled the statement in the patriarchal blessing given to him by the Patriarch Joseph Smith, Sr.: "The dead shall rise and come forth at thy bidding." Had he done so, he likely would neither have questioned the reality of that patriarchal promise nor foreseen the way in which it would be fulfilled years later in the case of Ella Jensen, a young girl in Brigham City.

Leaving Jerusalem, the Mormon tourists traveled north to

Nablous (once called Schechem), an ancient city rich in Israel-itish lore. It was here, Lorenzo reported in a dispatch home, that Abraham first pitched his tent in Canaan, and that Simeon and Levi avenged the dishonor of their sister Dinah by mass murder of Schechem's population. This beautiful site, located among the mountains of Ephraim and near the hills Ebal and Gerizim, is also where Joshua addressed the people (see Josh. 24:1); where Rehoboam was crowned in the hope of concili-ating the northern tribes (see Kgs. 12:1); and where the bones of Joseph are buried.

From Nablous, the party moved onward to Samaria, the one-time capital of the kingdom of Israel, a fortress city, where Gideon, the famous hero of Manasseh, was reared. In the nar-row passes north of the city the "ten thousands of Ephraim and thousands of Manasseh" stubbornly defended their city against the northern invaders. So well fortified was it and so ferociously did the Josephite tribes defend it, that the Assyrian invaders were able to capture it only after a siege of three years. (See 2 Kgs. 17:5-6.)

In rapid succession, the travelers, by now anxious to com-mence their homeward journey, visited Jenis; Nazareth, where the Savior was born and spent his childhood; and Cana, where he performed the miracle of converting water into wine at the wedding feast. From Cana, Elder Snow and his party traveled on to Tiberias, a community established by Herod on the Sea of Galilee as a resort that took advantage of the recreational facilities of the lake and the therapeutic bene-fits of the nearby hot springs, reputed to be one of the finest in the Middle East.

The Sea of Galilee, perhaps more readily than any other place in the Holy Land, aroused in Elder Snow powerful and poignant reflections about the Savior. Unlike most other his-torical sites that visitors had seen, this one had not been sub-stantially altered in its appearance by the passage of time. By ignoring the structures built or altered in the interim, Lorenzo realized he was looking upon the identical scene that presented itself to the Savior when he visited there during his earthly ministry. From Tiberias, which stands on the shores of Galilee, Lorenzo could see the same blue waters that greeted the eyes of Jesus hundreds of years before, the surrounding hills rising up from the edge of the sea, and, far beyond in Syria, the towering eminence of Mount Hermon, whose snow-capped summit reaches an elevation of nearly ten thousand feet. Moreover, as Lorenzo approached the margin of the sea, he could hear the lapping of the water, a sound that had continued intermittently and unabated since Jesus' time. He could smell the familiar odors emanating from the fisheries in the area, and, with some imagination, could have envisioned the terror that seized the Savior's disciples when their boat was struck by one of the sudden storms that occur frequently in the area, caused by the rush of cold air from the nearby hills to the hot surface of the lake, which lies 680 feet below sea level. (See Luke 8:22-24.)

While visiting this historic place, Eliza, moved upon by a poetic impulse, composed a poem that Lorenzo quoted in one of his dispatches to the *Deseret News*. Its content and import are suggested by this verse: "Again, when the shades on night were gone;/ In the clear bright rays of the morning dawn;/ I walked on the bank of this self-same sea;/ Where once our Redeemer was wont to be."

Before leaving this intriguing place, Lorenzo and several others of his party explored the shores of the lake on horseback. In the process, he was again exposed to the kind of historical vision he had encountered elsewhere in the Holy Land when he was shown places along the shore of the lake where Mary Magdalene presumably had lived and where the astonished disciples had witnessed the enormous catch the fishermen took when they heeded the Master's direction to cast their nets on the other side of the boat.

Ascending a mountain above the Fountain of the Fig Tree where the party had made camp, Elder Snow was caught up in a prayerful reverie as he admired the magnificent scenery—the Sea of Galilee, the plain of Gennesaret, and impressive Mount Hermon—and as he reflected upon the scenes and events that had come and gone there over the centuries.

Lorenzo wrote, "[The Savior] came down from the hilly country of Galilee and made his home upon these shores, chose his twelve apostles, taught the people in their towns and villages, and on the seaside as they flocked around him in multitudes." He noted with a tinge of regret that the thriving cities of Chorazin, Bethsaida, and Capernaum, which once stood proudly upon the shores of Galilee, had all but ceased to exist. He also alluded to the opulence and the decadence that had characterized Tiberias in the days of the Savior, to the numerous "palaces and temples" that had adorned its streets, to the citizens "revelling in splendor and luxury," and to the many priests, attired in "imposing costumes, full of studied systematic knowledge of the law and the Prophets, and glowing with pious zeal to entrap and destroy the apostles and the Savior of the world." And more relevant to his apostolic calling Lorenzo referred to the Savior's ministry at and around Galilee, where he spoke to "anxious multitudes, healing the sick, unstopping the ears of the deaf, giving sight to the blind, and raising the dead."

Leaving Galilee with a sense of nostalgic reluctance, Elder Snow and his Salt Lake party traveled northeasterly past the Fountain of Dan, a main source of the Jordan, to Cesarea Philippi. He recalled that here Jesus counseled with his disciples following their first missionary effort when he asked about the views of the people concerning his identity. Here Peter, answering the Lord's inquiry, boldly declared by revelation that he was "the Christ, the Son of the living God." (Matt. 16:16.) Elder Snow observed in his report to the *Deseret News* that every person had "the privilege of obtaining a like revelation."

From Cesarea Philippi, the party continued on its northeasterly course to Damascus, "the Pearl of the East," reputed to be the oldest city in the world and to have been founded by Uz, the son of Aram. Leaving Damascus, the Mormons traveled the fifty miles to Beirut (spelled Beyrout by Elder Snow) over what Lorenzo characterized as "the only decent road in Syria or Palestine," a macadamized road that had been constructed by a French company.

After several weeks of traveling by horseback and living in tents, Lorenzo luxuriated in the comfortable accommodations found in the modern Beirut hotel where his party stayed. Being the Mediterranean gateway to Damascus and the interior of Syria, this bustling port had attracted substantial investment

137

capital, which manifested itself in the modern and impressive stone structures and wide paved streets found in the newer part of the city. Elder Snow's sense of comfort and repose while waiting for the ship that would take the party to Constantinople is clearly evident in this excerpt from one of his dispatches: "Our hotel, situated close upon the shore commands a splendid view of the Bay of St. George, on which are floating ships and steamers; the Mediterranean; the finest portion of the city; and some of the picturesque scenery of Lebanon. It is a mental luxury to look from my window, or out from the open balcony, and contemplate these lovely scenes, wrought by the hand of God, and by his inspiration in men."

Embarking on an Austrian Lloyd ship on March 25, 1873, Elder Snow and his friends steamed slowly out of the busy Beirut harbor, entranced by the colorful array of flags and pennants that fluttered from the steamers and masted ships clogging the waterfront. Above and behind them could be seen the groves of pine and mulberry trees that grew on the rising hills of the Lebanon mountains behind Beirut, interspersed here and there with groups of palm and cypress trees. And in their minds loomed the trail they had followed through the land that had given birth to the Savior of the world, had nurtured and protected him, had seen him cruelly put to death, and, at last, had seen him resurrected to a perfected and glorified state.

Lorenzo's words and conduct during the quarter of a century of life that was to remain after his Palestine tour reflected the lasting impression this trip had made upon him. The experience transformed him into a man more sensitive to the reality of Jesus' earthly life and ministry, more anxious to please and to serve him, more willing to spend time and means to promulgate his teachings and to solidify his earthly kingdom, and more determined to qualify to see his face and to dwell eternally in his presence, sharing with him all that the Father has.

Given Lorenzo's sensitive and contemplative nature and his role as a special witness of Jesus Christ, we may be assured that these and other like thoughts occupied his mind as his steamer made its leisurely way westward through the

Mediterranean, following a course that was familiar to the ancient apostles.

Once the barrier leading to the Gentile world had been breached by Peter's vision at Joppa, Cephas and his brethren, especially the Apostle Paul, frequently plied the sea lanes that Lorenzo now traveled. In succession there came in view the islands of Cyprus, Rhodes, and Patmos, the latter being the remote outpost where John received his apocalypse. The ship then called at Smyrna, occasionally alluded to as the Ornament of Asia, at Mytilene, and passed through the Dardanelles into the Sea of Marmora and thence to Constantinople (now called Istanbul and orginally named Byzantium).

"The port was crowded with ships, steamers, barges, ferries and small boats," wrote Elder Snow, "so numerous that they appeared as if swarming on the waters, numbering many thousands. This magnificent bay accommodates twelve hundred sail, and is sufficiently deep to float ships of war of the largest magnitude."

Lorenzo Snow the historian, the educator, and the modern apostle was wholly intrigued by this cosmopolitan city. "For advantages of trade and commerce, and for beauty of situation," he wrote, "Constantinople undoubtedly excels all other cities in the world. It stands upon two continents, Europe and Asia, and upon two seas, the Black Sea and the Sea of Marmora. Its population is variously estimated at from five hundred thousand to eight hundred thousand; of these about three hundred thousand are Greeks and Armenians, sixty thousand jews, and thirty thousand Europeans. It contains forty colleges, one thousand mosques, many Jewish synagogues, and numerous catholic churches."

In Elder Snow's view, the most significant structure in this, the capital of the Ottoman Empire, was the famed Mosque of Saint Sophia, a mammoth building that was originally constructed as a catholic temple in the sixth century by the Emperor Justinian. Nine hundred years later, it was converted into a mosque following the conquest of Constantinople by Mohammed the Second. This conquest was symbolized at the time of Lorenzo's visit by two flags suspended on either side of the pulpit, one representing the victory of Islam over Judaism

and Christianity, and the other representing the victory of the
Koran over the Old and New Testaments.

The travelers departed from Constantinople on April 5 on
another Austrian Lloyd steamer destined for Athens. En route,
they stopped at Syra long enough to enable them to see the
sights, to shop, and to get some respite from the constant motion of the ship, which, it appears, had begun to wear upon
the Utah inlanders.

Any monotony their voyages had produced was dissolved
upon docking at Piraeus, Athens's ancient seaport. The five
mile carriage ride from the port to the capital across the plain of
Attica aroused Lorenzo's contemplative faculties to the highest degree. His mind reflected upon the glory that once had
shone upon this pleasant land, the cradle of many democratic
principles that had found their way into the fabric of American
government. The vast olive groves in the area reminded him
of Plato, one of Athens's intellectual giants, who often retired
to their seclusion for his meditations. He was impressed, too,
by the luxuriant verdure of the orange groves, the cypresses,
the pepper trees, and the Lombardi poplars, the latter reminding him of Brigham City and other Utah communities whose
broad streets were lined with these stately monarchs.

During his five-day stay in Athens, Lorenzo saw all of the
customary sights: the Acropolis, with its "stupendous and
melancholy ruins"; the Areopagus, or Mars Hill, where Paul
delivered his classic discourse on deity to the superstitious
Athenians; the Museum; and the King's Palace, which was the
most conspicuous contemporary building in the city. Of particular interest to the modern apostle, as they were to Paul, were
the numerous temples atop the Acropolis—the Parthenon
and the temples of Minerva, Propylaca, Wingless Victory, and
the Erectheum. These ancient, ruined structures caused Elder
Snow to marvel, both at the architectural and engineering
expertise of the builders and at their distorted understanding
of the nature and purposes of God.

Following a practice routinely observed during their pilgrimage, the tourists paid a courtesy call on the American
Minister, a Mr. Francis, who graciously invited them to spend
an evening at his residence. There they also met the consul

general of Constantinople, Mr. Goodenough, who was spending a few days in the Grecian capital. Rounding out his contacts with officialdom, Lorenzo, quite by chance, also met on the streets of Athens one day the king of Greece, "who was walking leisurely along the sidewalk, among the citizens, dressed in plain, ordinary costume." Elder Snow was impressed not only with this young Monarch's casual style, but also with his fidelity and high aims. "He has the reputation of honesty and frankness," wrote Elder Snow, "and his domestic life above reproach, and makes the welfare and improvement of his people a direct aim and constant study."

Ordinarily one is aware of significant events when they occur, as for instance an anniversary, a recognition, a promotion, or some other change in status. And usually such events are celebrated at the time so as to impart a sense of progress and achievement. But there are exceptions to this rule, one of which happened to Lorenzo Snow while he was poking through the ruins of Athens and pondering the reasons for the decay of the civilization suggested by the architectural litter on the Acropolis. Some time later Lorenzo learned that on the day after his ship docked at Piraeus, he was sustained as a counselor in the First Presidency at the forty-third annual conference of the Church held in Salt Lake City. At the same time, four other new counselors in the First Presidency were sustained, Brigham Young, Jr., Albert Carrington, John Willard Young, and George Q. Cannon. This action underscored both the burgeoning growth and vitality of the Church and the declining energy of its aging leader, Brigham Young. Seventy-two years old at the time, and having wielded ultimate authority among the Saints for almost thirty years, the Lion of the Lord felt the need to call younger, more energetic men to help carry the increasing burden of Church administration. And the first of the five new counselors called was Elder Snow, who had celebrated his fifty-ninth birthday just five days before while he was admiring the opulence and power of Constantinople.

It is not difficult to surmise why Brigham Young called Lorenzo Snow into the inner circle of Church leadership at this time. The new counselor brought experience, spirituality, and achievement to the assignment. He had served in the Twelve for almost twenty-five years, had demonstrated his aptitude in using the powers of the unseen world, and had shown himself to be a man of affairs through his leadership in establishing the Brigham City cooperatives. Moreover, Lorenzo was a man of intellect and social grace with the kind of discretion that would give President Young a sense of confidence in assigning any kind of sensitive matter to him. Finally, there was the familial tie through Eliza (who was bound to President Young by a time-only marriage), which provided another ground upon which the two could meet in unity and understanding. That this association fulfilled President Young's expectations is indicated by the fact that it continued until the day of Brother Brigham's death over four years later.

Unaware of the new mantle that had descended upon him four days earlier, Elder Snow and his companions left Athens the evening of April 12, bound for Trieste in another of the ubiquitous Austrian Lloyd steamers. They reached this busy Adriatic port on April 17 after a leisurely five-day voyage. From Trieste, they entrained to the Bavarian capital of Munich, traveling through the Brenner Pass by way of Verona, Italy. This scenic route took the party through a rich and highly cultivated agricultural area that drew this appreciative comment from Lorenzo's pen: "The landscape [was] covered with verdure and rich in luxurious foliage, the apple, plum, apricot, cherry and chestnut adorned with blossoms, and the vine clothed with leaves; patches of clover, grain in full growth, green pastures and meadows, and off in the distance a long range of mountains, with summits mantled in snow."

After crossing the spectacular Bavarian Alps, it came as somewhat of a surprise to Elder Snow to discover that Munich, the capital of Bavaria, lay on a barren plain astride the Iser River. And after spending several days touring Munich and studying its public buildings, its parks, its squares, its museums, libraries, and public gardens, two aspects of the city seemed to dominate his thinking. The first was the latent spirit of militarism that appeared to underlie the attitudes of the ruling class. Symbolic of this was a large obelisk he found in one of the city's many squares. It had been erected in honor of the Bavarians who were killed in the Russian campaign of 1812. This inscription on the monument is indicative of the martial impulses that ruled the Bavarian aristocracy and of their efforts to keep alive the enmities that had produced their wars: "To the thirty thousand Bavarians who perished in the Russia war, erected by Louis First, King of Bavaria, completed October 18, 1833."

While in Munich, Lorenzo was to experience firsthand the psychological impact of a monarchial reign. And, inferentially, the experience demonstrated to him how one could be caught up in the pomp and ceremony of it and impelled to do and accept things he might ordinarily refrain from doing, or might reject. Such were the feelings inspired by an imperial wedding in which the king and his royal court and equipage were involved. Learning of the ceremony, Elder Snow and Eliza decided to witness it, and, leaving their hotel, walked to a point where the procession would pass. Lorenzo wrote that they "submitted to half an hour's journeying, pressing and smashing by the enthusiastic citizens of Munich." At last reaching the point from which they intended to watch the procession, it soon came in view, treating the two American spectators to a scene that stretched their imagination. "Secured the honor," wrote Elder Snow, "of gazing a moment on the passing pomp and glory of His Royal Majesty, the King of Bavaria, and occupying a point toward which he smiled and civilly bowed."

As we have already seen, Lorenzo was no stranger to the importance and use of pageantry and symbolism. Indeed, he used them to a greater degree than almost any of the other early leaders to stir up enthusiasm for a cause, to foster self-improvement, or to inculcate knowledge about the history or aims of the Church. He considered these to be valid goals that justified what some condemned as mere theatrical display. But after watching the showy spectacle in Munich that seemed to have little purpose other than to exhibit the opulence and arrogance of the king, Elder Snow's views toward pageantry underwent some change: "After narrowly escaping being trodden down by the crowd," he observed, "I returned to my hotel, wondering how much mathematical skill or philosophical wisdom would be required to determine the exact value of what was gained by this exposure."

The second feature of Munich that claimed Lorenzo's special attention, and that softened his attitude toward the monarchy, was the Royal Library, a magnificently beautiful building that housed a treasure of eight hundred thousand volumes. The Mormon apostle and his sister, who shared a deep interest in intellectual things, would have welcomed the opportunity to stay longer in Munich if for no other reason than to delve into the literary wealth of the Royal Library.

The remaining part of the tour in Europe consisted of visits to Vienna, Berlin, and Hamburg. Aside from the customary objects attractive to tourists, Elder Snow was chiefly impressed with three things as the continental tour drew to a close. The first was the constant military presence that both oppressed and excited the man who, in his youth, had aspired to the military life as a career. In reporting his visit to Austria, he noted, "As in all other countries which we have visited, soldiers, in military costume, are seen almost everywhere in great numbers." And at Berlin, the military tide seemed to reach its crest. "We were surprised," he wrote from the Prussian capital on May 12, 1873, "to see the multitude of soldiers constantly parading the main thoroughfares and streets in this city. Every day they are marching past our hotel, in battalions, regiments, brigades and divisions, in the most imposing style, with magnificent flags and banners displayed—all led by instrumental bands of musicians in rich shining costumes—the whole performing their evolutions in the strictest order, skill and precision, presenting the finest and most splendid appearance of troops in any country we have visited."

Perhaps because of the less than friendly reception he had received in many places as a young missionary, Elder Snow was often amazed by the cordial and deferential way in which he and his party were received in the metropolitan cities of Europe. Checking in to what Lorenzo described as "the most fashionable and aristocratic hotel" in Berlin, the travelers were visited by many dignitaries who wished to welcome them and offer assistance. He wrote to the *Deseret News* rather self-consciously, "Considerable sensation was created among the aristocrats in our hotel, through the calls of distinguished gentlemen on our party. Our celebrity reached the public press, where we were creditably noticed, and perhaps somewhat flattered."

And the special attention they received at Hamburg far exceeded that which was lavished upon them at Berlin. "At the railroad station," Lorenzo confided to the *Deseret News,* "the proprietor of a commodious hotel, in the most respectful manner, solicited our patronage, conducted us into his best apartments, and bestowed upon us more than ordinary attention. The next day he officiated gratuitously as our guide through the city, taking particular pains and manifesting deep interest in pointing out and explaining every object of interest and curiosity. At first, we were a little suspicious that these extraordinary attentions were designed to establish heavy claims on the purse, but the mystery was at length revealed; this gentleman had read the German papers, and, at once, recognized us as the Distinguished Mormon Delegation from Salt Lake. Our notoriety here brought us acquaintances."

Lorenzo Snow, the realist, who had seen much of life in many parts of the world, knew that there was a seamy side to the cities he visited that was not apparent to the ordinary visitor. He provided his *Deseret News* readers with this insight into the underworld of Berlin, a city that at first glance gave little hint of what lay beneath its impeccable exterior. "Those fashionable institutions, 'houses of ill-fame,' " he wrote, "are said to flourish and command the patronage of nearly all classes here, as in Paris, the gay metropolis of France; and some of them are built at an immense cost, and fitted up in fabulous splendor and sumptuousness. The people of Berlin, viewed superficially, are remarkably intelligent, and appear interesting, lovely, beautiful and happy, as though all were conscientious, moral, upright and pure; but, in this city, as well as in most others we have seen, corruption, rottenness, demoralization and misery are underneath."

Leaving Hamburg on May 16, 1873, on the steamer *Iris,* the travelers moved up the Elbe River into and across the North Sea (called the German Sea by Elder Snow), arriving at

Blackwall, London, the evening of the eighteenth. After a few days in England, during which time Lorenzo addressed several gatherings of Saints, who avidly drank in all he said about the Holy Land, the party embarked for the United States. There it disbanded, leaving its members to make their separate ways home.

Although they had been away from Utah for seven months, Lorenzo and Eliza decided to make a side trip to Ohio before returning. Elder Snow had visited Mantua and the surrounding communities only once in the previous thirty-seven years, and Eliza had never been back. Their return, therefore, was full of memories for them, and a celebrity event for their relatives and friends who had been kept abreast of their doings through correspondence and the press. Wherever they went in Portage and the surrounding counties, Lorenzo and Eliza, the Snow children grown older and famous, were received with open-armed enthusiasm. "Indeed, it was one continual ovation, from first to last," wrote Eliza to the editor of the *Woman's Exponent*. And as the visitors observed the changes time had wrought and reflected on the forces that were inexorably at work altering the appearance and condition of relatives and acquaintances, Lorenzo's sister composed this poem that capsulized the feelings of both on returning home after so long an absence:

> *Our former loved associates*
> *Have mostly passed away.*
> *While those we knew as children*
> *Are crowned with locks of gray.*
>
> *We saw time's varied traces*
> *Were deep on every hand—*
> *Indeed upon the people,*
> *More marked than on the land.*
>
> *The hands that once with firmness*
> *Could grasp the axe and blade,*
> *Now move with trembling motion*
> *By strength of nerve decayed.*

The change in form and feature
And furrows on the cheek,
Of time's increasing volume
In plain, round numbers speak.

And thus as in a mirror's
Reflection, we were told,
With stereotyped impressions,
The facts of growing old.

The magnetic pull of Lorenzo to his natal home found parallel in the attraction he felt toward the home of his adoption—Utah, and, more particularly, Brigham City. Indeed, in assessing his feelings after an absence of almost nine months, the well-traveled apostle concluded that no place on earth was so congenial to his sensibilities and spirit as this rural, struggling community. And these feelings of "homeness" were intensified to a high degree by the elaborate welcome that was staged for him, a welcome in the best tradition of the pageantry Lorenzo himself had devised years before to honor President Young. It began at Brigham Junction on the Central Pacific line, four miles from town, where waited the mayor and city council, the bishop, the local judge, and a host of relatives, friends, and neighbors. Following a welcoming address delivered by Judge Wright, the Squire of Brigham City responded, commenting on his twenty-five thousand mile journey and alluding to some of the important places and people he had seen and met. Of all these, however, he said that none had been more meaningful to him nor had aroused greater feelings of gratitude and satisfaction than had the welcome extended to him by his family and friends.

The ceremonies at Brigham Junction were concluded with numbers by a snappy band whose music seemed even livelier because of the fluttering movements of a colorful banner, bearing a welcoming motto, that was held aloft by a group of Sunday School teachers. The entire procession then followed Elder Snow to his home, where waited an even larger crowd, anxious to show their love and respect for the man who had become a father-figure to all.

147

The impressions and insights Lorenzo Snow gained from this grand tour were to color and influence the remainder of his apostolic ministry to a marked degree. Thereafter, his sermons that developed themes of biblical history or doctrine would have greater depth of meaning because of his direct exposure to the ancient land of the prophets and the patriarchs. And his comprehension of the international role of the Church would be more precise because of his personal contacts with the leaders and peoples of many nations. But, more germane to his highest role as a special witness of Jesus Christ, were the spiritual assurances and illuminations he had received of the Savior's divinity and Godhood that had come to him as he had visited the historic places where the great Messianic drama had been enacted. These would ever be in his heart and his mind's eye in the years ahead as he served and bore testimony of the Master, and as he sought diligently, through his conduct, to qualify to return to the presence of God, there to be exalted and share with the Savior all the Father has.

Chapter Twenty-two

Counselor in the First Presidency

lder Snow took up his duties as a counselor in the
First Presidency with combined feelings of confidence
and trepidation. His confidence was rooted in his
basic faith in God, which had taught him over the
years that his Heavenly Father, whether acting directly or
through priesthood authority, would never require anything
of him but that a way would be opened up for its attainment.
He had surely seen this principle at work throughout his life,
whether searching for a testimony, proselyting in the nations
of the earth, groping in the chaos that followed the martyrdom of Joseph and Hyrum, struggling on the pioneer trail, or
striving manfully to establish the Saints in Brigham City. In all
these, as in many other difficult circumstances, he had gone
forward, one step at a time, taking advantage of the momentary light that guided his way and with conviction that when
he had taken the one step sufficient light and confidence
would come from God to enable him to take the next. His
training, his convictions, and his experience had qualified
him, therefore, to accept the heavy burdens of his new calling
with hardly a break in his stride or a ripple in the placidity of
his demeanor.

Yet there stirred within him a certain trepidation that agi-
tates anyone called to a position of high authority and responsibility. This emotion springs from a vague uncertainty as
to whether one can measure up to the requirements of the

position or to the expectations of the one who has called him to fill it. Lorenzo was well aware of the compelling force of President Young's personality and his powerful drives that were in large part responsible for the success of the exodus and the settlement of the Saints in the mountains. While Elder Snow had labored under President Young while serving as a missionary in England in the early 1840s and had been subject to his supervision since being called to the Twelve, he had never before been involved with him in the intimate kind of relationship that exists in the presiding quorum of the Church. So, there was an understandable uncertainty in Lorenzo's mind when he undertook his new duties about possible adjustments in his thinking or methods and about the role he would be expected to play in the new administration.

Any lingering doubts Elder Snow had about these two matters were soon dispelled. He found that no radical adjustments were necessary because it was not intended that he move to Salt Lake City. Thus, the personal relationship with President Young would continue on an intermittent basis, as it had during all the years since Lorenzo moved to Brigham City.

He found that he would continue to serve as president of the Box Elder Stake, and that his role in the First Presidency would be a specialized one, limited to teaching the theories and practices of cooperative enterprises and to organizational and ceremonial duties.

President Brigham Young's frequent praise of Brigham City's achievements in its cooperative enterprises and word-of-mouth reports by others who had personally observed their prosperity raised President Lorenzo Snow and his associates to an elevated status among the Saints. This was enhanced by the strong emphasis President Young laid on the cooperative movement at the time and by Lorenzo's special calling in the First Presidency. Many came to Brigham City to see for themselves what was being so widely discussed and applauded. "Church men came from near and far this year," wrote Vaughn J. Nielsen, Box Elder Stake's historian, "to have a looksee at the marvels of the co-operative movement smoothly carrying forth under Apostle Lorenzo's direction." The visitors included not only the rank and file of local leadership, but also many of the presiding brethren from Salt Lake City and elsewhere who wanted to learn the principles of cooperation and see them in practice. Elder Erastus Snow of the Twelve came in the autumn of 1873, and fellow-apostle Wilford Woodruff came the following spring. These brethren were intrigued by the efficiency of the hatter, blacksmith, and wagon shops, and by the tannery, boot, and woolen factories then in operation. The visits of these two members of the Twelve and the favorable reports they took back with them brought on a flood of visits by other dignitaries. "The brethren from Salt Lake seemed almost in perpetual attendance at Brigham City these days," wrote the stake historian, "witnessing the growth and operation of Lorenzo's cooperative movement. On Saturday and Sunday, June 27th and 28th, [1874] Presidents Brigham Young, George A. Smith, and Daniel H. Wells arrived, accompanied by Elders Orson Pratt, Wilford Woodruff, John Taylor and Erastus Snow of the Quorum of the Twelve and several gentlemen and a few ladies from Salt Lake City." The visitors were given the usual Lorenzo Snow greeting, with banners waving, the brass band playing smartly, and Sunday School children singing.

At services he directed during the June 1874 visit, President Young organized the Brigham City cooperatives into a branch of the united order. This became a conspicuous part of a network he envisioned would evolve into the society the Savior expects to find at his second coming. It seems to have been the Lion of the Lord's expectation that Brigham City would be the shining example to all other communities that were to be brought into the united order. "By fall," wrote historian Nielsen, "experts on cooperative institutions were in demand throughout the territory." Brethren from Brigham City who were schooled by Lorenzo Snow went out in all directions to preach the gospel of cooperation. As part of this educational effort, Lorenzo sent some of his brethren to Dixie to establish the Brigham City farm near the Virgin River.

Behind President Snow's energetic efforts to promote cooperatives and to foster temporal preparedness and independence was a gospel principle that far transcended the mere production and distribution of goods. Lorenzo knew that the temporal condition of the Saints was inextricably tied up with their spiritual development. On one occasion he declared, "The law requires us to seek *first* the kingdom of God, and . . . our time, talent and ability must be held subservient to its interests. If this were not so, how could we expect hereafter, when this earth shall have been made the dwelling-place of God and his Son, to inherit eternal lives and to live and reign with him? Who shall say that the rich, or those that possess many talents, have any better hope or prospect to inherit these blessings than the poor, or those who have but one talent? As I understand it, the man who works in the shop, whether a tailor, carpenter, shoemaker, or in any other industrial department, and who lives according to the law of the Gospel, and is honest and faithful in his calling, that man is just as eligible to the receiving of these and all the blessings of the New and Everlasting Covenant as any other man; through his faithfulness he shall possess thrones, principalities and powers, his children becoming as numerous as the stars in the firmament, or the sands on the sea shore."

These excerpts are typical of the admonitions and instructions Lorenzo gave in scores of talks delivered during the years he served as a counselor to Brigham Young. In them are evident the qualities of practicality, erudition, and spirituality that were so admirably combined in him. Although the themes he dwelled upon, as he instructed and admonished the people in the theory and practice of cooperatives, implied the most vigorous and exhausting kind of physical labor, yet they fell from his lips with the measured and objective detachment of a college professor. There was a sort of dreamy, abstracted quality in his conduct and delivery that could mislead one unacquainted with his background and achievements into the false belief that he functioned well only in the realm of thought and reflection. One acute observer defined the unusual merger of qualities in President Snow's personality by characterizing him as a "practical mystic." Another commented that "he could say and do the hardest things in the gentlest, quietest manner possible to man." As we see this aspect of Lorenzo's character, which is affirmed by the testimony of those who knew him and observed him in person and by the photographs that have come down to us, it is difficult to avoid the impression that we are witnesses to the steady progression of a man into godhood. Absent from his makeup were qualities we often associate with mankind, qualities of selfishness, envy, anger, and vaulting ambition. Instead, we find the Christlike qualities of liberality, charity, meekness, and self-effacement. Yet President Snow was neither a milque-toast, a doormat, nor a yes-man. On the contrary, he was a man of fire, spirit, and high intelligence who entertained strong views, who had his likes and dislikes, and who was as prone to anger, anxiety, and physical or spiritual affliction as anyone else. But over the years he had learned to control and mute these negative emotions and to channel them toward positive, productive ends. One cannot observe this process without relating it to the powerful compulsions that operated upon this man, compulsions that were rooted in spiritual phenomena. Lorenzo's patriarchal blessing, the spiritual witness that came to him in the woods near Kirtland and the revelation he received about man's potential for godhood never seemed to be far from his consciousness. These, along with his temple covenants and blessings, were a constant goad and reminder, daily giving him motivation and incentive to reach for a celestial character.

But, like any true disciple of Christ, President Snow had learned early that the road to perfection lies in the direction of service to others. And as already noted, his ecclesiastical service during this period had a dual purpose, to serve President Young as a counselor and to continue to serve as the president of the Box Elder Stake.

As time went on, Lorenzo found that his duties in the First Presidency made it necessary for him to delegate stake responsibilities to a greater degree than he had previously done. However, he continued to give strong leadership to the stake, both in temporal and spiritual matters. In 1876, he initiated the construction of the Box Elder Tabernacle, the building that stands as the most recognizable symbol of the community. Showing pioneer resourcefulness and ingenuity, the skilled European convert craftsmen who executed Lorenzo's design used native lumber and stone taken from the nearby mountains. Most of the labor was donated. The cash outlay of about five thousand dollars for imported fixtures and materials was raised chiefly by selling contributed produce, including "Sunday egg collections." Finally completed in 1890, the tabernacle burned in 1896, suffering the same fate as Lorenzo's woolen factory. But the sturdy walls withstood the blaze, and the building rose again out of the ashes of the tragic fire.

The year following the commencement of construction on the Box Elder Tabernacle, 1877, everyone in Mormondom knew they would again have the privilege of joining in the dedication of a house of the Lord, the first one in the west. President Young, who had wintered in Saint George, where the mild climate eased his rheumatic pains and where he could keep a watchful eye on the progress of the temple, had invited his counselors and the other general authorities to join him in Dixie for the dedication and for the April general conference, which was also scheduled there.

President Snow began his preparations for the trip in early March. Through the Brethren in Salt Lake City, arrangements were made for a large twelve-carriage convoy to transport the official party over the well-traveled but still rugged trails to Saint George. The existence of numerous Latter-day Saint colonies along the route ensured occasional lodging and meals for the travelers. But the distances between villages and uncertainty whether members and friends would have spare accommodations made it necessary for the party to carry ample bedding and provisions with them. This need was increased by the knowledge that hundreds of Saints would be flocking into Dixie for the temple dedication and the general conference, which likely would make it necessary to rely upon their own stores and equipment during their stay in Saint George. So the twelve carriages were heavily laden with food, camping equipment, and valises as they creaked their way out of Salt Lake City along the road toward Provo.

It was a congenial and joyous group that made up this large caravan. It included three of President Young's counselors in the persons of Lorenzo Snow and two of the President's sons, Brigham Young, Jr., and John W. Young. Although Brigham Jr. was eight years older than his brother, and had served as a member of the Twelve since 1864, the younger son had been called as the first counselor to his father at the October conference in 1876, filling the vacancy created by the passing of President George A. Smith, who had died in September 1875. Also in the party was another future president of the church, Joseph Fielding Smith, Lorenzo's self-confident companion on his mission to Hawaii, who had at this time served as a member of the Twelve for a decade. Among those in the party who were not of general authority status was John W. Taylor, the handsome nineteen-year-old son of President John Taylor.

Since their mode of travel dictated a leisurely pace, the members of the caravan had ample time to visit and meditate during the long stretches between towns. And to break the monotony, they often sang or engaged in games. One day, Lorenzo, who was driving one of the carriages, introduced a new and exciting diversion. Another carriage pulled abreast his own intending to pass. Instead of allowing it to do so, Elder Snow, on an impulse, clucked at his team and rapped their backs with the reins. The other driver promptly followed suit. The sixty-three-year-old member of the First Presidency responded by urging his team to an even faster pace. Soon the two ecclesiastical teamsters were racing pell-mell across the landscape, their hair flying and their arms gyrating. Now and then, the excited voices of the drivers could be heard above the din and the dust as they shouted commands to their teams.

Arriving in Saint George, the Brethren found that much more was afoot than a general conference and the dedication of the temple. President Young called the First Presidency and the Twelve into a special meeting at his office that adjoined his winter home. There he laid before them a plan that had been germinating in his mind for many months and that had been discussed intermittently in the high councils of the Church— the release of the members of the Twelve from their service as stake presidents and the restructuring of stakes to coincide with county boundary lines. Moreover, it was intended that the role of the Salt Lake Stake be diminished in the future, with each stake occupying an equal and independent footing in its internal administration. Having obtained the approval of the Brethren to these far-reaching proposals, President Young scheduled a special two-day conference to explain these changes to priesthood leaders before the general conference.

The meetings were held on the top floor of the temple, which had been fitted out to resemble the main floor of the Kirtland Temple. The First Presidency, the Twelve, and the Seventy, with other selected Melchizedek Priesthood leaders, were seated in the east end of the room on a tiered stand. President Young, Lorenzo Snow, and the other counselors were seated on or near the highest tier, which afforded a spectacular view of the multicolored hills to the southwest. On the west side of the room sat the presiding Bishopric and other leaders of the Aaronic Priesthood on a tiered stand identical to the one on the east.

As the brethren sat amidst the beauty and security of this holy edifice, their minds were led both backward and forward by the spirited oratory of those called on to speak. President Snow, who spoke at the morning session on the second day, accomplished this by an analytical treatment of a favorite theme—cooperation and consecration. He reminded his listeners of the Missouri era and of the revelations received there, whose object was to establish a celestial society. And he stressed the necessity of making adequate preparations in their mountain retreat for the Saints' ultimate return to the center stake of Zion.

"I assure you we will never go back to Jackson County, Missouri," he declared, "there to build up the New Jerusalem of the latter days, until there is a perfect willingness on our part to conform to its rules and principles." No one who had heard Lorenzo Snow speak in recent years had any doubt as to what these rules and principles were, or the direction his remarks would now take. "Many years have transpired since we received the revelation of the United Order," he continued, "and in one sense that long period of time bespeaks negligence on our part in not more fully obeying it. The very principles of that order, in my estimation, were given for our temporal and spiritual salvation. In order to derive the benefit that God designed should flow from them, they must be established and systematized on the principles of righteousness, each person learning to love his neighbor as himself. For us to undertake to deal with them on any other principle would virtually open the way to bitter disappointment. . . . Then will they enter into the spirit of the two great commands upon which, said the Savior 'hang the law and the Prophets,' namely, loving the Lord with all our might, mind and strength, and our neighbor as ourselves. This, in my opinion, is the foundation of our future success, temporally and spiritually in the United Order. Until we come down to the bedrock of honesty and sincerity in this matter, dealing with temporal or with spiritual things, wholeheartedly, holding all and ourselves sacred to the service of God, we may expect more or less failure."

In these words, and in others uttered in the same discourse, Lorenzo Snow revealed a facet of his personality, one that is shared by all converted Latter-day Saints and is difficult for an unbeliever to grasp. That is the reality and the immediacy of future, predicted events. A discussion of the Saints' ultimate return to Missouri had about it the same certitude as plans for next season's harvest. And as a harvest entails man's effort to plough, plant, fertilize, weed, and irrigate, leaving the miracle of growth to powers and influences external to man, so the return to Zion would entail concerted effort by the Saints and the spiritual blessings of God.

And here President Snow's fertile and scholarly mind used an analogy to connect his predominate interest in the United Order with the return to Jackson County. That analogy, quite appropriately, was the construction of Solomon's temple. "We read," said President Snow, "that the Temple which Solomon built was erected without the sound of a hammer being heard. There had been a previous preparation and an experience gained in some distant locality, and a proper training. The materials were accurately prepared elsewhere, and when brought together were ready for setting each piece to its proper place." The speaker saw essentially the same thing taking place as the Latter-day Saints prepared for their eventual return to Jackson County: "As knowledge and efficiency are obtained gradually, we may expect that the experience that we are getting now in learning how to built up cities in our present condition, conforming as near as possible to the holy order of God, is, in order to prepare us by and by to return to Missouri, whence we were driven, and there build up cities and Temples to the name of the Most High, upon which his glory will descend."

President Snow's analogy was apt, not only because of the similarity of the circumstances involved, but also because of the responsive chord struck in the minds and hearts of the Saints by his allusion to the ancient temple built by King Solomon. Even as Lorenzo spoke, his audience was keenly aware of the historic event that would occur the following day when the first temple to be constructed by the Church in the western United States would be dedicated. And this temple would stand apart from all others as being the first one in the world's history to witness within its walls the performance of vicarious ordinances for the dead. The Latter-day Saints had waited patiently and labored diligently looking forward to this day, and when it dawned bright and clear and warm, with the clean fragrance of their burgeoning orchards and gardens filling the air of a mild Dixie spring, their joy was unbounded.

April 6, 1877, was the day selected for the dedication of the temple. It marked the forty-seventh anniversary of the organization of the Church. Present were all of the members of the First Presidency and the Twelve except Albert Carrington. President Young honored his second counselor, Daniel H. Wells, by inviting him to offer the dedicatory prayer. There followed the traditional Hosanna Shout and the singing of "The Spirit of God like a Fire Is Burning," composed by W. W. Phelps and sung at the dedication of the Kirtland Temple.

The spiritual fervor of the dedication permeated the remainder of the conference, which extended through three full days, ending the evening of April 8. On April 8, President Young followed a procedure that was to be a pattern for Lorenzo and his associates in the First Presidency and the Twelve during the several months to follow—he reorganized the stake presidency in Saint George.

On the trip home from Saint George, Lorenzo had two opportunities to follow President Young's lead. On April 18, he directed the organization of the Kanab Stake, and on April 23, he organized the Panguitch Stake.

In addition to handling these organizational matters as he traveled homeward, Elder Snow took occasion to speak to the Saints along the way. Audiences at Salina, Monroe, and Lehi, among others, were treated to inspiring messages on the necessity of applying the principles of cooperation and the united order.

Reaching Salt Lake City the second week in May, President Snow participated with other members of the First Presidency in the reorganization of the Salt Lake Stake on May 12. In effecting this change, President Young made it clear to the new leaders that their jurisdiction would not extend beyond the boundaries of Salt Lake County, an instruction presumed necessary because of lingering though erroneous ideas of a residual control over areas carved from the parent stake that once encompassed the whole Utah territory.

Following the Salt Lake Stake reorganization, Lorenzo was able to spend a week at home in Brigham City recuperating from his strenuous trip, but a week later, he participated in the reorganization of the Cache Valley Stake. The following week he was in Ogden, where Elder Franklin D. Richards was released, and during the summer this old friend helped him organize a stake in Morgan City.

By this time, Box Elder Stake was like an island surrounded by stakes that had been organized or reorganized in line with the decision made in April at Saint George. Indeed, a tabulation showed that during this interval eighteen new stake presidences had been installed. It was as if President Young had delayed releasing his counselor until the very last.

Except for the ceremonies at Saint George and Salt Lake City, more Church officials were present at the reorganization of the Box Elder Stake than any of the others. President Young headed the group that traveled to Brigham City on Saturday, August 18, 1877. With him were his first and second counselors, John W. Young and Daniel H. Wells, in addition to Elders John Taylor, Franklin D. Richards, and Albert Carrington of the Twelve. Accompanying these general authorities were First

Presidency staff members George Reynolds, secretary to the First Presidency, and George F. Gibbs, Church reporter, who, according to the *Deseret News*, had "mastered the modern shorthand known as phonography."

Predictably, the Salt Lake visitors were treated to the usual fanfare of a Lorenzo Snow greeting. Bands, banners, and brotherhood were the order of the day. Soon after their arrival, they were ushered to the bowery, whose open-air features were more conducive to comfort in the summer heat than any enclosed building in town. A preliminary meeting was held there in the afternoon, and President Daniel H. Wells, Elder John Taylor, and brother W. C. Staines all spoke.

At the direction of President Young, Lorenzo had been busy for some time conducting interviews and extending calls to perfect the organization of the stake below the stake presidency level. A special leadership meeting had been scheduled for Saturday evening in which, it was expected, a decision would be made as to the new stake presidency. Before that meeting began, however, Elder Snow took President Young to his home, where a light supper was served. After the meal, the aging visitor delighted everyone present when he leaned back in his chair and, in a clear voice, sang one of his favorite hymns, probably the last vocal selection of his life.

The leadership meeting was held in the upper room of the Social Hall, where the stake leaders were assembled in an atmosphere charged with anticipation. After all, this was an event which, according to the tenure-in-office norms of the day, one might expect to witness only two or three times in a lifetime. There were, for instance, adults then in Brigham City approaching their thirties who had never known a leader other than Lorenzo Snow.

President Young did not keep the assembly in suspense long. He announced that Oliver G. Snow, Lorenzo's son, had been selected as the new stake president, "who being young would follow more easily in Lorenzo's footsteps." Said the Lion of the Lord, "The presidency all ought to be young men, who, unless I miss my guess, will be more likely to follow advice and counsel." With that admonition, Brigham left the decision about counselors to the new stake president, who designated two young men, Elijah A. Box, the husband of one of Lorenzo's daughters, and Isaac Smith, the son of Samuel Smith, who had served as Lorenzo's counselor for twenty-two years.

At the general session the following day, when the new stake officers were presented for the sustaining vote of the conference, President Young gave Lorenzo Snow a parting accolade for the distinguished service he had rendered: "Brother Lorenzo Snow, who has had charge of you, has set the best example for the literal building up of the Kingdom of God of any of our presiding elders. There is one man in the south who I think will come up to this standard, and continue on. But Brother Snow has led the people and guided them and counselled them in the way that they should go, apparently without their knowing anything about it, until he got them into the harness; and I like this very much. . . . Brother Snow has exhibited splendid talent in what he has done towards making this people self sustaining."

After the reorganization of the Box Elder Stake, Lorenzo directed the reorganization of the stake at Paris, Idaho. This was the twentieth and last stake to be reorganized under the policy adopted at Saint George the previous April.

On August 23, while Lorenzo's party was traveling from Franklin, Idaho, by carriage toward Paris to attend the conference, the Lion of the Lord had taken ill. He died on August 29, 1877, four days after his last great initiative as the head of the Church was completed. With Brigham's death, Elder Snow was automatically released as a counselor to the First Presidency, and at that moment, John Taylor, who had been his subordinate at Paris, became his presiding officer.

Chapter Twenty-three

Years of Trial and Maturing

The events of 1877 and of the several years that followed brought an increased maturity to Lorenzo Snow. His release as stake president and as a member of the First Presidency foreshadowed radical changes in his life. So long had he been the presiding authority in Brigham City that it was difficult not to assume the direction of affairs that now were the responsibility of his son. While Oliver was amenable to the counsel of his father and showed him every consideration and respect, these attentions and peripheral involvement in the ecclesiastical life of the community could hardly fill the void created by Lorenzo's release. And the extent of that void was magnified by his release from the First Presidency, the two events occurring within a fortnight of each other. However, any sense of letdown these changes may have created were skillfully masked behind his kind and courtly manner. In fact, from all we can learn from the available evidence, Elder Snow accepted these changes with the same detachment and unconcern that greeted his calls to service. He was seemingly devoid of any ambition for place or power. Nor did he seem to require the trappings of authority and status to convince him of his self-worth. It was enough, apparently, that he was a spiritual son of God, and that he had the promise of exaltation in the presence of God conditioned upon his diligence in keeping the commandments. So it would appear that once the historic events of

August 1877 were behind, Lorenzo picked up the remaining threads of his life and began to weave them into his mortal tapestry with the same diligence and steadiness of purpose that were evident in the earlier phases of his career.

The underlying philosophy that guided Elder Snow along the way and that enabled him to accept any change with poise and dignity is reflected in a sermon he delivered not long after Brigham Young's death. In it, he developed the themes of desire, repentance, and perseverance, showing them to be instruments of progress that lead to perfection.

"We are no better than the rest of the world," he declared, "if we do not cultivate the feeling to be perfect, even as our Father in heaven is perfect." To negate any idea of impropriety in aiming toward God's perfection, he quoted these words of the Apostle Paul: "Let this same mind be in you which was also in Christ Jesus: who being in the form of God, thought it not robbery to be equal with God." Lending encouragement to those who, burdened with weaknesses, feel unworthy or incapable of pursuing such a high purpose, he cited the examples of revered biblical characters. "There was the Apostle Peter, for instance," he told his Salt Lake Tabernacle audience, "a man valiant for the truth, and a man who walked before God in a manner that met with his divine approval; he told the Savior on a certain occasion that though all men forsook him he would not. But the Savior, foreseeing what would happen, told him that on the same night before the cock crowed, he would deny him thrice, and he did so. He proved himself unequal for the trial; but afterwards he gained power, and his mind was disciplined to that extent that such trials could not possibly affect him." And, drawing an inference from Peter's experience, Elder Snow showed that his was not an isolated case, and that, indeed, everyone falls short of the goal to one degree or another: "If we could read in detail the life of Abraham, or the lives of other great and holy men, we would doubtless find that their efforts to be righteous were not always crowned with success. Hence we should not be discouraged if we should be overcome in a weak moment; but, on the contrary, straightway repent of the error or the wrong we may have committed, and as far as possible repair it, and

then seek to God for renewed strength to go on and do better."
Later he expounded on the dangers of discouragement, and of
the need to apply the antidotes of repentance and perseverance: "If the Apostle Peter had become discouraged at his
manifest failure to maintain the position that he had taken to
stand by the Savior under all circumstances, he would have
lost all; whereas, by repenting and persevering he lost nothing
but gained all, leaving us too to profit by his experience. The
Latter-day Saints should cultivate this ambition constantly
which was so clearly set forth by the apostles in former days.
We should try to walk each day so that our conscience would
be void of offense before everybody. . . . We must not allow
ourselves to be discouraged whenever we discover our weakness. We can scarcely find an instance in all the glorious examples set us by the prophets, ancient or modern, wherein they
permitted the Evil One to discourage them; but on the other
hand they constantly sought to overcome, to win the prize,
and thus prepare themselves for a fulness of glory."

With only the single precedent of Joseph's death to guide
them, the Twelve were reluctant to move promptly to install a
new president. And so it was decided that the Twelve would
govern for the time being.

Lorenzo traveled regularly to Salt Lake City for the meetings of his quorum, in which policies were adopted and necessary delegations of authority were made to committees of the
Twelve and to others. After a while, the work settled into an
orderly routine, with most of the decisions about the operations of the Church being left with President Taylor. But one
matter of business intermittently occupied the attention of the
entire Quorum of the Twelve during most of this apostolic in-
terregnum—the settlement of the estate of President Brigham
Young. A lack of understanding by some members of Brigham's family and others as to what was Church and what was
Brigham's property created a legal controversy.

A settlement was reached in the latter part of 1879 that
adequately protected the legitimate interests of both the
Church and the heirs of the deceased president.

While the year 1879 thus saw the satisfactory resolution
of a sensitive internal problem, it also saw the beginning of

a serious external problem. On January 6, 1879, the United States Supreme Court upheld the constitutionality of the first of the so-called antipolygamy acts in the landmark case *U.S. v. Reynolds*, in which the defendant was Elder George Reynolds, Lorenzo's good friend, who served as the secretary to the First Presidency.

In 1862, the first federal legislation striking at polygamy, the Morrill Act, was passed by Congress. Asserting that this act was unconstitutional, the Saints deliberately ignored the law, but when at last the constitutionality of the Morrill Act was upheld in the *Reynolds* case, the Saints were stripped of legal justification for the practice.

The political opposition to polygamy extended all the way to the White House, manifested in four presidential statements made by three separate chiefs of state. In two annual messages to congress in December 1879 and December 1880, President Rutherford B. Hayes castigated the Mormons severely, advocating that the political rights and privileges of the Latter-day Saints "who violate or oppose the enforcement of the law" on polygamy be withheld or withdrawn. He also advocated that the territorial form of government be abolished and replaced by an administration consisting of a governor and judges or commissioners appointed by the President. In his inaugural in March 1881, James Garfield said that polygamy destroyed family relations and endangered the social order. And Chester A. Arthur, who succeeded President Garfield, urged "vigorous measures" against the Church during his message to Congress in December 1881.

An Episcopal convention in New York in April 1881 adopted a resolution against the Church, which stated in part: "The filth of its abominations is overflowing into other territories, and in conjunction with communism threatens, in effect, the nation. The people's neglect in this matter has already become a national wrong, if not a crime."

Fed by a stream of invective that flowed regularly from the press of the day, the crusade mounted by the politicians and the clergy culminated successfully with the passage of the Edmunds Act in the spring of 1882. This act declared polygamy to be a felony punishable by imprisonment of up to five

years or a maximum fine of $500 or both. It also declared "un-
lawful cohabitation," polygamous living without formal marriage, to be a misdemeanor punishable by imprisonment not
to exceed six months and by a fine not to exceed $300 or by
both imprisonment and fine at the discretion of the court. The
act excluded all polygamists or cohabs from jury duty and
vacated all registration and election offices, transferring their
duties to a board of five commissioners to be appointed by the
president with the advice and consent of the Senate. The
Church hierarchy could see that the sanctions of the Edmunds
Act would be enforced with pitiless rigidity.

In this state of affairs, Lorenzo and his brethren set on a
course of deliberate civil disobedience, believing that it was
better to obey the laws of God than the laws of men.

The leading brethren who were exposed to the sanctions
of the Edmunds Act decided to drop from sight so that service
of legal process upon them would be impossible. Thus, one by
one, the apostles began to disappear from the scene, some to
places of exile away from Utah and others to furtive, underground living within the territory. In order to remain as close
as possible to Church headquarters, President Taylor remained near home, moving from one place of refuge to the
other as circumstances required. Joseph F. Smith, who, along
with George Q. Cannon, had been sustained as a counselor to
John Taylor when the First Presidency was reorganized, spent
considerable time in Hawaii, while Daniel H. Wells went to
England, and Elder Wilford Woodruff roamed far and wide in
the Arizona territory. Because of his notoriety as a senior
member of the Twelve and as a former member of the First
Presidency, Lorenzo was a prime target of the zealous federal
officials. To minimize the chance of being apprehended, Elder
Snow spent considerable time in Northern California during
this period, where he wrote copiously and endeavored as best
he could to instruct and motivate the few members there who
were organized into scattered branches.

While in San Francisco, President Snow received a letter
from President John Taylor dated July 2, 1885, in which the
President called him to "visit the various [Indian] tribes to
which you can get access." The letter referred to previous dis-

cussions about such an undertaking that had involved Elder Snow and his fellow apostles Franklin D. Richards and Moses Thatcher. At that time, President Taylor had expressed anxiety about the need to undertake missionary work among the Indian tribes. "I was greatly moved upon by the spirit of the Lord," he wrote to Elder Snow, "to lay before the Twelve the duty of opening the gospel to the Lamanites and furnishing them with teachers to enable them to progress in the knowledge of its principles."

Lorenzo accepted this assignment, and advised President Taylor of an "anxiety" he had to visit the Nez Perce Indians, whose reservation was in the northwestern part of the Idaho Territory. "They are the most intelligent tribe on the Pacific coast," Elder Snow wrote, "a fine, noble race of Indians. Some of them have been educated in schools and colleges in the east. Many of them live in comfortable houses; very industrious—farm extensively—have good schools etc. etc. A mission established there would prove of invaluable advantage in obtaining opening to other tribes."

Having received approval of his plan, Elder Snow left San Francisco on August 8, destined for his new field of labor. Embarking on a coastal steamer, he traveled first to Portland, Oregon, via the Columbia River. Then he took a train eastward to Pendleton, Oregon. Finding himself within a few miles of the Umatilla Indian reservation, Lorenzo paid it a visit that accomplished little other than to confirm his feeling that his first effort should be among the Nez Perce.

Traveling by railroad and stagecoach, and finally by steamer up the tortuous Snake River, Lorenzo made his way to Lewiston, the gateway to the Nez Perce reservation. There he was fortunate to obtain the services of a Mr. Whitman, generally regarded as the most able and reliable interpreter in the area.

With his interpreter, the Mormon apostle went to the nearby reservation, where he conferred with the Indian agent, Mr. Montieth, who turned out to be the interpreter's son-in-law, and later attended a tribal meeting where about two hundred had assembled for a worship service. He found the audience neatly dressed, attentive, and intelligent, and noted

particularly in his report home that the closing song, the Dox-
ology, was sung in English.

After appraising the situation among the Nez Perce, and
visiting with tribal leaders and government administrators,
Elder Snow traveled westward to Walla Walla, Washington,
where he collected his thoughts and wrote a lengthy report to
President Taylor. Although his initial impression about beginning the work among the Nez Perce had not changed, he now
felt inclined to tie in that effort with an approach to the
Umatillas as well, due to the proximity of their reservation and
their similarities in background and customs.

He envisioned the purchase of a farm that would serve as
a Mormon base of operations in the area, so situated as to
provide easy access to both tribes. "Let a suitable person with
a proper assistant start at once," Lorenzo urged President
Taylor, "with wagon, good hardy team, an extra animal, small
tent, Etc, and proceed to the Nez Perce reservation, spending
one, two, or more weeks if necessary before purchasing."

Due to sensitive conditions that had evolved in the past between the Indians and the representatives of other churches established there, Elder Snow saw wisdom in acquiring property
in the name of individuals, not the church. "The farm would
[then] be worked and improved," he wrote, "made a pleasant
and delightful home and self-sustaining. The Indians have
homes of their own and these could be visited and instructed
and return those visits as they pleased without hindrance."

Lorenzo nominated as president of the mission Abraham
Zundel, one of his protégés from Willard, Utah, near Brigham
City, who thirty years before had served as a "colonization
missionary" in the Salmon River country of Idaho. As Brother
Zundel's assistant, he nominated another Box Elder product,
Bishop George Facer of the Willard City Ward, whom Lorenzo
commended as being "wise, prudent, industrious and a good
financier."

Having laid the foundation for work among the Nez Perce
and Umatilla tribes, Elder Snow left Walla Walla on September
10, traveling 500 miles southeast to Neeleyville, a small Latter-
day Saint settlement a few miles west of the Fort Hall Indian
Reservation in Idaho. Accompanied by Bishop William Neeley,

a former bishop of the Bear River City Ward in the Box Elder Stake, Lorenzo attended a meeting on the reservation, where he found that many of the Blackfoot Indians there had already been baptized as the result of an earlier missionary effort. Learning that Brother Thomas Richardson, a member who owned land nearby, would be willing to donate a site for the purpose, Lorenzo recommended that the Church construct a modest building for use by the Indians and that the affairs of this Lamanite branch be administered by Bishop Neeley and the bishop of the nearby Rock Creek Ward.

As he had mentioned in reports to Church headquarters, Elder Snow also intended to survey the possibilities for further proselyting among the Arapahoes and Shoshones on the Wind River Reservation in Western Wyoming. Before proceeding there, however, he made a brief undercover trip to Brigham City, where he visited quietly with his family and arranged with a number of dependable brethren to accompany him to the Wind River Reservation.

Departing on September 24, 1885, Lorenzo and his party had to battle early autumn snows along the well-marked trail leading to their destination. Arriving there on October 3 after a tiring trip in inclement weather, Elder Snow made camp and almost immediately sought an interview with chiefs of the Shoshones and Arapahoes. To his disappointment, however, the latter failed to send representatives, and the former was represented by two minor chiefs instead of by Washakie, the supreme leader of this proud tribe. Interestingly enough, the two Shoshones who did appear were baptized and endowed members of the Church, but their understanding of gospel principles was quite poor. "Though they have honest and warm hearts," Elder Snow observed in his report to President Taylor, "they are extremely ignorant, and if one wishes to do them permanent good, he must be fortified with much patience and perseverance."

Lorenzo recommended that Bishop Amos Wright be appointed as the president of the Shoshones and Arapahoes on the Wind River Reservation, with James Brown, a Latter-day Saint Indian, as his counselor. "Should you think proper," he added, "I will select a small company subject to your approval and start next spring as early in the season as possible, visit the Shoshones and Arapahoes, . . . and give them such counsel as the circumstances and spirit at the time may incline you to suggest." Lorenzo also proposed that the Church then look into the acquisition of a farm on the northern boundary of the reservation "to help the missionaries, and to facilitate the preaching and establishing the gospel among the northern tribes. After this we can continue our journey some 250 miles, visit the Crow Indians, and see what measures can be adopted to introduce among them the principles of the gospel."

Given the anti-Mormon bias in Utah's Gentile community at that day, it comes as no surprise that a malevolent purpose was seen in Lorenzo's mission to the Lamanites. In a harsh and misleading article, the *Salt Lake Tribune* editorialized on Elder Snow's work among the Indians: "Apostle Snow of Brigham City has been looking after the Indians up north. He has been around the agencies in Idaho, notably that of Rosse Fork, accompanied by one of his bishops, an interpreter and has visited the various camps for some purpose. It is well known that the Mormons sell ammunition and guns to Indians, and that they class these Red Men as the Battle Axes of the Lord who are ready to do the bidding of the Priesthood. Would it not be well for the government to make some inquiry into the cause of these visits by Apostle Snow and learn what mischief he might be concocting in the interest of the Mormon church?"

Had Uncle Sam acted upon the *Tribune's* admonition, he would have found Lorenzo's so-called "mischief" to be nothing more grievous than to bring the elevating effects of Christianity to a deprived people. And had it not been for some mischief of its own the government had concocted for Elder Snow upon his return to Brigham City, he would have continued with his humane work among "the Indians up North." As it turned out, his mission to the Lamanites was cut short by a series of dreadful events that were to see him arraigned before a vindictive court, convicted by a hostile jury, and cast into prison. A universal search likely would not have uncovered a less qualified candidate for a convict's role than Lorenzo Snow, the gentle apostle.

Chapter Twenty-four

Into the Pit

Months of guarded living, even during his work among the Lamanites, had conditioned Lorenzo to the need for caution and constant watchfulness in his daily activities. So devious and resourceful were the federal officials who sought to enforce the Edmunds Act that the ingenuity and skill of the Saints who lived on the underground were taxed to the limit. They devised elaborate schemes to avoid detection, and the process of warning against the approach of lawmen, or of concealing loved ones from their prying searches, almost became an art form. Secret rooms, closets, or cubby holes became a standard feature of the homes of polygamists constructed during this era.

Elder Snow's place of refuge in his Brigham City home was a small cubicle located directly beneath the master bedroom, access to which was gained through a trap door concealed beneath the carpet. Equipped with a chair and makeshift bed, and ventilated by a grating in the foundation of the home, the Squire of Brigham City could retire there promptly on notice that U.S. marshals were in the area and could wait in comparative comfort until the danger of detection had passed.

After completing his visit to the Wind River Reservation in the autumn of 1885, Lorenzo received word that things were quiet at home, so he spent several weeks there in late October and early November, keeping to the house, for the most part, and maintaining contact with the Brethren and with his subordinates in the Northern Indian Mission through voluminous correspondence.

On Thursday, November 19, 1885, seven U. S. marshals, learning through the grapevine that Elder Snow had returned to Brigham City, obtained warrants to search his home and arrest him should the search reveal his whereabouts. To avoid tipping their hand prematurely, the officers traveled from Ogden by train, arriving at Brigham City under cover of darkness. After dawn, the officers went unannounced to the Snow residence and, after exhibiting their search warrants, were admitted. Upon examining every room in the house, poking into closets, pantries, and attic spaces, beneath beds and behind couches, and after thoroughly searching the cellar, the marshals decided either that their intelligence had been faulty or that their quarry had been warned in time to escape. However, as they left the house in disappointment, one of the several guards, who had been posted outside to prevent Lorenzo's flight, should he be flushed out by the searchers, called attention to the Snow's faithful and indiscreetly stupid watch dog, Nero, sniffing at the small, previously unnoticed ventilator grating in the foundation of the house. Correctly deducing that Nero detected a familiar odor wafting from the vent opening, the officers returned to the room above it and discovered the trap door, the place of refuge, and its famous occupant, who willingly submitted to arrest after satisfying himself that the warrant was in proper order.

Word spread quickly that Brigham City's venerable leader, now a dignified seventy-one years old, had been arrested. Immediately a throng gathered to watch the unfolding drama, and, presumably, to respond to any instruction that Elder Snow might be inclined to give them.

However, he submitted quietly and accompanied the marshals to Ogden, where he was taken before U. S. Commissioner F. T. Black, who set bond at $1,500. A preliminary hearing was held the following day, and Lorenzo was bound over for trial on three separate indictments for unlawful cohabitation, a misdemeanor that carried a maximum penalty of six months imprisonment and a $300 fine. "It was gratifying," wrote one reporter, "to observe that Brother Snow appeared as calm and dignified in his demeanor as he does on ordinary occasions. The tenor of his disposition was unruffled, and he exhibited no trace of excitement whatever."

The three trials, which were held between December 30, 1885, and January 5, 1886, were a mere farce. In substance, the only evidence presented to sustain the charge of unlawful cohabitation was testimony that Elder Snow and one of his polygamous wives had been seen walking together on a Salt Lake City street. Unlawful cohabitation was inferred from the fact that both parties were alive and had been seen together; hence, they were deemed to be "living together."

Despite the fact that the alleged misconduct grew out of the same set of circumstances, the defendant was found guilty in each of the three suits, and in each one, the maximum penalty was imposed, which totaled eighteen months in jail and fines of $900.

Appeals were promptly made to the territorial supreme court, where anti-Mormon judges as promptly handed down decisions of affirmance. They decreed that "the offense of cohabitation is complete when a man to all outward appearances is living and associating with two or more women as his wives."

While all these legal shenanigans were in progress, Elder Snow was free on $15,000 bail. As if to compensate him for all the anguish and anxiety the litigation produced, the Brigham City Saints immersed him in an outpouring of love and support. Just before appearing to be sentenced, he was surprised by a visit from thirty beautiful girls representing the Young Ladies Mutual Improvement Association of Brigham City. Their spokesman read a tribute to the venerable leader that said, "Dearly beloved and highly respected President Snow, . . . you always make the young feel and realize your great anxiety for their improvement and welfare—not only spiritually, but morally and intellectually. No other man has exercised such an influence of true nobility and refinement in our midst. We estimate you in the character of a true gentleman."

Not to be outdone by the Young Ladies, the Relief Society sisters feted Elder Snow at a special dinner on January 27, 1886.

The next day, arguments began in Elder Snow's case before the territorial supreme court. When that court affirmed the judgments of the trial court, an appeal to the United States Supreme Court was pressed immediately. At the same time, an effort was made to have his case advanced on the calendar, not only to serve the interests of the aging apostle, but also to expedite a final decision that might overturn the harsh interpretations made by the territorial court. Learning that it would not be possible under the rules of the court to advance the case on the calendar as long as he remained at liberty on bonds, Elder Snow elected to go to prison immediately.

March 12, 1886, was the day set for Lorenzo's imprisonment. Desiring to save the feelings of his family, he bid them good-bye at home and was accompanied to the territorial prison only by his attorney, F. S. Richards. The prison, located at the mouth of Parley's Canyon in Salt Lake Valley, had the appearance of an ancient castle or fortress with high, dingy, red brick walls and jutting turrets at the corners, which housed armed guards.

This cold, forbidding place housed inmates whose offenses ranged from those of questionable validity, like the one of which Elder Snow stood convicted, to the most heinous felonies, rape, incest, and murder. Among them were men of every race, creed, and nationality intermingled in crowded, drafty, insect-infested quarters that reeked constantly of foul odors.

To reduce the hygienic problems as far as practicable, the prison staff enforced quite rigidly the rule that all prisoners be clean shaven with closely cropped hair. Elder Snow's doctors, John D. Carnahan and J. P. Allen, had written a letter to the prison officials pleading that certain concessions be made in his behalf. "In consideration of the advanced age [seventy-two years] of the bearer, Lorenzo Snow," it read, "and also of his usually delicate condition, we the undersigned, take the liberty of stating that we fear his health would be seriously jeopardized by depriving him of his hair and beard, as he has worn the latter 16 years on this account." The doctors then asked for a waiver of the usual rule in his case, which, they concluded, "would, in all probability avoid the risk of serious consequences to Mr. Snow."

Unlike the harsh treatment given to some other convicted

polygamists, the warden granted this request and in other ways saw to it that Elder Snow was treated with as much consideration and respect as the unpleasant conditions allowed.

Lorenzo discovered that the prison community was divided roughly into two categories of inmates, the "toughs" and the "cohabs," the former being the hardened criminals imprisoned for the commission of major felonies, and the latter being the Mormon polygamists. By the time of Elder Snow's incarceration, there was, for the most part, an actual physical segregation of the prisoners, with the cohabs occupying most of the upper terrace of the cell block and the toughs occupying the lower terraces. The cells, measuring about five by seven feet, each accommodated two men, who slept on canvas strips hung lengthwise in a manner resembling sailors' hammocks. Slop pails served as the only sanitary accommodations within the cells. Even at noon, a pall of darkness hung over the interior of the cell block, broken occasionally by shafts of light that fought their way in from the outside or by dim lamps or candles. Weekly baths were allowed the prisoners, using water they hauled from a stream that flowed through the prison compound. Each man did his own laundry, although it was permissible for family or friends to bring fresh clothing to the prisoners.

Menus were skimpy, consisting chiefly of the cheapest cuts of tough meat immersed in tasteless gravy, small potatoes in jackets, and bread and coffee. Orthodox Mormons like Elder Snow forsook the coffee for cold water. The only departures from the monotony of this diet were mush or soups, often served for supper, and beans, considered to be a delicacy served as the main meal on Sundays.

Once Elder Snow had been given his prison garb, a suit marked with horizontal alternating black and white stripes and matched by a round striped hat, and had been assigned to his cell, he began to appraise his situation. He discovered that while he had been robbed of physical freedom, his mind and spirit remained free. He also discovered that the more than forty other cohabs who were in the penitentiary when he arrived had already begun to create a prison society of a kind previously unknown. Some wrote, some painted, some sculpted, and some composed. Some banded together to study languages, mathematics, or history, or to learn the manual arts. And all of them regularly devoted substantial time to studying the scriptures and to fasting and prayer.

Elder Snow was an illustrious addition to this community of convicts, which included Abraham H. Cannon, who was then a member of the First Council of Seventy; Rudger Clawson, who would later be called as a member of the Twelve, as a counselor in the First Presidency, and as the President of the Twelve; James Moyle, an English convert from Cornwall, England, who would become the patriarch of a large, influential Latter-day Saint family; and Andrew Jenson, a future assistant church historian. No sooner had Lorenzo arrived than he slipped easily into the role of leader of the Latter-day Saint convicts, he being the ranking priesthood leader then in the penitentiary. He participated in a Sunday School that had been organized at the prison, and, as the opportunity arose, counseled and instructed the younger prisoners who came to him from time to time. So intimate and constant was the prisoners' relationship that Lorenzo was once heard to say, half in jest, "I have always wanted to live the United Order," alluding to their common housing and board.

On April 8, 1886, Elder Snow assembled the Mormon prisoners as if to compensate them for having missed the recently concluded general conference. He said, "We have been sent to this place and are associated together in prison. It will be our privilege, if we so desire, to express our feelings to the Lord by offering up unto him the sacred shout" (alluding to the Hosannah Shout, traditionally given as the culmination of a temple dedication). Elder Rudger Clawson later said of this incident, "He informed these prisoners for Christ's sake that it would be their privilege to raise their voices to the Lord in the sacred shout, if they felt the spirit of it. An expression was taken, and it was the unanimous feeling of the brethren that they avail themselves of this great and glorious privilege. The sacred shout was then offered up within those prison walls—a great and mighty shout to God and the Lamb. The foundations of the prison seemed to shake, and the shout ascended to heaven. I testify to you it is my belief that that great shout was acceptable to the Lord and is recorded in the library of the Celestial Kingdom."

During May 1886, Lorenzo had two interviews with the new territorial governor, Caleb W. West. The first occurred on May 8, only three days after the governor arrived in Salt Lake City.

Caleb West was an upright Kentucky judge and former confederate officer who had been appointed by President Grover Cleveland to attempt to bring order out of the legal chaos in Utah. Correctly assessing that a satisfactory resolution of Elder Snow's case would have a moderating effect upon all the others, Mr. West decided to confer with the aging apostle immediately.

The governor, who was accompanied to the prison by three aides, Arthur Pratt, J. Barnett, and Bolivar Roberts, lost little time in getting to the point once the interview had begun. He admonished Elder Snow, and through him all other Latter-day Saints, to place themselves at once in harmony with the laws of the country.

"I infer from your remarks," Lorenzo answered, "that you now recommend the abandonment of our doctrine of plural marriage, and the abandonment of our wives. But as that doctrine is a fundamental principle of our religion, we could not consent to relinquish it."

The governor said he did not expect the Saints to renounce their "religious belief and opinions," but only that they give up the "practice" of polygamy. He cited the secessionists, of whom he was one, to illustrate what he had in mind—men who, at last, had yielded themselves to the law of the land, but who still retained their view about states' rights.

"I think, Governor," answered the apostle, "that yourself and your political friends acted wisely; but our cases are widely different. Your belief of State rights was of human source and direction, whereas our doctrine of celestial marriage is divine, revealed to us from heaven."

The nonplussed governor could only mumble that he "did not wish to bring religion into the question."

Elder Snow posed a hypothetical question: "Governor, suppose we adopt your suggestions and relinquish plural marriage, what guarantees have we of enjoying peace and being unmolested in our religious rights and liberties?"

The governor assured Elder Snow that the Supreme Court would provide the umbrella of protection the Saints fervently sought: "Surely in that court prejudice or partiality cannot appear—the decision will be just and should be honored and obeyed by all good citizens."

The governor must have been surprised by Lorenzo's frank response: "You are aware, as well as ourselves, this is far from the fact, which is forcibly demonstrated in my own case as well as in many others."

Undeterred by his failure in this first discussion, the persistent governor made a second attempt to win Lorenzo over to his views a few days after the U. S. Supreme Court declined to consider Elder Snow's appeal on the questionable ground that it lacked jurisdiction. The shaky premise of this decision is revealed by the fact that before rendering it, the court recalled and reversed itself in an earlier similar case, in which it had originally assumed jurisdiction. The dialogue between Elder Snow and his importunate visitor during their second interview shows the competitive and tenacious aspects of the prisoner's character, and sheds light on the cruel dilemma the Mormon polygamists faced during the dark days of the underground: "Mr. Snow, I suppose you are advised of the action of the Supreme Court in your case?"

"Yes, sir, I heard they concluded they had no jurisdiction in my case."

Getting a concession from the prisoner that this made the judgments of the territorial court final, the governor said, "I conceived that it would be a very opportune time to call and submit to you a proposition. . . . Upon consultation with Judge Zane and Mr. Dickson, and their supporting the view I have suggested, I have come to say to you and your people here that we will unite in a petition to the Executive to issue his pardon in these cases upon a promise, in good faith, that you obey and respect the laws, and that you will continue no longer to live in violation of them."

The prisoner's answer was that he had been convicted without valid supporting evidence, and that it was inappropriate, therefore, to ask that he refrain from alleged misconduct in the future of which he had not been proven guilty in the past.

Unwilling to accept that premise, the governor pressed the point: "I am not talking about the past, I come to propose that the Federal officials unite in asking the President for a pardon for you and for others, to relieve you from any punishment you may have incurred, if you, in good faith, for the future submit yourselves to the laws as interpreted and construed by the courts."

"But I have no confidence in the courts. Even if I [were] to make a promise I have no idea in the world that the courts would administer us justice. Let them first administer us justice, and administer the laws correctly, and then we will see."

Following his interview with Elder Snow, the governor met with the other Mormon prisoners and repeated the offer he had made to Lorenzo. On May 24, the prisoners directed a letter to the governor, formally rejecting it. The style and content of the document suggest that it was the literary product of the first signatory—Lorenzo Snow. They wrote: "Of the forty-nine Elders of the Church of Jesus Christ of Latter-day Saints now imprisoned in the Penitentiary for alleged violation of the Edmunds Law, all but four had plural wives from its passage to thirty-five years prior to its passage. We were united to our wives for time and all eternity by the most sacred covenants, and in many instances numerous children have been born as a result of our union, who are endeared to us by the strongest paternal ties. So far as compliance with your proposition requires the sacrifice of honor and manhood, the repudiation of our wives and children, the violation of sacred covenants, heaven forbid that we should be guilty of such perfidy; perpetual imprisonment, with which we are threatened, or even death itself, would be preferable."

Rejection of his compromise veered the governor toward the enemies of the Church, who were chiefly responsible for the later passage of the more repressive Edmunds-Tucker Act. In the meantime, Lorenzo and the other Mormon prisoners settled down into the monotonous and degrading routine of prison life, confident that their freedom would be purchased only by serving out their sentences or by future proceedings in the courts.

Lorenzo now began to diversify his prison routine by writing numerous letters to family, friends, and Church associates. His letters were filled with optimism and hope, and reflected intellect, culture, and spirituality that were the dominant features of his character. This excerpt from a letter written to the First Presidency is typical: "I am very thankful to the Giver of all Good, for the bodily health and buoyancy of spirit which He so confers on me that I feel perfectly resigned with calm submission to the inevitable and am enabled, fully, to acknowledge the hand of God, and His overruling Providence in whatever has or may occur." The only thing remotely resembling a complaint that found its way into his writings related to his inability to perform his apostolic duties as usual: "It requires an effort to suppress regrets that I am under the necessity of so abruptly closing my missionary enterprise." However, he hastened to negate any idea that he was remorseful or discouraged by adding, "But if I can serve the Holy Cause, which is dearer to me than life, and promote the glory of God by passing through the ordeal of incarceration in a penitentiary, I am perfectly willing."

Perhaps the most accurate expression of the resigned attitude Lorenzo maintained toward his imprisonment is this excerpt from a letter home in which he mentions a comment he had made to a companion inside the prison: "I said that I considered that I had no reason to complain and felt quite reconciled to my situation. Had made up my mind from the moment of my arrest to accept, without worry, whatever might be the results; being convinced that important good would surely come of it both to myself and the Great Cause, to promote which, during the course of fifty years, I had been industriously engaged. God requires us to stand by it at whatever cost, or personal sacrifice, like a beacon light from upon its rocky basis amid the howling storm and dashing waves, yet calm and unmoved, its glittering light directing the observant mariner with unmistakable certainty to the desired haven of safety and rest."

For over five months after the Supreme Court rejected his appeal for want of jurisdiction, Elder Snow quietly and uncomplainingly lived the life of a model prisoner. In October 1886, however, it was decided, on advice of counsel, to make another attempt to prove the illegality of his imprisonment through a habeus corpus proceeding that raised the issue of whether he was being held illegally. To no one's surprise, the territorial court promptly denied the petition. But the United States Supreme Court promptly allowed an appeal and assumed jurisdiction. The matter was argued on January 20, 1887, and the following month on February 7, the court handed down an unexpected decision that granted the petition, thereby freeing Elder Snow. The high court decreed that there was but one offense and that, therefore, the trial court had no jurisdiction to impose sentence. "The division of the two years and eleven months [into three periods] is wholly arbitrary," ruled the Supreme Court. "On the same principle there might have been indictments covering each of the thirty-five months, with imprisonment for seventy-four years, and fines amounting to $44,400; and so on, ad infinitum, for smaller periods of time."

The news of this decision spread rapidly throughout the territory, carried by wire, the press, and word-of-mouth. It brought joy and hope to the numerous polygamists who had been convicted or charged under the procedure rejected by the Supreme Court decision, and it produced some consternation among the enemies of the Church.

On February 8, 1887, the day after the Supreme Court decision was announced, Lorenzo Snow walked out of the penitentiary a free man. "Eleven months I had been incarcerated within the walls of a gloomy prison," he wrote later. "Imagine for yourselves how like a dream it seemed when, suddenly and unexpectedly the prison gate flew open and clad in my striped convict suit, I was at once ushered into the presence of a multitude of warm-hearted friends, anxiously awaiting my appearance. O, what warm clasping and shaking of hands. What hearty greetings and expressions of congratulation."

After this happy reunion, Elder Snow went to the prison's

tailor shop, where he traded the striped convict uniform for a "new black broadcloth suit," and, as he put it, "Richard was himself again."

Lorenzo was shown to a waiting carriage by his attorney, F. S. Richards, where he was greeted by his daughter Eliza, his son, Alvirus, and a large number of friends and associates who had assembled to pay their respects. "It was a matter of astonishment," he wrote appreciatively, "that so large a gathering should put in an appearance on the spur of the moment. Included in the number were Heber J. Grant and John W. Taylor, of the quorum of the Twelve Apostles, . . . Abraham H. Cannon, representing the Seven Presidents of Seventies [who had had his own 'coming out party' only a short time before], John Nicholson and George C. Lambert, representing the *Deseret News,* a representative of the *Salt Lake Herald,* President L. W. Shurtliff of the Weber Stake, and many others—ladies and gentlemen—noble men and women of God, of whose society I am justly proud."

The day after his release, Elder Snow was the guest of honor at a gala party held in the Social Hall, hosted by the Salt Lake Tabernacle Choir. In addition to refreshments, dancing, and brief remarks by Elder Snow, the evening featured the choir singing, appropriately, "Home Again."

The first Sunday following his release, the celebrated apostle addressed a capacity crowd in the Salt Lake Tabernacle. "Who shall separate us from the love of Christ?" he asked rhetorically, quoting the Apostle Paul. "Shall tribulation, or distress, or persecution, or famine, or nakedness, or peril, or sword?" (Rom. 8:35.) In his scholarly and eloquent way, yet with a new fire ignited by his unjust imprisonment, the speaker proceeded to answer this query negatively. He first traced early incidents in his own life, held up as a type of what had happened to the entire Church, showing the tragic consequences of persecution. But these, he assured his audience, were but the badge of Christian discipleship, a badge they must be prepared to wear openly and fearlessly throughout life. So, for the future, he held out to them the prospect of more of what they had endured in the past. He assured them that the Saints "must pass through the narrows and learn by sacrifice." Lest any of them misunderstand, Elder Snow cited Job as an example of the endurance the Saints must cultivate in order to withstand the pressures the future doubtless held for them. But, he did not fail to draw attention to the reward that awaited at the end of their trials. This reward, the speaker advised his listeners, was of such a transcendent nature as to be beyond his power to describe.

Significantly, this talk was devoid of any criticism of the government at whose hands he had suffered. Indeed, he expressed gratitude for the blessings and privileges he enjoyed by reason of his American citizenship, an asset he seemed to prize as highly as his mentor, Paul, valued his Roman citizenship. He did, however, denounce in somewhat mild through explicit terms certain corrupt officials whose acts were a betrayal of the form of government Lorenzo regarded as being of divine origin.

The celebrations in Salt Lake City were duplicated in Brigham City when Lorenzo returned home. He settled into a more comfortable and secure routine, confident now that his conviction and imprisonment would, in light of the Supreme Court's decision, provide immunity against further harassment. Evidence of his return to a normal life is found in this entry in the history of Box Elder Stake: "By April 2nd, 1887, Lorenzo was revived and going strong, urging the saints in Brigham City to attend to the cleanup of the Tabernacle Square, which should be fixed up before any other in town."

On the day following this entry, Elder Snow celebrated his seventy-third birthday. Practically all of Brigham City turned out to pay homage to this beloved leader, whose recent imprisonment had added a martyrlike quality to his already rich and varied character. Included on the program was a poetic welcome delivered by his son Orion, which seemed to capsulize the reverential feelings his family and friends entertained toward him: "Gaze but a moment on the wondrous past/ The youth, the man, The Saints; his trials, last/ Our loved aged apostle, seeking all to bless/ Can gaze on life— pronounce it a success."

Chapter Twenty-five

President of the Twelve

The euphoria created by Elder Snow's legal victory and release from prison was soon followed by the leaden reality of the newly passed Edmunds-Tucker Act. While the final version of this legislation hardly measured up to what its sponsors had originally aimed for, the result was so extremely harsh and punitive as to create deep forebodings in Elder Snow and other knowledgeable members of the Church. Among other things, it abolished the Emigration Fund Company, the Nauvoo Legion, and women's suffrage. It also created a federal board to take charge of the re-registration and election machinery of the territory, dissolved the Church as a legal entity, and escheated its property to the federal government. All this was done because of an expressed abhorrence of polygamy, but what the enemies of the Church actually feared was the influence of Church members on Utah politics.

Despite the uncertainty raised by the Edmunds-Tucker Act, Elder Snow went about his apostolic duties as usual. Soon after his release from prison, he attended the semi-annual conference of the Young Mens' Mutual Improvement Association of the Utah Stake. His recent legal triumph gave him an influence with the youth of the Church that few leaders could match.

With his newfound immunity from legal harassment, Lorenzo was able to move about in public without fear of arrest. On this account, he was assigned by President Taylor to preside at the annual conference of the Church to be held in Provo, Utah, on April 6, 1887. Accompanying him were junior members of the Twelve Franklin D. Richards, John Henry Smith, Heber J. Grant, and John W. Taylor, whose personal circumstances were such as not to place them in legal jeopardy by their attendance. All the other general authorities of the Church were either in exile or away on assignment.

At Provo, the Saints met in the seclusion of the new but only partially completed stake tabernacle, away from the legal bitterness and intrigue that agitated Salt Lake City.

The theme of the conference was set by Elder Snow in his principal address. The newly liberated apostle made it clear that the Spirit of the Lord had been with him in prison to the same extent that it had been with him in freedom. From the book of Daniel, Elder Snow quoted Daniel's answer to the king, who had asked whether the Lord had been able to deliver him from the lions: "My God hath sent his angel, and hath shut the lions' mouths that they have not hurt me: forasmuch as before him innocency was found in me; and also before thee, O king, have I done no hurt."

Within less than four months after he assigned Elder Snow to preside at the 1887 April general conference, President John Taylor was dead. The exiled leader passed away on July 25, 1887, at the home of Thomas F. Rouche in Kaysville, Utah, a small village in Davis County about fifteen miles north of Salt Lake City. Just thirteen days before his death, President Taylor's second counselor, Joseph F. Smith, had returned from the Hawaiian Islands, where he had lived in exile for two and a half years. President Smith's return marked the first time since December 1884 that all three members of the First Presidency had been together.

President Taylor's death elevated Wilford Woodruff to the leadership of the Church (as President of the Twelve) and placed Elder Snow next in line to occupy that position once the First Presidency was reorganized. Since he did not enjoy Elder Snow's immunity from arrest, however, it became necessary that President Woodruff remain on the underground, a fact that thrust Lorenzo more into the public eye than his presiding officer. So while Elder Snow was able to play an open and prominent role in the conduct of President Taylor's funeral, President Woodruff had to be content to watch the funeral procession from the veiled windows of the Church historian's office. And he had to maintain a similarly low profile at the dedication of the Manti Temple in May 1888. However, on this historic occasion, he did actively participate by holding a private dedication on May 17, attended by Elder Snow and other members of the Twelve, and by a few of the local leading brethren.

On May 21, four days after the private gathering, Elder Snow led out in the public dedicatory services, which continued over a period of three days. At each of the several sessions, Elder Snow spoke briefly and then read President Woodruff's comprehensive prayer of dedication, which referred to practically every part of the building and to every aspect of the worldwide work of the Church. At the conclusion of each session, the assembled Saints joined in the Hosannah Shout, which likely reminded Lorenzo of his last participation in this sacred ordinance while in prison. Following the shout came the Hosannah Anthem, as a part of which the entire congregation joined in singing "The Spirit of God like a Fire Is Burning."

Some of the more spiritually sensitive members of the congregation witnessed spiritual phenomena during the dedication. This statement, signed by fourteen members of the Church, appeared in the May 30, 1888, issue of the *Deseret News:* "A bright halo of light was seen by a number of persons over and around the heads of the following speakers—viz: Lorenzo Snow, Jacob Gates, Robert Campbell, John Henry Smith, Francis M. Lyman, John W. Taylor and A. M. Cannon. Brother Canute Peterson, of Ephraim (a very reliable and able man of affairs), observed this halo around the heads of all the speakers. While the public dedicatory prayer was being offered by Brother Lorenzo Snow, near the middle of the prayer, during a pause, the words 'Hallelujah, hallelujah, the Lord be praised' was uttered by a voice in a very soft and melodious tone, heard by brother Lewis Anderson, one of our assistant recorders here. On the 21st of May, before the opening exercises commenced, Brother A. C. Smyth, the chorister, seated himself at the organ, and rendered a piece of sacred music, a selection from Mendelssohn at the conclusion of which, persons sitting near the center of the hall, and also on the stand at the west end, heard most heavenly voices and singing—it sounded to them most angelic, and appeared to be behind and above them, and they turned their heads in the direction of the sound, wondering if there was another choir in some part of the temple."

Others reported that they saw the spirits of Brigham Young and one of his counselors, Jedediah M. Grant, and President John Taylor in the temple at various times during the dedication.

Even as the Saints enjoyed the spiritual outpourings at the dedication of the Manti Temple, they were aware that the larger and as yet uncompleted temple in Salt Lake City was then in the hands of United States Marshal Frank H. Dyer, who had been appointed as the receiver of Church property under the escheat provisions of the Edmunds-Tucker Act. Mr. Dyer had not only taken charge of the Salt Lake Temple, but of all the facilities on Temple Square, the President's offices, and most other possessions of the Church in the territorial capital. Elder Snow and the other Church leaders had no way of knowing whether the temple they had just dedicated would soon be taken over by Mr. Dyer. By October 1888, a few months after the Manti Temple dedication, and following lengthy negotiations between counsel for the Church and the government, a stipulation was reached as to the Church property subject to the escheat provisions of the Edmunds-Tucker Act. This formed the basis of the test case that ultimately decided the constitutionality of the act. It was not until 1893 that the Church's personal property was returned, and not until 1896 that its real property was returned. The confused and complex conditions that existed during these years created the financial problems Lorenzo Snow would face later as President of the Church.

But all these trying events lay in the dim future as President Woodruff and Elder Snow and the other apostles prepared for the annual conference in April 1889. Great excitement preceded the event because of the decision the Twelve had made to reorganize the First Presidency and to present the new leaders to the conference for a sustaining vote. It came as no surprise when Wilford Woodruff, in being sustained as the new President of the Church, presented George Q. Cannon and Joseph F. Smith as his counselors. These brethren, who had ably served as counselors to President John Taylor, were skilled administrators and had rendered important service to President Woodruff during the interim following President Taylor's death.

The elevation of his longtime friend and fellow-apostle to the prophetic chair brought about Lorenzo Snow's installation as President of the Quorum of the Twelve. Having turned seventy-five just a few days before, the new quorum president could look back with a sense of satisfaction upon more than half a century of devoted service to the Church.

Despite his elevation to the second-highest office in the Church, President Snow continued to reside in Brigham City and to commute to and from Salt Lake City as the needs of his office required. On December 23, 1889, he concurred with the First Presidency in a call to "all the Latter-day Saints throughout these mountains" to join in a day of fasting and prayer. The object of the fast was to invoke God's blessings upon the Saints as a witness that he was still with them; to seek for a softened attitude toward them on the part of their enemies; and to plead for more just and merciful treatment by government leaders. In doing this, the Saints were admonished to reflect an attitude of meekness and faith. The Church leaders exhorted in the *Deseret News*, "There ought to be no expression or desire for wrath and judgment upon those who have persecuted, reviled, and falsely accused us, and who seek to oppress us, but rather that they may turn from their wicked ways and be led to do right."

While there were no immediate visible fruits from this spiritual exercise, which was undertaken on the eighty-fourth anniversary of the birth of the Prophet Joseph Smith, it presumably had a significant impact upon events the following year.

In the interval between this special fast and September

1890, Lorenzo joined with President Woodruff and the other Brethren in the most agonizing reappraisal of the status of the Church and the course it should follow that had occurred since its organization. This journal entry made by President Wilford Woodruff, following consultation with Lorenzo Snow and other members of the Twelve, reveals the culmination of this effort: "I have arrived at a point in the history of my life as the president of the Church of Jesus Christ of Latter-day Saints where I am under the necessity of acting for the temporal salvation of the church. The United States government has taken a stand and passed laws to destroy the Latter-day Saints on the subject of polygamy, or partriarchal order of marriage, and after praying to the Lord and feeling inspired, I have issued the following proclamation which is sustained by my counselors and the twelve apostles." Then followed the document known as the Manifesto, which was presented to the general conference of the Church convened on October 6. Following the reading of this historic instrument, President Lorenzo Snow rose to say, "I move that, recognizing Wilford Woodruff as the President of the Church of Jesus Christ of Latter-day Saints, and the only man on the earth at the present time who holds the keys of the sealing ordinances, we consider him fully authorized by virtue of his position to issue the Manifesto which has been read in our hearing, and which is dated September 24th, 1890, and that as a Church in General Conference assembled, we accept his declaration concerning plural marriages as authoritative and binding."

This motion carried unanimously, and with the adoption of the Manifesto, the road was opened for the eventual resolution of problems that had harassed the Saints for several decades.

As he divided his time between Salt Lake and Brigham City, Lorenzo continued to exert a strong but indirect influence upon ecclesiastical affairs in Brigham City, despite the fact he had been formally released as stake president over ten years before. Brigham Young had installed Lorenzo's son, Oliver, to succeed him in the expectation that the apostle would continue to provide over-all guidance through the willing and loyal submission of the son to the desires of the father. Oliver served ably until July 1887, just a few months after his father was released from the territorial prison. Then, because of personal considerations, Oliver stepped down as stake president and was temporarily replaced by his first counselor, Elijah A. Box, who served as acting president until February 1888.

When Oliver relinquished the reins of leadership, his permanent successor, Rudger Clawson, was still in prison, well on the way to becoming the man who served more time in prison for the sake of his religious convictions than any other Latter-day Saint.

Freed from the penitentiary on December 12, 1887, Rudger was called as president of the Box Elder Stake eleven days later in a letter signed by President Wilford Woodruff. The call was instituted by Lorenzo Snow, however, who remembered the young prisoner from his own penitentiary days and who looked upon him as "just about the finest disciple of Christ" he had ever met. Further evidence of that appraisal is seen in the fact that Rudger Clawson was the first apostle called after Lorenzo Snow became president of the Church; and when George Q. Cannon died in 1901, President Snow called Rudger as his second counselor, although the president passed away before his young protege could be set apart.

It is likely that one of the facets of Rudger's character that attracted President Snow was a characteristic that had dominated Lorenzo's own life—a certain diffidence or unconcern about status or place accompanied by an overriding interest in the welfare of the Church and its members. We see this in Lorenzo when, during the Reformation, he told Brigham Young of his willingness to step down from the Quorum of the Twelve if the President felt there was another who could better fill the position. And we see it in Rudger's comment that had the matter been left to his own judgment, he would have refused the call to serve as the Box Elder stake president.

These two men, kindred spirits, and presumably tied together by premortal as well as earthly relationships, comprised an unusual and unlikely pair—the aged, erudite, and well-traveled apostle who, when he first became closely associated with his young friend (who was forty-three years his junior) had been in the priesthood harness for half a century, and the young, Utah-born polygamist, who had once defied a mob to shoot him after it had killed his missionary companion. But, despite vast differences in age, education, and experience, this duo worked together like a team of choice thoroughbreds. Having complete confidence in President Snow and loving him like a father, Rudger Clawson was amenable to the direction of his mentor, and apparently would spring into action or refrain from it at the merest hint from the apostle that something ought or ought not to be done.

Perhaps the most significant thing they did together as a team, certainly the most dramatic, involved a priesthood administration in which a young woman in Brigham City, Ella Jensen, was brought back to life after having been dead for more than two hours. This unusual case is not only one of the few well-documented incidents in which a person has been called back from the dead, but it also was the fulfillment of a prophetic promise made to Elder Snow more than fifty years before the event: "If expedient the dead shall rise and come forth at thy bidding," Joseph Smith, Sr., had told Lorenzo in his patriarchal blessing. Like so many of the other extraordinary promises made at that time, this one had to await the maturing of events for its fulfillment.

Chapter Twenty-six

Raising the Dead

In the early part of 1891, Elder Snow's niece Ella Jensen came down with a fever accompanied by a sore throat and headache, symptoms of a late winter cold. However, two or three days later, Ella broke out in a rash and red spots appeared on her palate, and the illness was diagnosed as scarlet fever. Since the patient was almost twenty years old and, except for her sickness, in good health, no great concern was shown over her condition. However, as the disease hung on and she failed to respond to the usual remedies of the day, complications set in and her condition rapidly worsened until her life hung in the balance. She oscillated between life and death for several weeks, being attended around the clock by her concerned family and by helpful neighbor volunteers. In early March, Leah Rees, a family friend, came on duty at 8:00 P.M., intending to stay until morning. "Ella asked me to sing and play for her," Leah reported, "but goodness, I was so worried about her condition, I felt more like crying." Stifling her melancholy feelings, Leah played the old-fashioned harmonium in the Jensen home and sang until the patient fell asleep. She then lay down on the couch to rest. About 3:00 A.M., the volunteer nurse was awakened by Ella's calls. Ella asked her for a comb, brush, and scissors, explaining, "They are coming to get me at ten o'clock in the morning." She told Leah that she wanted to look presentable for "them." When Leah inquired about the identity of these unknown visitors, she was told by Ella that her deceased Uncle Hans Jensen and certain "messengers" had appeared to her. "I am going to die," she said, "and they are coming at ten o'clock to get me and take me away."

Assuming that this improbable story was merely the jumbled product of a fevered brain, the nurse tried to soothe her patient and coax her back to sleep, but to no avail. When the request for comb, brush, and scissors escalated into a somewhat angry demand, Leah complied.

Having received the things she had so imperiously demanded, the sick girl found that she lacked the strength to fix her hair and so prevailed upon her friend to do it. As Leah brushed her hair, the girl asked that her parents be awakened so she could tell them about Uncle Hans and the messengers. Leah protested that it was very early and that her parents were tired and needed rest, but soon gave in to the daughter's demands. When the sleepy pair appeared at her bedside, Ella recited the astonishing facts about the visitation. If anything, they were more incredulous about Ella's story than Leah had been and, fearing their daughter was delirious, tried to placate her and to tempt her back to sleep. "No," she announced with finality, "I am not going to sleep any more. I know I am going to die and that they are coming to get me."

Leah left the Jensen home about 8:00 A.M., confident that her friend was near death, not so much from Ella's story about the nocturnal visitors as from her frailty.

The dying girl's father, Jacob, later recounted the events that occurred between Leah's departure and ten o'clock. "[Ella] wanted to see all the folks and bid them good-bye. All who were near came in, all but Grandma Jensen. She was in town and I sent for her. She arrived just when the others of us had said good-bye. Ella put her arms around her grandmother's neck and kissed her good-bye. It was not more than a minute after that when her pulse stopped and she passed away. I was holding her hand and felt her pulse stop."

Jacob and his wife decided to advise Lorenzo Snow, who had married Sarah E. Minnie Jensen, Jacob's sister. Since Lorenzo was then in a meeting at the Brigham City Tabernacle, Jacob hitched up his team and drove to town. Tethering his horses nearby, he entered the tabernacle and, finding that Elder Snow was speaking, wrote a note to him and had it placed on the pulpit. "President Snow stopped his talking," Jacob later reported, "read the note and then explained to the Saints that it was a call to visit some people who were in deep sorrow and asked to be excused." In the vestry, the dead girl's father told his brother-in-law what had happened. After meditating for a moment, the apostle said, "I will go down with you." But as the pair was leaving, Elder Snow told his companion, "Wait a moment, I wish you would go into the meeting and get Brother Clawson. I want him to go also." (Lorenzo was very close to Rudger Clawson and once called him "just about the finest disciple of Christ" he had ever met.) The three then left the tabernacle together and rode the mile and a half to the Jensen home.

On arriving there, they found that Annie Cecilia Nelson, a nurse and midwife who had served the community for many years, had made initial preparations for the burial by "laying the body out," washing it, and dressing it in clean linen.

After entering the room where the body lay, Ella now having been dead for about two hours, the apostle stood for a while in deep meditation and then asked for some conse- crated oil. This "surprised" Jacob Jensen who, nevertheless, complied with the request. When he had received the oil, Lorenzo handed it to Rudger Clawson, requesting that he anoint the girl, which he did. The two of them then laid their hands on Ella's head as Elder Snow sealed the anointing. "During the administration," Jacob Jensen reported later, "I was particularly impressed with some of the words which he used and can well remember them now. 'Dear Ella, I com- mand you, in the name of the Lord, Jesus Christ, to come back and live, your mission is not ended. You shall yet live to per- form a great mission.' He said she should live to rear a large family and be a comfort to her parents and friends."

Elder Rudger Clawson left this account of the incident: "We then laid our hands upon her head, and the anointing was confirmed by President Snow, who blessed her and among other things, used this extraordinary expression, in a commanding tone of voice: 'Come back, Ella, come back. Your walk upon the earth is not yet completed, come back.' Shortly afterward we left the home."

Ella's body remained lifeless for more than an hour after Elder Snow and Elder Clawson had left. Then, as her parents sat near her bedside, Ella suddenly opened her eyes. "She looked about the room," her father reported, "saw us sitting there, but still looked for someone else, and the first thing she said was: 'Where is he? Where is he?' We asked 'Who? Where is who?' 'Why, Brother Snow,' she replied. 'He called me back.' "

At first Ella was not overjoyed with what Elder Snow had done. "Why did he call me back?" she asked complainingly. "I was so happy and did not want to come back. At ten o'clock my spirit left my body. It took me some time to make up my mind to go, as I could hear and see the folks crying and mourning over me." Once Ella had received a glimpse of the other world, however, she went willingly and enthusiastically. She said that at the moment her spirit passed through the veil, "all care and worry left me." She first beheld an extremely large room or hall, so large she could not see the end of it, thronged with happy, smiling people. "It was like going along the crowded street of a large city," she wrote, "where you meet many people, only a very few of whom you recognize." Among those whom she did recognize was her grandfather Hans Peter Jensen and his son and namesake Hans Jensen, Ella's uncle. With Uncle Hans was his wife, May Ellen Valentine Jensen.

When Ella reached the end of the large room she had first seen, she entered a smaller room filled with children, who were being supervised by Eliza R. Snow. While listening to the singing of these children, Ella heard the voice of Lorenzo Snow, calling her back to mortality. "Sister Ella," said the voice in a commanding tone, "You must come back as your mission is not yet finished here on earth." Obedient to that command, Ella walked back through the large hall, advising relatives or acquaintances along the way that she was going back. However, she had no enthusiasm about the prospect. "It was very much against my desire," the young woman wrote later, "as such perfect peace and happiness prevailed there; no suffering, no sorrow. I was taken up with all I saw and heard; I did hate to leave that beautiful place.

"As I returned I could see my body lying on the bed and the folks gathered about in the room. I hesitated for a moment, then thought, 'Yes, I will go back for a little while.' I told the folks I wanted to stay only a short time to comfort them."

The "little while" Ella referred to stretched into a period of over sixty-five years. Four years after her brief sojourn in the spirit world, she married Henry Wight, and they produced a family of eight children. After having loved and cared for this large brood and having lived a productive life, Ella Jensen Wight passed away on October 23, 1957 at age eighty-six.

Chapter Twenty-seven

Salt Lake Temple President

T he high degree of spirituality that raising Ella
Jensen from the dead necessarily implies qualified
Lorenzo Snow for the Church position that, perhaps, requires as much spirituality as any other—
that of temple president. Being the place where work for both
the living and the dead is performed, the temple is a connecting link between the spiritual and the temporal worlds. And,
occupying that vital position of linkage, the one who heads it
should, therefore, reflect in his character and works the qualities necessary to meet the challenges emanating from either
world—qualities, for example, enabling him to direct efficient-
ly the work of a large staff and, at the same time, to cope with
the powerful spiritual forces in performing vicarious work for
the dead.

If ever a man satisfied in precise detail every requirement
of this sensitive position, it was Lorenzo Snow. Approaching
eighty years of age when the Salt Lake Temple neared completion, this viril and venerable leader had been toiling in the
vineyard for almost six decades, during which he had filled
practically every position and had confronted practically every
problem known to the Church. He had proselyted vigorously
at home and abroad despite illness and fatigue; had challenged and banished the powers of evil; had been shepherd
and father to struggling pioneer communities on the plains of
Iowa and in the mountain valleys of Utah; had instructed and

inspired the Saints from the pulpit and in the classroom; and, more recently, had even challenged and temporarily suspended the power of death.

Given the requirements of the position and the qualifications of the man who ultimately filled it, we are led to wonder whether President Snow received advance hints, by spiritual means, that he was to be the first presiding officer of the Salt Lake Temple. If so, he failed to divulge it in his records.

Great excitement and anticipation gripped the Latter-day Saints as the time for the completion and dedication of the Salt Lake Temple drew near. The Manifesto had relieved much of the pressure under which the Church had suffered for so long, and had cleared the way for the finishing touches to be put on the temple.

As the April 1892 conference approached, it became apparent that the capstone would be ready for laying during the conference. The temple had been under construction so long it was difficult for some to realize that the great event was at hand. Indeed, some Salt Lake City residents in their early forties or late thirties had never known a time when Temple Square was not a scene of turmoil and unsightliness because of the construction in progress there. So, the completion of the temple represented a historic milestone in the lives of the people, and it was a symbolic watershed for the Church, marking the commencement of an era of reconciliation and redirection.

In harmony with the nature of the event, the preparations for the capstone laying were elaborate and dramatic. A large platform was constructed on the south side of the temple, appropriately festooned with bunting and flowers, to accommodate the general authorities and other Church leaders and a special choir. An electrical device made it possible for the aged President of the Church, Wilford Woodruff, to lay the capstone merely by throwing a switch. Several bands formed a procession and led the way to Temple Square, where thousands were assembled, jamming every part of the square or watching from the windows of nearby buildings.

Following an opening prayer by President Joseph F. Smith, a counselor in the First Presidency, and the singing of an appropriate hymn, President Woodruff stepped forward to say in a loud voice, "Attention all ye house of Israel, and all ye nations of the earth. We will now lay the capstone on the Temple of our God, the foundation of which was laid and dedicated by the Prophet, Seer and Revelator, Brigham Young." So saying, President Woodruff pulled the switch, and the granite capstone moved slowly into place. At a signal from his leader, President Lorenzo Snow then led the vast multitude in the Hosanna Shout, after which the multitude, estimated by some to total as many as 40,000, sang "The Spirit of God like a Fire Is Burning." At the conclusion of this stirring piece, Elder Francis M. Lyman of the Quorum of the Twelve proposed that those present "pledge themselves, collectively and individually, to furnish, as fast as it may be needed, all the money that may be required to complete the temple at the earliest possible time, so that the dedication may take place on April 6, 1893." This proposition being loudly and enthusiastically approved, the choir rendered "The Song of the Redeemed," and the benediction was offered by President George Q. Cannon, the First Counselor in the First Presidency.

The year preceding the dedication of the Salt Lake Temple was filled with feverish work and high anticipation. It was no small task to raise the funds to finish the interior work and to furnish this huge edifice. Selected to oversee the work, under the direction of the First Presidency and the Twelve, was John R. Winder, second counselor in the Presiding Bishopric, who would later be associated with Lorenzo Snow in the presidency of the temple. As the work moved rapidly toward completion, the excitement grew apace. The symbolism of the forty-year period of construction was not lost on the Saints. As their biblical forebears had been required to wander forty years in a desert wilderness before being allowed to enter the promised land, so the Mormons of the nineteenth century had struggled for an equal period of time in a political wilderness before being able to enjoy the blessings of their mountain temple. With the polygamy problem on the way to solution, with their property being returned to them, with improved prospects for statehood, and now with the dedication of the temple near at hand, the Latter-day Saints sensed that a new day was dawning for them. The First Presidency and the Twelve admonished the Saints to purge themselves of all iniquity for the important day ahead. The result was what Elder James E. Talmage called "a general cleansing of mind and soul" and "a veritable jubilee."

By April 5, 1893, all was in readiness, and the temple was opened for a brief inspection by selected members and non-members of the Church. Then, on the following day, the sixty-third anniversary of the organization of the Church and the fortieth anniversary of the laying of the cornerstone, the first dedicatory session of the Salt Lake Temple was held in the spacious assembly room. The hundreds of eager Saints, who filled the main floor and the balconies, were admitted on recommends from their bishops. Shortly before 10:00 A.M., the general authorities entered the southwest door of the temple, mounted the circular granite steps leading to the fifth floor, and filed into the assembly room. The First Presidency, the Twelve, the Patriarch, and the Presidents of the Seventy took their places on the east stand facing west, and the Presiding Bishopric took their seats on the west stand facing east.

Unlike the dedication of the Manti temple several years before, President Woodruff was able to play the leading role openly at Salt Lake City because of the relaxed attitude of the federal officials since the Manifesto. So President Woodruff, instead of Elder Snow, read the dedicatory prayer at the first general dedicatory session on the morning of April 6, 1893.

Once the dedication ceremonies were behind him, President Woodruff moved promptly to complete the organization of the temple presidency and staff. The selection of President Snow as the temple's president was met with uniform and enthusiastic approval. Upon John R. Winder, Lorenzo's first counselor, lay the task of the physical arrangements and maintenance of the building. And Adolph Madsen, the other counselor, was an experienced Church administrator, having served as a bishop and as a counselor to Rudger Clawson in the presidency of the Box Elder Stake.

President Snow settled down comfortably into his new responsibilities. At the outset, a primary task was to call, set apart, and instruct the large number of ordinance workers necessary to operate the temple. Since the other temples in Utah already operating were some distance from Salt Lake City, very few Saints in the Salt Lake Valley were trained temple workers. President Snow doubtless received satisfaction from the process of molding a group of willing but untrained workers into a corps of efficient and highly motivated temple specialists.

An indication of the loyalty Lorenzo's leadership inspired among his co-workers is a celebration they staged for him less than a year after his call on the occasion of his eightieth birthday. Without his knowledge, the temple staff gathered in the temple's assembly room after work one evening. Unaware of what was afoot, Lorenzo went to the assembly room on invitation, where he was surprised and pleased to receive the compliments and best wishes of his coworkers. John R. Winder spoke for the group in invoking blessings upon the white-haired prophet. He also presented to President Snow, as a gift from the staff, an ebony black, gold-handled walking cane, reported to be the "handsomest" in the city, bearing on its top the inscription "Lorenzo Snow, President Salt Lake Temple, April 3, 1894." The front of the handle bore the words, "Presented by Officers and Workers, Salt Lake Temple on his 80th Birthday."

In his response, the aging leader, spare, erect, and alert, typically diverted attention from himself to those around him. He expressed love and appreciation for his coworkers, and invoked the blessings of God upon them. A eulogy in the April 3, 1894, issue of the *Deseret News* painted a fleeting word picture of the accomplished octogenarian who was still very much on the move: "He has travelled in many lands and has lifted up his voice among strange people as a messenger of salvation, and now in the evening of his days, still busy and earnest in the great cause to which he has given his earlier years, he is continuing within the sacred precincts of the temple the glorious labors to which he and his associates have consecrated themselves."

Perhaps by way of reciprocating the thoughtfulness of his staff, President Snow arranged an outing for the Salt Lake Temple workers the June following his birthday celebration. To make it plain that the outing was not merely an entertainment or holiday, the host characterized it as "a sacred excursion."

The party, which entrained from Salt Lake City in the early afternoon of Friday June 22, 1894, included not only the Salt Lake Temple presidency and staff, but also the First Presidency and other general authorities. Arriving to a typical Brigham City welcome shortly after 5:00 P.M., the visitors were driven to the homes of members, where they were to stay as honored guests. The procession, as it left the depot, included nearly a hundred vehicles and, according to a *Deseret News* reporter, "took its way up the shade-skirted avenue for which Brigham City is noted, to the town, where the United Order came very nearly to perfection."

Lining the main street, shyly but proudly waving their hellos, were several hundred Sunday School children, whose faces reflected the awe and reverence with which they regarded the distinguished guests.

After freshening up at the homes of their hosts, the visitors were feted at a grand, old-fashioned Mormon Ball in the evening. They were welcomed by stake president Rudger Clawson, and then enjoyed the spirited dancing that was the distinguishing feature of such gatherings. Throughout the evening, the dancing gave way now and then to impromptu speeches by the leading hosts or by some of the distinguished guests. "Owing to your labors for the good of the human race," Rudger Clawson said approvingly, "we consider it a great honor to open our homes to you and to welcome you to the best our stake affords." President Snow responded to his protégé with appropriate remarks of acknowledgment and appreciation.

Early the next morning, the visitors were loaded into carriages and driven eastward in a long, serpentine procession to the Alpine-like village of Mantua. As the column reached the mountain bowl that shelters the small town bearing the name of Lorenzo's birthplace, the passengers were treated to a sight that brought tears to the eyes of many. Lining the roadway leading to the meetinghouse was another group of Sunday School children, waving shyly.

Inside, the townspeople were treated to a spiritual feast

the likes of which they had never tasted before nor would again, for all the members of the First Presidency addressed them in their humble chapel. Especially significant to them were the words of the prophet, Wilford Woodruff, who said that in the assembly seated before him he saw a fulfillment of the centuries-old prophecy about the gathering of the Saints to the tops of the mountains in the last days.

After this meeting, the Mantua Saints and their guests, one hundred and seventy strong, moved from the chapel to an adjacent hall where an elaborate banquet was served.

Before leaving Mantua, the First Presidency held a meeting with the Sunday School children of the town and spoke briefly and simply on elementary gospel themes.

Returning to Brigham City late Saturday afternoon, the guests were treated to an evening in the town's famous opera house.

On Sunday, three meetings were held in the stately tabernacle, similar in tone and content to the meetings held the day before in Mantua; and on the next day, the visiting party traveled to nearby Willard City, where Saturday's events at Mantua were duplicated. On Monday evening, the travelers returned to Salt Lake City by train, ending what for many was undoubtedly the most memorable outing of their lives, enjoyed in the presence of the First Presidency of the Church and the President of the Twelve.

Lorenzo's preoccupation with temple work during the several years he served as Salt Lake Temple president influenced him to concentrate more upon the well-being of his own family. He took positive steps toward creating a family organization that would bind his progeny together and provide a forum where family traditions and ideals could be preserved and family genealogical and other projects could be done. "When visiting Brigham City the other day," he noted in a letter written during this period, "I called the family together who were living there, about thirty, and urged upon them the necessity of becoming more united as a family. . . . The family now numbers two or three hundred, and the numbers of dead in the line of our ancestory whose names we already have runs into the thousands."

In a November 1897 letter, Lorenzo wrote to his son Leroi, who was then serving a mission in Germany, "I knew it to be the will of the Lord that I should set my household in order; unite the members of my family that they may be a worthy example to the families of Israel."

This suggests, as do the actions and other statements of President Snow, that his role as a leader, a teacher, and an exemplar of the Saints was seldom out of his mind. As much as he might have wished it otherwise, Elder Snow's family was constantly in the public eye and was, therefore, subject to the hazard of public scrutiny. So any proposed actions of the Snows invariably had to be measured by a standard that did not apply to many—the effect they would have upon others, whether by way of emulation or justification. To see in the apostle's family a laudable example of organization and discipline would doubtless impel many to follow suit, while neglect of their duty would afford an excuse for some to be disobedient or dilatory. It is inferred that this aspect of his leadership role was more distasteful to Elder Snow than any other. To exhibit himself or to push himself forward ran against the grain of this inherently private man, especially if to do so would imply any sense of superiority in him or would impart any hint of egotism or self-seeking. It is assumed that he reached an accommodation with himself on this point by recognizing that actions often speak more eloquently than words and that it was incumbent upon him to use this and every other honorable means of teaching true principles.

During this period Elder Snow took one of the few pleasure trips of his life. While some Church assignments occupied him intermittently and briefly along the way, these seem to have been from his puritanic sense of duty, which urged him incessantly to be up and doing.

Accompanied by his wife, Minnie, and their daughter, Mabelle, the vacationing apostle left Salt Lake City on August 1, 1896, traveling first to San Francisco, California, in the comfort of a luxury train. Because of the Church's interests in railroads and its resurgent influence in Gentile society, now that polygamy had been abandoned and Utah had been admitted to statehood, the Brethren always received preferential treatment when traveling by train. So every want of the Snows was catered to as the train paralleled the course of Lorenzo's rough and dirty stage coach trek to San Francisco, more than thirty years before, en route to a near-drowning in the Pacific and the showdown with the apostate Walter Gibson.

The travelers remained in the Bay area for almost three weeks, relaxing, sight-seeing, and visiting with members, friends, and a relative. The latter was Lorenzo's younger brother Samuel, whom he had not seen for twenty-four years. Seven years younger than his brother, Samuel, according to the observation of his wife, appeared to be seven years older, attesting to the renewing process that apparently had taken place in Lorenzo's eighty-two-year-old body as he had struggled against the forces of evil. And the difference lay not alone in the physical appearance of Oliver's two sons, but in their achievements as well.

Descending from the same parentage and reared in the same rural environment, Samuel could not have helped but speculate to himself about the causes that had produced such disparate results in two brothers, who had begun life's journey with essentially the same qualities and opportunities. The difference at the end could be accounted for by differences of inherent spiritual qualities, of human intelligence or discipline, or of the way in which opportunities or resources were used. Had such a question been put to President Snow, however, he doubtless would have answered that the gospel and his struggling attempts to live its principles had made all the difference. He had been striving for perfection, and that concentrated focus had inevitably carried him into a sphere of thought and action foreign to his younger brother, whose mind and actions had been mostly on a lower plane. And the physical and spiritual attributes of the two men partook of the qualities of their spiritual and physical environments.

But any analysis or introspection as to the long and winding trails the two men had traveled since their days on the Snow family's Ohio farm were overshadowed by the happiness they felt in being reunited and the love they felt toward each other. "[Samuel] was overjoyed to see me," Lorenzo wrote in a letter to one of his sons, a feeling he wholeheartedly reciprocated.

President Wilford Woodruff and his first counselor, George Q. Cannon, arrived in San Francisco a week before Elder Snow departed. In that interval, the three apostles counseled at length with Henry Tanner, the president of the California mission, who was headquartered in San Francisco. Earlier, Lorenzo had accepted President Tanner's invitation to speak in a meeting attended by some of the missionaries and by local members and investigators. There, the apostle, excited and aroused by once again being in the mission field, bore powerful testimony of the reality and divinity of Jesus Christ, whose special witness he was.

Lorenzo took great delight in showing his wife and daughter the sights of picturesque San Francisco—the Bay, Chinatown, Fisherman's Wharf, and the Presidio—and to introduce them to the exciting and somewhat frightening cable cars that crawled and clanged up and down the city's precipitous hills. Lorenzo had become well acquainted with this metropolis during the days of the underground, when he spent much time in Northern California, an exposure that must have given him a somewhat proprietary feeling as he guided Minnie and Mabelle around Baghdad by the Bay.

The Snows left San Francisco on August 21 on the steamer *Walla Walla*, destined for Victoria, B. C., on Vancouver Island. Passing smartly through the Golden Gate, whose portals were a familiar sight to Lorenzo but new and strange to his wife and daughter, the ship soon surmounted the heavier ground swells near shore, and, after reaching a point to the west far enough from land to avoid all navigational hazards, veered northward toward its destination some nine hundred miles away. The several-day trip afforded the usual pleasures of sea travel, with deck games, promenading, visiting, reading, and ocean-gazing to fill the daylight hours, interspersed, of course, with gargantuan meals—for those who had the appetite for them. Entertainments marked the evenings, held in the ship's dining room, where burnished silver place-settings and sparkling crystal gleamed against crisp linen tablecloths, and where tasteful floral center pieces added a touch of elegance. In these surroundings, served by accommodating and formally attired waiters, the Snow women were introduced to a world quite foreign to the utility-oriented community in which they had been reared. It undoubtedly was reassuring to them to discover that their host, their husband and father, was unawed by these touches of opulence and seemed as much at ease as if he were eating bread and milk in the rustic surroundings of his Mount Pisgah cabin.

At Vancouver Island, the travelers transferred to a smaller vessel that carried them to the mainland, where they boarded a train that took them to Lethbridge, Alberta, Canada. From there, they were driven by coach to their ultimate Canadian destination, Cardston.

The trip from Vancouver to Lethbridge opened Lorenzo's eyes to a stupendously beautiful part of the world as the train snaked its way through the towering Canadian Rockies. Passing through Banff and near world-famous Lake Louise, Lorenzo, always a careful observer, could not have helped but note the marked similarity between the breathtaking vistas in these mountains and those in the Alps. It is somewhat anomalous that this western-bred American, who, in terms of one accustomed to the broad reaches of prairie and desert, lived only a stone's throw from Southern Canada, was much more familiar with the Alpine grandeur of Central Europe than with the massive, jutting peaks ringing Banff and Lake Louise.

After spending a few days in Cardston, Lorenzo departed for home to attend to his duties at the temple, leaving Minnie and Mabelle with friends. "One week ago last Wednesday," Lorenzo wrote to a missionary son in a letter dated September 22, 1896, "I left your mother and Mabelle at Cardston, Canada, in good health and fine spirits, to remain there till about the first of January and will then expect to return." Before returning to Utah, Minnie gave birth to a daughter, Lucille, the last child fathered by President Lorenzo Snow, then eighty-two years old.

Her birth completed the circle of forty-one children born to nine wives. In addition, Lorenzo raised and educated the three children of Mary Adaline, fathered by her first husband,

George W. Henderson. These wives and mothers, whom President Snow loved and respected, through efficiency and managerial ability in directing their children and households, made it possible for Elder Snow to devote most of his time to the ministry. Lorenzo's frequent absence caused his wives to develop initiative and independence lacking in many other women. While they knew that Lorenzo would always respond to any call for assistance, they asked for his help only when absolutely necessary, and worked out their problems in counsel with other wives and the older children. This interdependence cemented Lorenzo's family into a single, unified whole, although his children took pride in their maternal ancestry within that larger family.

Charlotte Squires, the first wife, had two children, Leonora Charlotte and Roxcy Armatha. *Mary Adaline Goddard,* wife number two, bore Lorenzo three children, Rosetta Adaline, Oliver Goddard, and Isadore Percy. The three children fathered by her first husband, whom Lorenzo loved as his own, were Hiram Ackley, Orville Daniel, and Jacob Wayne. The third wife, *Sarah Ann Prichard,* bore Lorenzo five children, Eliza Sarah, Sylvia, Lorenzo, Jr., Parintha, and Laurin Alvirus. Wife number four, *Harriet Amelia Squires,* had five children, Abigail Harriet and Lucius Aaron; Alonzo Henry and Amelia Henrietta, twins who died in infancy; and Celestia Armeda. The fifth wife, *Eleanor Houtz,* was the most prolific of all the wives, giving birth to eight children, Amanda Eleanor, who died in infancy, Ida, Eugenia, Alphonso Houtz, Susan Imogene, Roxcy Lana, Hortensia, and Chauncey Edgar. *Caroline Horton,* the sixth wife, bore three children, Clarissa Caroline, and twins Franklin and Sarah Augusta (who died only two weeks after her birth). *Mary Elizabeth Houtz,* wife number seven, was the mother of six children, Lydia May, Jacob E. Fitzroy (who died in infancy), Virginia M. Marian, Mansfield Lorenzo, Mortimer Joseph, and Flora Bell Birdie. The eighth wife, *Phebe Amelia Woodruff,* one of President Woodruff's daughters, gave birth to five children, Mary Amanda (who lived only two days), Leslie Woodruff, Orion, Milton, and Phebe Augusta Florence. And *Minnie Jensen,* the ninth and last wife, gave birth to four children, Clarence Leroi, Minnie Mabel, Cora Jeane, and Lucille.

One cannot fully grasp the magnitude of President Snow's family without seeing a tabulation of his wives and children. Nor can one comprehend what this family meant to him without understanding his conceptions of eternity and life's purpose.

Chapter Twenty-eight

President of the Church

As the nineteenth century wound down, the Church found itself in a state of acute financial embarrassment. The cause was not hard to find. Several decades of battling with federal officialdom over polygamy, culminating in the dissolution of the Church as a corporate entity and the confiscation of its assets, had left the Mormons in economic chaos. Following the Manifesto, positive steps had been taken to pick up the pieces, but the magnitude of the job, coupled with depressed economic conditions throughout the country, had slowed the process to a snail's pace. And after statehood, when the economic picture brightened, extensive borrowings to develop the local economy placed the Church deep in debt.

Thus, through most of his administration, during the 1890s, money problems created more woe for President Wilford Woodruff than anything else. "I don't sleep nights," he wrote plaintively on August 8, 1894, "and am weary by day. As trustee-in-trust and the presidency of the church we have taken such a load upon us [that] it is difficult for us to carry it." President Woodruff's journal entry the next day was much the same: "There is a heavy load resting upon us in church affairs, our debts are very heavy." And the passage of two years did nothing either to ease the debt or the President's feelings of concern over it. "The presidency of the church are so overwhelmed in financial matters," he wrote on December 30,

1896, "it seems as though we shall never live to get through with it unless the Lord opens the way in a miraculous manner. It looks as though we shall never pay our debts." Four months later President Woodruff seems to have repented of this fatalistic mood when he wrote, hopefully: "I [do] not want to die until the church and myself as trustee-in-trust are out of debt."

The prophet was not permitted to see this wish fulfilled. In August 1898, he went to San Francisco, seeking relief from a chronic asthmatic condition. While there, Wilford the Faithful, the indefatigable missionary, the persistent diarist, the ceaseless worker and the spiritual powerhouse, passed away quietly at the home of Colonel Isaac Trumbo, where he was staying as a guest. President George Q. Cannon, who was in San Francisco at the time, promptly notified President Joseph F. Smith in Salt Lake City, requesting that he, in turn, notify the other general authorities. The word reached Lorenzo in Brigham City, where he had gone to handle family and business affairs. Although the news was shocking, it was not wholly unexpected. Indeed, Wilford's advanced age and frail condition had impelled Lorenzo to engage in special prayer in the temple, imploring the Lord to extend the prophet's life. "Nevertheless," he told the Lord, "Thy will be done. I have not sought this responsibility but if it be Thy will, I now present myself before Thee for Thy guidance and instruction." As he walked through a hallway, after leaving the special room where he had prayed, back to an apartment where he often stayed in the temple overnight, the aged saint was startled to see, standing before him in the air, the Savior of the world, who gave him detailed instruction about the reorganization of the First Presidency.

This electrifying experience revolutionized Lorenzo's thinking, which, until that time, seemed to be drifting away from the challenges of mortality toward the afterlife. Those who heard him speak at the April 1898 general conference might have inferred that he was preparing to leave for the world beyond. "I suppose it would be with Latter-day Saints generally as with me in regard to this point," he told the congregation, "that as we advance in years and come nearer to what we generally consider as the time of our departure into

211

the other life we are more inclined to devote our thoughts and reflections upon those things that we may receive in the next life, the circumstances that may surround us there, and the proper preparations that we have made, and are making, to reach that which we anticipate. I know it is so with me." Little did he realize, when these words were uttered, that in less than six months the ultimate responsibility for the affairs of the Church would rest upon him, and he would then be struggling beneath the heaviest load he had ever carried.

On September 4, 1898, two days after President Woodruff's death, his body arrived at the Ogden depot, where it was met by President Snow and several other members of the Twelve, including Joseph F. Smith, a counselor in the First Presidency. Elder Smith willingly deferred to Lorenzo Snow, since Wilford's passing had automatically dissolved the First Presidency and relegated his former counselors to membership in the Twelve, subordinate to Elder Snow, its presiding officer.

From Ogden, the body was taken by train to Salt Lake City, accompanied by President Snow and other general authorities, who also went with the casket to President Woodruff's home, where it remained until the burial four days later.

On September 8, President Snow presided at the funeral, but honored George Q. Cannon, President Woodruff's first counselor, by assigning him to conduct the services. The huge tabernacle was practically filled an hour before the 10:30 A.M. meeting. The general authorities, who had accompanied the casket to Temple Square, entered the building in single file, solemnly taking their places on the stand in order of their seniority. Directly in front of the stand was the casket, and behind it in the center section were members of President Woodruff's large and loyal family. Beyond them, extending to the rear of the building and on each side of the main floor, as well as the balcony, sat friends and admirers of the deceased Prophet, packed snugly together on the tabernacle's hard, wooden benches. Behind the general authorities sat the Tabernacle Choir, which had come to sing its last tribute to the man who had never wavered from a course of strict rectitude during his long and fruitful ministry.

As President Snow sat in the tabernacle that day, he must

have felt a great loneliness. Wilford Woodruff, with whom he had associated for sixty-two years, was the last of the apostles who had been ordained during the life of the Prophet Joseph Smith. The general authorities seated with Lorenzo on the stand either had not been born or were mere children or teenagers when Lorenzo joined the Church in 1836. Gone were those who had exerted such a powerful influence upon him during the early years—Joseph the Prophet and his father, Hyrum, Brigham, Heber, Willard, and John. Gone, too, was Eliza, one of his mentors, and other close members of his family.

In his brief, concluding remarks at the funeral, President Snow extolled the virtues of his predecessor, the virtues of diligence, faithfulness, and spirituality. He also calmed the fears of any who were troubled by the temporary lack of a First Presidency, assuring them that the Twelve would promptly and conscientiously handle all administrative matters during the interim.

Fulfilling that commitment in part, the Twelve met the following day when Elders George Q. Cannon and Joseph F. Smith were received back as members of the Twelve, occupying the positions in the quorum to which they were entitled by seniority. The reconstituted quorum then unanimously gave full authority to President Snow to handle all Church affairs until the First Presidency should again be organized. Despite the knowledge he had received from the Savior that he was to lead the Church, President Snow, in apparent deference to the principles of free agency and common consent, offered to step down from the leadership of the quorum and to yield to anyone whom his brethren might designate. The Twelve ignored this suggestion in unanimously sustaining Elder Snow as their president.

Four days later, Lorenzo called the quorum to an executive meeting in the offices of the First Presidency. All fourteen members were in attendance, the enlarged number being explained by the induction of the two former counselors at the previous meeting. The president was prompted to call the brethren together by a problem that would agitate his administration more than any other—the financial embarrassment of the Church. Frank J. Cannon, who, before President Woodruff's death, had been negotiating with financiers in the east for a $1,500,000 loan to the Church, was invited in to explain the status of his negotiations. It soon became apparent that nothing could be done to obtain the loan until a new trustee-in-trust was appointed. This, plus the remembrance that President Woodruff had strongly counseled against delay in reorganizing the First Presidency, resulted in Lorenzo Snow then and there being sustained as the President of the Church and trustee-in-trust. He, in turn, designated Elders George Q. Cannon and Joseph F. Smith as his counselors. In accepting the burdens of the prophetic office, President Snow told of the heavenly manifestations he received in the temple a few days before, during which it was revealed he was to be the new President of the Church. He explained he had not previously told anyone of this sacred experience, as he wanted to see if the same spirit of revelation was in the Twelve.

In that intimate setting, President Snow also spoke of the revelation he received early in his ministry, showing man's capacity to become like God. This had been his guiding star throughout his life, he told the Brethren, and had inspired him to try, as far as possible, to live like God while in the flesh. He also expressed confidence that this goal was within the ability of all mortals.

A *Deseret News* article on September 14, 1898, announcing Lorenzo's call as the President of the Church, summarized his qualifications for his new responsibilities: "His entire life has been a school—God's school—fitting him for the exalted position he now occupies among his brethren. His long experience in the service of the church, his intimate acquaintance with the founders thereof and above all integrity and Apostolic zeal qualify him for the position he has been called to occupy as the fifth president of the Church of Jesus Christ of Latter-day Saints."

Despite these accolades and many others, Lorenzo accepted his call with the same sense of diffidence that had characterized his demeanor throughout life. "If I had had the power to escape it honorably," he told a Salt Lake Tabernacle audience on September 19, "I would never have been found in my present position." The speaker went on to say, however, that since it had been revealed to him that he would be called to preside over the Church, he would not shirk the responsibility.

The word, seeping into the Gentile world, that his call had been revealed to him, soon presented President Snow with a challenge in diplomacy and tact. It came in the form of a telegraph from the managing editor of the *New York World* that contained several questions, including this one: "What sort of revelation is responsible for your appointment?" Not wanting to reveal sacred things to one who would not appreciate or understand them, and who, likely, would give them light or derogatory treatment in his paper, President Snow gave this accurate but not wholly enlightening answer: "A revelation given March 28, 1835, which clearly defines the relationship the Twelve bear to the First Presidency. When a vacancy occurs in the presiding council, such as has occurred by the death of President Woodruff, the Twelve Apostles become the presiding quorum of the church, and it has been the rule for the President of that body, if he be the senior apostle by ordination, to succeed to the presidency when the Council of Apostles decides that the First Presidency should be reorganized. He, with two counselors whom he may select, are then presented to the body of the church in general conference. If accepted by the church they become the First Presidency thereof. In this manner I have been selected as the President of the Church."

Prior to the October general conference, where he would be sustained as the fifth president of the Church, Lorenzo made a nostalgic trip to Brigham City. Anticipating his attendance for Sunday services, the first since his call as the president of the Church, the local leaders had outdone themselves in decorating the "new" tabernacle, which had been rebuilt after fire had destroyed it in 1896. Behind the rostrum was a huge arch fashioned from evergreens intertwined with late summer flowers. It bore the motto "Our Prophet." As a mark of respect, the audience stood when their bearded, white-haired townsman entered, singing for him "We Thank Thee, O God, for a Prophet." One can imagine the joy that filled the new president of the Church when he saw that President Clawson, probably in emulation of his mentor, had arranged for the presence of a group of Sunday School children carrying bouquets of flowers. Alluding to the children, the flowers, and the decorations, President Clawson said they were "emblematical of the love and esteem of the people for the president." In his response, President Snow acknowledged with gratitude the honor bestowed upon him by his friends and neighbors, and explained that a chief purpose in his coming to Brigham City at that time was to seek the faith and prayers of the Saints there to lend strength to his administration.

Although there is little solid evidence to support the conclusion, it seems likely that President Snow's search for someone to fill the vacancy in the Twelve also took him to Brigham City. This selection was the first major ecclesiastical decision to be made, and since Rudger Clawson, his protégé from prison, undoubtedly was high on his list of candidates, it is logical that Lorenzo wanted to gauge whether his initial impressions of the man were confirmed by observations of him in action.

If this speculation is well-founded, President Snow came away from Brigham City with positive feelings about the young stake president. But, as in the case of his own call, he wanted the counsel and input of the Twelve. So, upon returning to Salt Lake and prior to the general conference, he invited the Twelve to submit nominations of brethren whom they considered to be qualified to fill the vacancy in their quorum. Thereafter, according to the journal entry of Heber J. Grant, made on October 8, 1898, President Snow told the Twelve, "I know that we have the mind of the Lord, and I know it just as perfectly as I have ever known anything. The man we [the First Presidency] have chosen and upon whom we are perfectly united is Rudger Clawson." When the Council of the First Presidency and the Twelve had unanimously approved this choice, President Snow told them that after he met Rudger in prison and had the opportunity to observe him and appraise his character, "it was manifested . . . that Brother Clawson should be chosen to preside over the Box Elder Stake." Later, when Elder Clawson was called to this position, his father protested, saying his son "would be a pauper." Yet, according to President Snow, Rudger accepted willingly, though "he had had no experience in preaching." Heber J. Grant's journal entry describing this incident concluded, "Brother Snow said he did not know any young man who had improved as Brother Clawson had done."

The spiritual sensitivity shown by President Snow in making this decision on the threshhold of his presidency is typical of his entire administration. This quality surfaced again at the general priesthood meeting held on October 8 when the new president expressed the conviction that the Lord was "looking upon" the assembly, as were Abraham, Isaac, Jacob, Joseph Smith, Brigham Young, John Taylor, and Wilford Woodruff. Lorenzo said that these beings, who had played such prominent roles in the great religious drama over the centuries, were "deeply interested in this assembly of men" because of the great authority entrusted to them.

In the same talk, President Snow reflected upon his earlier life and upon the individuals who had helped to mold his character, and upon the events that had given him seasoning and important insights. He alluded to his strict upbringing and mentioned his early yearning to be a military man, his pursuit of a college education, his conversion and the spiritual witness that accompanied it, and his revelation about man's capacity to become like God. The frequency with which Lorenzo recounted these experiences and the depth of feeling that was so evident when he related them to the powerful influence they exterted upon him throughout his life.

Elder Snow was set apart as the fifth President of the Church on October 10, 1898. All of the apostles, including Rudger Clawson, who had just been called and ordained, joined in laying their hands on the prophet's head. President George Q. Cannon acted as mouth in the blessing.

Later President Snow gave wise counsel to his young protégé about the way he should conduct himself as a member of the Twelve. The junior apostle was reminded that his experience was quite limited compared to that of the senior members of his quorum, suggesting that at first he should listen more and talk less. He also told Rudger that his call had come from the Lord, not man, that God would reveal his mind and will according to Rudger's needs, and that success would depend largely upon his own exertions. Then, revealing a key that would unlock the door to peace and contentment, the aged prophet told his young disciple to move along slowly, pausing now and then to enjoy the journey, and promising that if he would do that, the Spirit of the Lord would be with him always and would show him how to act in all circumstances.

When the ceremonial functions connected with his installation as the head of the Church had been completed, President Snow promptly turned his attention to the most pressing problem that faced his administration—money, or the lack of it. Following up on the negotiations commenced during the life of President Woodruff, Lorenzo, with the concurrence of the other leading brethren, authorized the issuance of short-term, 6-percent bonds in the amount of $1,000,000 instead of the $1,500,000 for which Frank J. Cannon had been negotiating. At about the same time, the Church abandoned certain unprofitable mining and milling ventures and railroad enterprises. These measures gave President Snow some breathing room, and time to reflect and pray about the course of action he should take to bring about a permanent solution to the financial dilemma facing the Saints. Obviously, the Church could not continue indefinitely to operate on borrowed money, and economies and budget-cutting could be carried only so far.

By the spring of 1899, an answer to this complex problem still had not been found. However, at the April general conference, the Brethren did not share with the membership their overwhelming concern about the issue that dominated their private councils, but instead focused upon the basic doctrines and principles of the gospel, faith, repentance, and spirituality.

Within a few weeks after the April general conference, President Snow received the first glimmerings of light that would lead to a solution of the Church's critical financial problems. These came in the form of a vague, yet positive impression that he should go south to St. George and there hold a special conference with the Saints. Neither the purpose nor the content of the conference was made known to Lorenzo. But the Spirit prompted him to go.

Selected to accompany President Snow were his wife, Minnie, and their son Leroi; President Joseph F. Smith and his wife, Alice Kimball Smith, a daughter of Heber C. Kimball; Elders Franklin D. Richards, Francis M. Lyman, and Abraham O. Woodruff of the Twelve, and their wives; Elder Rudger Clawson, the junior member of the Twelve; Elder Seymour B. Young of the First Council of the Seventy; Presiding Bishop William B. Preston; and Arthur Winter of the First Presidency's staff.

Associates and family members bid farewell to the President and his party at the Salt Lake train depot, Monday, May 15, 1899. At the McCune station, just south of Milford, the visitors were met by the presidency of the St. George Stake and other men of prominence from that community. The following day, the visitors and their hosts traveled in a caravan of twelve carriages to their destination in Utah's pleasant Dixie.

As the party moved onward toward St. George, the feelings of the Saints seemed to build in intensity. A reporter for the *Salt Lake Herald* who was in attendance tried to paint a word scene for his readers in a dispatch dated May 17: "The visit of President Snow is regarded as a most notable event in the history of the stake as is evidenced by the manner in which his party is greeted on every hand. The streets are lined with wagons from adjoining settlements bringing visitors to the special conference which began today. The tabernacle is taxed to its utmost. The Rio Virgin Mills at Washington and all the stores in the city are closed and everybody seems to be in attendance at the meetings."

At the time of President Snow's visit, Southern Utah was plagued with a severe drought. Nephi Savage, a resident of St. George who attended this special conference, described the conditions in these pessimistic terms: "Eighteen months prior to the coming of President Lorenzo Snow and his party, there had not been enough moisture fall at any one time to lay the dust in the streets; as a result many of the streams and wells of the country had dried up, and starvation seemed to face the people."

Some of the St. George residents must have hoped that President Snow would give them some counsel about how to solve the problem of the drought. At first, he spoke on various gospel topics, but of all the subjects touched upon by the prophet during this conference, none was of more lasting significance to the Saints in Dixie and throughout the Church than was his admonition about the law of tithing. Leroi Snow, Lorenzo's son and clerk of the conference, has provided us with this important account of his father's address: "It was during one of these meetings that my father received the renewal revelation on tithing. I was sitting at a table reporting the proceedings, when all at once father paused in his discourse; complete stillness filled the room. When he commenced to speak again his voice strengthened and the inspiration of God seemed suddenly to come over him, as well as over the entire assembly. Then he revealed to the Latter-day Saints the vision that was before him. God manifested to him there and then the purpose of the call to visit the Saints in the south. He told them that he could see, as he had never realized before how the law of tithing had been neglected by the people, also that the Saints, themselves, were heavily in debt, as well as the church, and now through strict obedience to this law— the paying of a full and honest tithing—not only would the church be relieved of its great indebtedness, but through the blessings of the Lord this would also be the means of freeing the Latter-day Saints from their individual obligations and they would become a prosperous people."

Having learned the reason for going to St. George, President Snow elaborated upon the theme of tithing and shared with the conference the course he would follow in implementing this "new" but old revelation for the benefit and blessing of all. "The word of the Lord to you is not anything new," he told his listeners, "it is simply this: The time has now come for every Latter-day Saint, who calculates to be prepared for the future and to hold his feet strong upon a proper foundation, to do the will of the Lord and to pay his tithing in full. That is the word of the Lord to you, and it will be the word of the Lord to every settlement throughout the land of Zion. After I leave you and you get to thinking about this, you will see yourselves that the time has come when every man should stand up and pay his tithing in full. The Lord has blessed us and has had mercy upon us in the past; but there are times coming when the Lord requires us to stand up and do that which He has commanded and not leave it any longer. What I say to you in this Stake of Zion I will say to every Stake of Zion that has been organized."

President Snow lost little time in executing his plans. On the return trip to Salt Lake City, which began shortly after the conference ended, he held special meetings along the way. Washington, Leeds, Toquerville, Kanarra, Cedar City, Summit, Parowan, Beaver, Meadows, Fillmore, Holden, Scipio, Juab, and Nephi all heard the prophet's call to pay tithing. He reminded his listeners that tithing was not a mere option the Saints could ignore. Rather, it was a commandment from God to the Church members, who were obligated by their baptismal and temple covenants to comply. He also described glowingly the blessings that would be realized through obedience to the law of tithing.

Arriving home on Saturday, May 27, President Snow went directly to his office to read the mail and to be briefed by his staff about events that had transpired during his absence. President Snow also looked forward to the annual conference of the Young Men's and Young Women's Mutual Improvement Association scheduled for the following Monday and Tuesday. As it turned out, he would use an officer's meeting of the Young Men's Association on Tuesday afternoon as a forum in which to expound his views on the severe financial problems facing the Church, and the solution that had been revealed to him. In attendance at that meeting were Young Men's leaders from practically every stake in the western United States. The prophet was well aware, therefore, that any sparks of enthusiasm kindled at that meeting would be carried throughout much of the Church and would, in turn, fire anew the commitment and dedication of the Saints to the principle of tithing.

"A poor woman . . . has ten dollars," President Snow told

the audience. "It is hard for her to support her children; she has ten dollars and goes and pays one dollar tithing, which is used for the benefit of the temple, or for other purposes. Here, on the other hand, is a man who has thousands of dollars and pays no tithing . . . but they go into the temple just as the poor woman, and they are given the same privileges as she, they receive the same blessings; her dollar goes to pay the expenses of the temple and they pay nothing toward it."

Turning his attention especially to the Young Men's leaders who were in attendance, the prophet said, "The Lord has raised you up and fitted you to come to the rescue. If we fail to get that assistance from you we shall have to—no I shall not say it, for we would not give it up, we will remain faithful to the Lord and try to execute his will." Finally, President Snow shared with his young followers the plans he had formulated to carry his plea to the Church membership and the role he hoped they would play: "Now Brethren," he said, "we shall visit all the stakes in Zion and we shall see you again in the parts where you reside. We wish you to consult yourselves and the Spirit of the Lord in reference to this principle."

While President Snow was delivering this sermon, Elder Brigham H. Roberts, a member of the First Council of the Seventy, scribbled the following resolution and afterward presented it to the assembly: *"Resolved:* That we accept the doctrine of tithing, as now presented by President Snow, as the present word and will of the Lord unto us, and we do accept it with all our hearts; we will ourselves observe it and we will do all in our power to get the Latter-day Saints to do likewise." What followed was reported by an eye witness as being "very impressive and dramatic." All present unanimously adopted the resolution by "rising to their feet and shouting 'Aye.' "

Elder Francis M. Lyman of the Twelve then went to the pulpit and said, "President Snow, I believe this body of men are as clear upon this law and have about as faithfully met the obligation in regard to tithing as any body of men in the Church. It is a splendid thing, brethren, for us to be always in shape to accept the will of the Lord when it comes."

Rising with the deliberation his advancing years made mandatory, the frail, bearded, white-haired prophet moved slowly to the pulpit, where he pronounced his blessing upon the congregation: "Brethren, the God of our fathers, Abraham, Isaac, and Jacob bless you. Every man who is here, who has made this promise, will be saved in the Celestial Kingdom. God bless you. Amen."

On June 2, Lorenzo attended conference in the Millard Stake, where he dedicated a new chapel and spoke on tithing. He reported later about this visit, "Yesterday we held two meetings. I shook hands with 700 people, travelled thirty miles in a carriage, and attended a reception in the evening. I did not sleep much last night as we were on the train all night, but I am feeling well and ready for another journey. I shall likely attend the Morgan Stake Conference next Sunday, and I am thinking of visiting the Malad country the latter part of the month." He also attended a quarterly conference of the Davis Stake held in Centerville.

In all these stake gatherings, including those held after the solemn assembly, the principle of tithing dominated the minds of speakers and listeners alike. And we can be assured that many, if not most, of the Saints who attended them reappraised their attitudes and practices about tithing.

On July 2, all forty stakes of the Church were represented at a solemn assembly in the temple, as were most of the four hundred and seventy-eight wards. These, added to the twenty-six general authorities who were present and some representatives of the auxiliaries brought the total attendance to 623. This was the core of Church leadership, who received directly from President Snow instructions about tithing, both in its theoretical and practical aspects. Following the pattern set at the recent Young Men's meeting, a resolution to support the Prophet was presented and unanimously adopted.

After the solemn assembly, Lorenzo continued his tours to the stakes as he had promised, attending stake conferences in Provo on July 22; Logan, August 6 and 7; Heber City, August 12; Soda Springs, Idaho, August 20 and 21; Paris, Idaho, August 26 and 27; San Pete, September 4; and Farmington, September 9 and 10.

A year later in 1900 at the October general conference, President Snow reported to the Saints, "They have paid twice the amount of tithing this year and last year than they paid two years ago." And in the same sermon, President Snow said, "I do not wish to say very much about tithing, for I think I have said enough. In the settlements that we have travelled through coming from St. George, I talked very strongly about it, because I knew it was a command of the Lord that the people should repent and reform from the great neglect that we had all been guilty of more or less. I felt determined about it then with all my heart and soul, and I did not know but that the Saints might think I was going a little too far. To ease their minds upon this I told them that I should never come again to talk to them as I talked at that time. But I said they must do what they had been told if they calculated to be Latter-day Saints. The reformation in this line has been effected."

The "reformation" referred to by President Snow had taken less than eighteen months to achieve. While the Church did not become free of debt until some time after Lorenzo's death, the initiative he set in motion guaranteed that complete solvency was merely a matter of time.

Heber J. Grant said years later, "I know that Lorenzo Snow was a prophet of God. . . . Lorenzo Snow came to the presidency of the church when he was eighty-five years of age, and what he accomplished during the next three years of his life is simply marvelous to contemplate. He lifted the church from the financial slough of despond, so to speak, from almost financial bankruptcy—when its credit was hardly good for a thousand dollars without security, when it was paying 10 percent for money—he lifted the church out of that condition and made its credit A No. 1, so that people solicited and asked for the privilege of buying the bonds of this church at 6 per cent. . . . And in three years this man, beyond the age of ability in the estimation of the world, this man who had not been engaged in financial affairs, who had been devoting his life for years to laboring in the temple, took hold on the finances of the church of Christ, under the inspiration of the living God, and in those three years changed everything financially from darkness to light. I know that Lorenzo Snow was God's mouthpiece upon the earth; that he was the representative of the Lord, and that he was in very deed a prophet of God."

Chapter Twenty-nine

Taking Hold of the Reins

Heber J. Grant's allusion to the way in which President Snow "took hold" of Church finances could apply equally as well to every other facet of Church administration. With little fanfare, yet with a sure, deft touch, the new president began from the outset to make his influence felt in every phase of the work.

He was the first president of the Church who had had extensive experience in the lower echelons of Church administration. His more than twenty years service as a stake president had given him insights and understanding none of his predecessors had possessed. And during that long tenure, he had also had an unparalleled view from the top, first as a member of the Twelve, and during the last three years as a counselor to the First Presidency. This experience, added to good mental discipline, determination, spirituality, and imagination, equipped him well for the task. And so ably did he perform it that some observers have rated him alongside Brigham Young in administrative ability. Orson F. Whitney, the historian who later became a member of the Twelve, and who was a witness of President Snow's achievements, made this comparison: "It was to be expected that the business acumen and executive ability which founded and carried on the United Order of Brigham City—a cooperative system the nearest and most successful approach to the United Order projected by the Prophet Joseph Smith yet realized—would do something

225

towards relieving the tension under which the church was laboring at the time of President Snow's advent to power; but that such an impetus as has been manifested would be given, particularly at his time of life, was altogether unlooked for. Not since the days of President Young, of whose firm-handed puissant administration, the present one is strikingly reminiscent, have the Latter-day Saints been so stirred by the preaching of their leaders as during the first year of Lorenzo Snow's presidential incumbency—a year of tithes preaching and tithe-paying almost unprecedented, and, already resultant in a better condition of affairs, temporally and spiritually, than the church has known for years."

Coincident with his drive to increase the revenues of the Church through a reemphasis on tithing, President Snow took steps to control more tightly the handling and disbursement of Church funds. A year before President Woodruff's death, preliminary steps had been taken to create "a comprehensive plan of church finance" which contemplated "the formation of responsible committees to regulate and manage the business affairs of the church." Once Lorenzo had been briefed on the plans to diffuse the authority over finances and in effect to deprive the president of control over the funds of the Church, he moved promptly to cancel them.

We can gauge the decisiveness of Lorenzo's action in this matter, and the results it produced, from the writings of Frank J. Cannon, who apostatized and was excommunicated after the death of his father, George Q. Cannon. "At once upon his accession to power," Frank J. Cannon wrote of President Snow, "he notified us that he did not intend to carry out any such plan as we had suggested for the administration of the church's finances. It meant a diffusion of authority; and he held that the best results had been obtained by keeping all power in the hands of the Prophet, Seer and Revelator, and of those whom he might appoint to work with him."

Showing the difference in temperament and character between this feisty, ungovernable maverick and his thoroughbred father, who never wavered in his loyalty to President Snow, is this revealing comment: "My father," wrote Frank J. Cannon, "necessarily bowed to the President's decision. 'It is within the authority of the Prophet of the Lord,' he counselled me, 'to determine how he will conduct the business of the church. President Snow has his own ideas.' "

In less than three months after being sustained as the president of the Church, Lorenzo took another far-reaching administrative action. He assumed control of the *Deseret News*, the official organ of the Church, which had been leased to George Q. Cannon & Sons since October 1892.

During this period, President Snow also took a lively interest in politics, at least to the extent of encouraging able people to seek office. An indication of the concern he had about the U. S. senatorial race is a decision he made to allow George Q. Cannon to run for that office. In furtherance of his counselor's candidacy, he made an unsuccessful attempt to persuade President Cannon's son, Frank J., to withdraw as a candidate opposing his father. The meeting where this attempt was made was held in the evening at President Snow's home. It followed by a few days a tumultuous rally held in the Salt Lake Theatre, where Frank J. had spoken on the subject of "Senatorial Candidates and Pharisees," in which he had denounced certain members of the Twelve whom he derisively called "financial apostles." The bitterness and recalcitrance of the speaker, and the passions that had been aroused by the political campaign, doomed President Snow's effort to failure. The son refused bluntly to withdraw from the race.

While Mr. Cannon's account of a nocturnal visit to President Snow's home is undoubtedly colored by the writer's combative personality and highly partisan views, the general purpose and outcome of it seem to be as he stated them: that the President was anxious that his counselor be elected to the Senate and that the counselor's son was unwilling to withdraw his own candidacy in favor of the father. And in the process of painting what he obviously intended to be an unflattering word picture of the Prophet, his objectives and his methods, the writer left us this invaluable insight into the domestic life of the eighty-five-year-old Mormon leader: "He excused himself a moment to go to an infant [three-year-old Lucille, his youngest child] whom we could hear crying in an inner room; and, when he returned, he had the child in his arms—a little

227

girl in a night gown. He sat down, petting her, stroking her hair with his supple lean hand, affectionately, and smiling with a sort of absentminded tenderness as he took up the conversation again. This memory of him sticks in my mind as one of the most extraordinary pictures of my experience. I knew that I had come there to hear my own or some other person's political death sentence. I knew that he would not have invited me at such an hour, with such secrecy, unless the issue of our conference was to be something dark and fatal. And in the soft radiance of the lamp he sat smiling—fragile of build, almost spirituelle, white haired, delicately cultured—soothing the child who played with his long silvery beard and blinked sleepily."

Lorenzo's confrontation with Frank J. Cannon was only one element in a complex political melange that often claimed President Snow's attention during the first year of his administration. About the time Lorenzo became president of the Church, Brigham H. Roberts, a member of the First Council of the Seventy, was nominated by the democratic state convention as a representative to Congress. Because of the so-called "Political Manifesto," which the First Presidency and the Twelve had adopted several years before, and under whose strictures a General Authority was precluded from engaging in political contests without approval of the Brethren, Elder Roberts's candidacy obviously had President Snow's approval. This, coupled with his later consent for George Q. Cannon to run for the Senate, indicates Lorenzo's anxiety about the caliber of men to be elected as Utah's representatives in Congress. Undoubtedly, that anxiety was made more acute by a series of articles that appeared in May and June 1898 in *The Kinsman*, a sectarian publication, under the caption "Polygamy and Inspired Lies." The articles charged that the leaders of the Church were secretly reverting to both the teaching and practice of polygamy. Also, the Church was accused of controlling the political action of the Saints and of interfering in the political affairs of the state. These accusations were aired by the presbytery of the Presbyterian Church at its semiannual meeting held in Manti, Utah, on August 29, and were later disseminated by it. This touched off a national debate about the alleged "Mormon Perfidy."

The fact that the two men Lorenzo supported for national office were both General Authorities and polygamists (circumstances which gave some credence to the charges being leveled against the Church) seemed not to trouble the president. Given his intelligence and shrewdness, a reasonable inference is that he decided that these detriments were outweighed by other considerations, such as the presence in Washington of able elected officials who could plead the case of Utahns, most of whom were the much maligned Mormons.

Whatever the reason for doing so, President Snow vigorously supported President Cannon and Elder Roberts in their candidacies. This undoubtedly helped to fan into flame the smoldering resentments and animosities that many non-members harbored against the Church and its leaders. Another powerful manifestation of this is seen in the work of a group of twenty-four sectarian ministers who convened in Salt Lake City on December 6, 1898, and who made an appeal to others throughout the United States to protest the admission of Elder Roberts to the House of Representatives. The ground of their appeal was that polygamy was still being taught and practiced by the Church and that this violated "the covenant made between the Mormon leaders and the government when Utah was admitted to statehood." President Snow promptly telegraphed the *New York World* denying these charges, except as to polygamous relationships that had been formed before the 1890 Manifesto. At the same time, President Snow made this explanation, which, while implying his personal support of Elder Roberts, differentiated individual support for Church institutional support: "Non-Mormons participated in his nomination in the regular convention of his party. Non-Mormons also aided in his election. Many Mormons not being of his party, voted for his opponent. He was not a church candidate in any sense of the word. The church had no candidate. He was elected as an American citizen by American citizens and the question of religion did not enter into the purely political contest."

President Snow's voice was hardly audible in the clamorous demands that were raised nationwide to deprive Elder Roberts of his seat in Congress. The industry and animosity of the opposition is suggested by a "monster national petition" they presented to Congress bearing the signatures of seven million who opposed the seating of the Utah representative.

While the Roberts drama was being enacted to a national audience on the boisterous stage of Washington politics, President Snow was quietly formulating a new international policy for the Church in the cloistered councils of the Mormon heirarchy. In reality, the policy was not a new one, but was a reversion to a concept that had underlain the basic mission of the Church from the beginning—that the Twelve and the Seventy were to take the lead in proselyting throughout the world. Although this role was well defined in the revelations, the exigencies of establishing and building up the stakes of Zion in the mountains had necessitated a temporary alteration of this traditional role. The altered policy had resulted in Lorenzo being assigned to preside in Brigham City for so many years, and for other members of the Twelve to be similarly assigned to other localities. While this condition existed, it was not feasible for the Twelve to lead out in aggressive international proselyting.

After President Snow saw that the Church was on a relatively secure financial basis, and after necessary adjustments had been made in certain business interests of the Church, he turned to the task of rechanneling the efforts of the Twelve into their traditional role. His first step was to open a new mission in Japan. To head this mission he appointed Elder Heber J. Grant of the Twelve, who had played a conspicuous role in the business and financial affairs of the Church but who had never been on a mission. Elder Grant, who had received his call February 14, 1901, and who was given several months to put his personal affairs in order, departed for his field of labor on July 24, 1901.

Not long thereafter, President Snow elaborated his views on the international scope of the work of the Twelve and the Seventy in a meeting of the Council of the First Presidency and Quorum of the Twelve. Joseph F. Smith later reported

President Snow's instructions in an editorial that appeared in the *Juvenile Instructor:* "I want to say, here are the Apostles and the Seventy," Lorenzo told the Brethren, "their business is to warn the nations of the earth and prepare the world for the coming of the Savior. They have been engaged in this more or less. Now we find ourselves in a compact, gathered condition, the church divided into stakes, and we come together from time to time in a council capacity to consider the interests of the cause generally, and make appointments for brethren to visit the stakes when holding their conferences. It looks to me that our minds ought to extend somewhat, and we get out of the beaten track, and a little change be made. For instance, we have started in this direction by sending Brother Grant over to Japan, but this is only a start. Things seem to be going on favorably with him; but whether he will accomplish much or not matters not in one sense; it is for the Apostles to show to the Lord that they are His witnesses to all the nations, and that they are doing the best they can."

To channel the work of the Twelve in this new direction entailed a significant shift in administrative authority and responsibility in the stakes. For decades the members and local leaders had become accustomed to having the Twelve assume stake duties.

In general conference, Lorenzo counseled, "You presiding officers of the various stakes of Zion, the time is coming when you will not have to call and depend so much upon the Twelve Apostles. They will be directed in other channels, and I want you to distinctly understand it; and do not seek to throw responsibilities that belong to you upon these Twelve Apostles and upon the Seventies. The presidents of these fifty stakes should consider the people in their respective stakes [as being] in their various dominions. They should regard them as their own family, as their sons and daughters; and take as deep an interest in them as they ought to take in their own wives and children. It should be their thought by day and by night, how and in what way they can be most serviceable to their respective charges. You presidents, when you retire to your rest, you probably can spend half an hour before you go to sleep, and let your thoughts run over your several jurisdictions. See wherein, either physically, financially or spiritually, you can help, and what can be done best in advancing the interests of your official family. These bishops, however wise and energetic they may think themselves—and the most of them certainly are very wise and energetic—need to be looked after."

Chapter Thirty

The Curtain Falls

Many years lay upon the head of President Lorenzo Snow, but he was not old. There were signs of age—the white hair and beard, the measured pace, the deliberate speech. But these masked the energetic spirit within. At the threshhold of his ecclesiastical career, Joseph Smith, Sr., had told Lorenzo, "Thou shalt have long life. Age shall not come upon thee. The vigor of thy mind shall not be abated; and the vigor of thy body shall be preserved."

As the October 1901 general conference approached, President Snow reached the halfway point of his eighty-eighth year. Judged by the standards of the day, he had lived a long life.

Until shortly before the conference, he had been in excellent health and spirits. He had attended to his duties each day in the office of the First Presidency. But Lorenzo's routine was interrupted by a heavy chest cold that produced a rasping hoarseness. To avoid aggravating his condition, he heeded his family and physician and did not attend any of the sessions of the conference except the last. The strain of trying to make himself heard in the great tabernacle, without amplifying devices, returned him to his sickbed.

On October 9, following a sleepless night of retching and vomiting, Lorenzo's condition became critical. Minnie, alarmed at her husband's weakened condition, sought Joseph

F. Smith to administer to the prophet. She found the counselor in the presidential suite holding a meeting with MIA leaders. Joseph F. went immediately to President Snow's bedside in the adjoining building, taking John Henry Smith of the Twelve with him. There the two apostles administered to their leader while his physicians, Doctors Wilcox and J. S. Richards, were summoned, who later diagnosed the illness as pneumonia.

Lorenzo was much worse the following day. Minnie, carrying out what she understood to be her husband's wishes, summoned the Temple Choir to sing to him. She also called for his counselors. Arriving about the same time as the choir, the counselors found that President Snow was decidedly against the choir singing but welcomed another administration. Joseph F. anointed, and the prophet's protégé, Rudger Clawson, sealed the anointing. Even in this extremity, Lorenzo, aware that the choir members might have been disappointed in not being able to sing for him, invited them to sing at his funeral.

President Lorenzo Snow passed away quietly at 3:55 that afternoon, October 10, 1901. He was conscious until near the end, lucidly answering questions from those at his bedside.

Word of the prophet's death spread rapidly. President Joseph F. Smith, the senior apostle, took charge, appointing President Rudger Clawson and Elder Abraham O. Woodruff to work with the Snow family in making funeral arrangements.

Because of Lorenzo's long association with the place, it was decided to inter him at Brigham City, in sight of the mountains he loved. But the memorial services were to be held in the Salt Lake Tabernacle, at the headquarters of the Church. Sunday October 13, 1901, was selected as the date.

The body lay in state in the main parlor of the Beehive House. Thousands of admirers, member and nonmember alike, filed past the bier to see and to pay their last respects to the deceased prophet, who, only a few days before, had delivered a powerful sermon in the Tabernacle. At 9:30 A.M. the casket was closed, and with only relatives and the general authorities present, a family prayer was offered. The casket was then carried out to a horse-drawn hearse waiting at the curb on South Temple Street. With family and associates

Funeral of Lorenzo Snow in Salt Lake Tabernacle

forming a procession behind, the body of the venerable leader was driven to Temple Square, passing on the way the First Presidency's offices, the Lion House, and the old tithing office and yard located on the corner east of the square where the Hotel Utah now stands.

On Temple Square were hundreds of mourners who could not find seating in the Tabernacle, which was already filled to capacity. These moved aside in respectful silence as a way was opened up for the hearse. The pallbearers carried the casket to an elevated, flower-decked catafalque near the pulpits that had been constructed especially for the occasion.

The scene inside the building would have aroused Lorenzo's imaginative and dramatic instincts. The base of the massive organ in the west end of the building was covered with white, draped bunting. In the center of the base hung a floral tribute in the form of the Salt Lake Temple, above which, framed in white, was a full-sized painting of President Snow, which now hangs in the annex of the Salt Lake Temple. Above

235

the picture was the word *UTAH,* and still above that hung a star of David. These last two objects symbolized the power of Caesar and the power of Christ, the positions of the two suggesting the preeminence of the latter.

The elevated stands where the general and other authorities were seated were similarly draped with bunting, as were the balustrades of the choir loft and the front portions of the balcony on both the north and south sides of the building. Also, the four front columns supporting the balcony on either side of the building were wrapped with the white bunting in barber pole fashion. Numerous floral displays adorned all levels of the stand, the most significant one bearing the motto "As God Is, Man May Be."

President Joseph F. Smith conducted the services, which commenced with the choir singing "O My Father," whose lyrics were composed by Lorenzo's sister Eliza. The speakers included Elders Brigham Young, Jr., John Henry Smith, and John W. Taylor of the Twelve, and Presidents Rudger Clawson and Joseph F. Smith. Of the many eulogies spoken, the most significant was the one offered by Joseph F. Smith (who had known all of the early Church leaders), who said that with the exception of the Prophet Joseph Smith, he doubted there had ever been one who had borne more powerful and precise testimony of the Savior than Lorenzo Snow.

After the services, instead of making the customary trek to the city cemetery, the funeral cortege proceeded directly to the train depot, where a special train, provided through the courtesy of officials of the Oregon Short Line Railroad Company, waited to take the body and the funeral party to Brigham City. At its destination the train was met by what appeared to be the entire population of Brigham City.

The casket was placed in a black hearse whose windows were partially veiled by fringed and tasseled white drapes. Pulling the vehicle was a beautiful team of four matched white horses, all wearing black blinders.

Behind the hearse, carrying the floral tributes brought from Salt Lake City, followed a wagon whose work-a-day employments were only partially concealed by a white plat-

Horse-drawn hearse at Brigham City cemetery

Wagon bearing floral arrangements

Final resting place of Lorenzo Snow at Brigham City cemetery

form attached to its bed, and behind it trailed dozens of carriages filled with Lorenzo's Brigham City admirers and the more than one hundred and fifty mourners who had accompanied the body on the train. The mile-long route to the cemetery was lined with well-scrubbed children, attired in their Sunday best, who strewed the path of the cortege with autumn flowers.

The unrecorded graveside ceremony and dedication of the grave was conducted by the new head of the Church, Joseph F. Smith, whom Lorenzo had predicted would one day wear the prophetic mantle. While President Smith's words have been lost to us, we can imagine his having uttered sentiments to this effect, which would have been entirely appropriate and true: "Today we lay at rest one of God's noblemen who taught us how to live in the world yet not be of the world, who always placed obedience to his apostolic calling above all else, and who inculcated the principles of faith, integrity, and discipline through a long life of service to others. He also taught us how to live a life of culture and refinement despite poverty in the midst of a desert, how to convert the commonplace into something of uncommon beauty, and how to channel the skills and efforts of many toward laudable goals. And he achieved and taught all this with a poise and dignity that made it seem natural and effortless, like the imperceptible growth of a beautiful plant."

In contemplating the life of Lorenzo Snow, and in seeking to emulate him, one is led to look to the source of his power and accomplishments. This leads to the realization that God was his chief mentor and confidant. Moreover, we are brought to the realization that God is our own heavenly parent who loves and is interested in us, and that through our faith, our obedience, and our diligence, we can ultimately attain to the status he now occupies, being his spirit children and having the seeds of Godhood and perfection within us.

Epilogue

I t was a warm, clear summer day when the author visited the cemetery where President Lorenzo Snow's mortal remains lie in peace. Present was one of Brigham City's distinguished native sons, Elder Boyd K. Packer of the Quorum of the Twelve, who, earlier in the day, had conducted several of us on a tour of the historic sites in Brigham City and neighboring Corinne. As we examined President Snow's headstone, discussed some of his unusual qualities, and reflected upon the impact he has had and will have upon millions of Latter-day Saints, there came an inner peace and a spiritual whispering that this man was and is a true prophet of God. His life conformed in every detail with the high principles he taught during a ministry that spanned sixty-five turbulent years. There came, too, a greater insight into the nature and importance of his apostolic calling, reflected in the demeanor and comments of our guide, Elder Packer, whose love and admiration for the deceased prophet are shown in the fact that his own future burial plot lies adjacent to the burial place of President Lorenzo Snow.

Index

241

Index

Index

India, 67; in France, 68; in Malta, 70-71; in Sandwich Isalands, 97-102; in northern California, 166, 206; among Indians, 166-70; as responsibility of Quorum of Twelve, 230-31
Missions of LS: first mission, 11-15; second mission, 22-27; mission to England, 29-38; mission to Italy, 60-71; special mission to Sandwich Islands, 89-102; voyage to Holy Land, 120-28; pilgrimage through Palestine, 129-37; voyage from Holy Land, 138-46; mission to Indians, 166-70
Mobocracy, 14-15, 24, 47, 66-67
Morrill Act, 165
Mount of Olives, 130-32
Mount Pisgah, 50-52
Munich, 142-44

Nablous, 135
Naples, 126-27
Nauvoo, 39-40, 42, 48-49, 61
Nauvoo Temple, 48-49
Neeley, William, 168-69
Nettie Merrill, 92
Nez Perce Indians, 167-68

Oberlin Collegiate Institute, 2-4

Packer, Boyd K., 240
Palestine, 129-37
Pamphlets and tracts of LS, 36, 46, 64-65
Paris, 68, 124-25
Patriarchal blessing of LS, 9-10
Patten, David W., 2-4
Perpetual Emigration Fund, 37, 58-59
Peter, example of, 163-64
Piedmont, 63-65, 125
Pioneer Day celebration, 57-58
Plural marriage: at Nauvoo, 40-42, 45; presidential statements against, 165; publicity against, 165, 228-30; during antipolygamy legislation,

165-66, 179, 181, 184, 189; law enforcement during, 171-74; penitentiary for those convicted of, 174-76, 179-81; govenor's views on, 177-79; favorable judicial decision concerning, 181; decision of Manifesto concerning, 189; wives and children of LS under, 208-9
Polysophical Society, 73-74
Pratt, Parley P., 35
Prichard, Sarah Ann (wife of LS), 48, 72, 208
Prison, territorial, 174-76, 179-82
Promontory Summit, 114-18

Quorum of Twleve Apostles, 34, 56, 213-17, 230-31

Railroad, transcontinental, 114-17
Ramleh, 130
Rees, Leah, 192-93
"Reformation," 84-86
Repentance, principle of, 21
Revelation of LS on godhood, 28-29, 214
Reynolds, George, 165
Richards, Franklin D., 115
Roberts, Brigham H., 222, 228-30
Rocky Mountain Saints, The, 114, 117
Rome, 126

Saint George conference, 219-21
Saint George Temple dedication, 154-58
Salt Lake Stake, 155, 159
Salt Lake Temple, 74-75, 187, 198-203, 207, 211
Salt Lake Valley, 55-56
Samaria, 135
San Francisco, 91-92, 101, 166-67, 204-6
Sandwich Islands, 92-100
Sawmill, problems with, 111
Sea of Galilee, 135-37
Seixas, Joshua, 4
Shalersville, 26
Shannon, 61-62

243